Writing Logically,
Thinking Critically

Writing Logically, Thinking Critically

FIFTH EDITION

Sheila Cooper
Rosemary Patton

PEARSON
Longman

New York   Boston   San Francisco
London   Toronto   Sydney   Tokyo   Singapore   Madrid
Mexico City   Munich   Paris   Cape Town   Hong Kong   Montreal

Publisher: Joseph Opiela
Executive Marketing Manager: Ann Stypuloski
Senior Supplements Editor: Donna Campion
Production Manager: Ellen MacElree
Project Coordination, Text Design, and Electronic Page Makeup: Nesbitt Graphics, Inc.
Cover Design Manager: John Callahan
Cover Designer: Laura Shaw
Cover Illustration: *Luce di novembre # 3, 2003,* by Nancy Genn, Takada Gallery, San Francisco
Photo Researcher: Ilene Bellorin
Senior Manufacturing Buyer: Dennis J. Para
Printer and Binder: R.R. Donnelley & Sons, Inc.
Cover Printer: Phoenix Color Corp.

For permission to use copyrighted material, grateful acknowledgment is made to the copyright
holders on pp. 245–246, which are hereby made part of this copyright page.

Library of Congress Cataloging-in-Publication Data

Cooper, Sheila, 1946–
    Writing logically, thinking critically / Sheila Cooper, Rosemary Patton.—5th ed.
        p. cm.
    Includes index.
    ISBN 0-321-41431-4
        1. English language—Rhetoric. 2. Critical thinking. 3. Academic writing. 4. Logic. I.
Patton, Rosemary. II. Title

PE1408.C5485 2005
808'.042—dc21   2007044484

ISBN 0-321-41431-4

5 6 7 8 9 10—DOC—09 08

He who will not reason, is a bigot; he who cannot, is a fool; and he who dares not, is a slave.

—LORD BYRON

A mind that is stretched to a new idea never returns to its original dimension.

—OLIVER WENDELL HOLMES

The vital habits of democracy: the ability to follow an argument, grasp the point of view of another, expand the boundaries of understanding, debate the alternative purposes that might be pursued.

—JOHN DEWEY

BRIEF CONTENTS

DETAILED CONTENTS

CHAPTER 3

The Structure of Argument 54

CHAPTER 4

Written Argument 81

CHAPTER 6

CHAPTER 7

CHAPTER 8

GUIDE TO READINGS

PREFACE

Good Writing is Good Thinking.

—NEW YORK TIMES MAGAZINE

Once again we have designed this new edition as the central text in a course devoted to composition with an emphasis on argumentation and critical thinking. We have updated essays, examples, and exercises for relevancy. We have also added some fresh cartoons, as we believe these visual images with punch lines reinforce the text. In response to helpful suggestions from those who have used previous editions, we have tightened, rearranged, and clarified material throughout the book. We have also added writing assignments (for a total of eighteen) and a number of new readings. A feature of this text that makes it stand out among others in its field is the inclusion of fiction and poetry. For all readings, we provide a separate list for quick reference.

CONTENT CHANGES

In Chapter 1, "Thinking and Writing—A Critical Connection," we have added a discussion of e-mail and expanded our section on metaphor.

In Chapter 2, "Inference—Critical Thought," we've added new exercises on inference, including a new poem and short story.

In Chapter 3, "The Structure of Argument," we have new essays to sharpen the distinction between argument and explanation, and new cartoons to examine for hidden assumptions. We have moved "Summary" and "Plagiarism" to Chapter 9, where they complement research and documentation.

Chapter 4, "Written Argument," continues as the center of the book, describing all aspects of a well-written argument. We have updated topics in both examples and writing assignments. To increase students' understanding of rhetorical strategies, we have introduced two new readings for analysis. We have created additional exercises on sentence joining and rhetorical choices, and on coherence. And we have replaced an essay by a professional writer with one by a student demonstrating current documentation.

In Chapter 5, "The Language of Argument—Definition," we emphasize the role of specificity in good writing with an exercise distinguishing levels of specificity. In order to give students a strategy for defining terms, we moved our section on appositives from Chapter 8 to this chapter. We have revised our approach to written definition first in an exercise analyzing two new readings and then in two new writing assignments focused on argument.

Chapter 6, "Fallacious Arguments," Chapter 7, "Deductive and Inductive Argument," and Chapter 8, "The Language of Argument—Style," remain much the same except for new cartoons and a few updated examples.

Chapter 9, "Research, Summary, and Documentation," is reorganized and condensed to meet the needs of students conducting research for assignments in this text.

SEQUENCE

We suggest that instructors follow the sequence of chapters in order, with the possible exceptions of Chapters 8 (sentence polishing) and 9 (research), which can be referred to throughout the course. Some instructors, however, prefer to create their own order to suit the needs of their particular class.

As before, we assume that *Writing Logically, Thinking Critically* will be most effective in classes where the students have already completed an introductory semester or quarter of composition. But many find the book works well as the foundation text in first-year writing classes. Some secondary school instructors have been enthusiastic about its success in their advanced composition classes. Upper division college students preparing for the LSAT, the qualifying exam for law school, have also found the text useful.

PEDAGOGY

As in previous editions, we include a number of collaborative activities to encourage an interactive approach to learning. Most of the exercises and assignments can, in fact, be approached collaboratively, as can many writing projects in the business world. Writing assignments and exercises invite a broad range of responses that should cover the demands of writing across a diverse curriculum.

INSTRUCTOR'S MANUAL

We suggest you turn to the Instructor's Manual to find more strategies for each chapter and a few additional student essays related to select writing assignments. We have printed these essays on separate pages so you can copy them for your students.

ACKNOWLEDGMENTS

We remain grateful to our students, a few of whom are represented here, and to those who have used *Writing Logically, Thinking Critically* and offered invaluable advice for this revision.

Sheila Cooper
Rosemary Patton

CHAPTER 1

Thinking and Writing—
A Critical Connection

*It is doubtful whether a man [or woman?] ever brings his faculties to bear
with their full force on a subject until he writes upon it.*

—Cicero

It would hardly seem debatable that to write well we need to think clearly.
And the evidence is strong for concluding that writing about ideas can help
to clarify them. Taking this notion a step further, many would argue that the
act of writing can create ideas, can lead writers to discover what they think.
Language, according to many scholars, can give birth to thought, and written
language provides a way to refine our thoughts since, unlike speech, it can be
manipulated until it accurately reflects our thinking.

THINKING MADE VISIBLE

Consider writing then as thinking made visible, as thinking in slow motion, a
process whereby we can inspect and reflect on what we are thinking about.
As novelist E. M. Forster put it, "How can I tell what I think till I see what

Cartoon by Richard Guindon—Reprinted by permission of the Detroit Free Press.

I've said?" Roger Traynor, a former Chief Justice of the California Supreme Court, agreed when he spoke of writing and the law:

> I have not found a better test for the solution of a case than in its articulation in *writing,* which is *thinking at its hardest.*

Writing doesn't simply convey thought; it also forges it. It is a two-way street, both expressing and generating ideas.

Writing and thinking, when taken seriously, are not easy—a reality that led painter and critic Sir Joshua Reynolds to comment, "There is no expedient to which we will not resort to avoid the real labor of thinking." And many writers have groaned over the pain of writing. New York writer Fran Lebowitz takes an extreme position on the subject: "Writing is torture. It is very hard work. It's not coal mining, but it's work."

After visiting the Galapagos Islands in the 1830s, evolutionist Charles Darwin wrote to his sister from his ship, the *Beagle,* about the special challenge of reasoning on paper, the kind of writing we emphasize in this book.

> I am just now beginning to discover the difficulty of expressing one's ideas on paper. As long as it consists solely of description it is pretty easy; but where reasoning comes into play, to make a proper connection, a clearness and a moderate fluency, is to me a difficulty of which I had no idea.

THE POWER OF WRITING PERSUASIVELY

Although writing and thinking may be difficult, mastery and success in both can be well worth the effort. Indeed, clear writing is often essential. If we are not able to articulate a request, a complaint, or an endorsement in precise, forceful language, we may find ourselves settling for less than we deserve. If we can't write a persuasive application, the job or graduate school position may go to someone else. Linguist Robin Lakoff, in her book *Talking Power: The Politics of Language,* puts it this way:

> In a meritocracy such as ours, we believe that those who best demonstrate the ability to think and persuade should have the lion's share of power. Articulateness according to the rules goes a long way; and its possessors are assumed to possess intelligence and virtue as inseparable concomitants. People who say things right, who plead their cases well, will be listened to and their suggestions acted upon. They will make the money, win the offices, find love, get all the goodies their society has to give.

The Advent of E-Mail

Many today fear that the importance of writing is in decline. First the telephone and then the computer saw the status of letter writing diminish. But now, the letter has been reborn as e-mail; the written word lives on. Written communication has become quick and easy, most of us eager to respond to the call of "You've Got Mail."

Increased informality encouraged by the computer, however, can put students and business employees at risk. Language now flies through cyberspace, and impressions are made quickly. Getting it right in an e-mail is becoming important in the academic and business worlds, where persuasive writing remains important. A recent *New York Times* article, which addressed the concerns of many corporations, stressed the high cost to American companies of poorly written e-mails. A university professor, who now heads an online business writing school, quoted an example of a request he received:

> i need help I am writing a essay on writing I work for this company and my boss wants me to help improve the workers writing skills

No punctuation, no attention to the sentence. How far is this employee going? How can he help others?

The cry for improved writing instruction in schools and colleges keeps growing louder. In a recent report, The National Commission on Writing found that companies all over the country are complaining that college graduates are unable to write clearly or concisely. Editorial writer Brent Staples claimed that the information age "requires more high-quality writing from more categories of employees than ever before." A writing resource teacher wrote in response to his column: "Teachers must give students specific tools that will encourage them to explore the craft of writing and to become critical thinkers by shaping words on paper." Our thinking precisely.

Linguist John McWhorter fears that the replacement of written English with more casual oral language has led to "a steep and steady decline in the quality of political oratory . . . and ultimately thinking." He cites the broad variety of constructions and vast vocabulary in formal English as the natural idiom for expressing nuance and logical argument. Not everyone, however, would agree with McWhorter's position.

EXERCISE 1A

Thinking About Language

1. In class, write a quick list of reasons why you support or disagree with the following propositions and then as a class **discuss** your findings. Some of you may not agree with the claims made by the writers quoted above.

    a. Spoken English is degrading the quality of written language and thus thinking too.

    b. The ability to write accurately and persuasively remains important.

2. Write an e-mail introducing yourself to your instructor. You will need to include information useful to your instructor, such as why you are taking this class, what writing or logic courses you have already completed, what you expect to gain from the class, and anything else bearing on your participation during the semester or quarter. If your instructor wants you to be in direct contact by e-mail, send this assignment over the Internet; if not, turn in a printout.

CRITICAL THINKING

If, as we maintain, there is a strong relationship between thinking clearly and writing well—if one skill strengthens the other—then integrating the two as a course of study makes sense. But what do we mean by "thinking clearly"? For our purposes, we have found it helpful to narrow our focus and concentrate on the phrase **critical thinking.** This term has assumed a central position in both academic and public life and is variously defined today.

EXERCISE 1B

Defining Critical Thinking

Before you read further in this chapter, put this book aside, take a piece of paper, and write a few sentences discussing what you think the phrase *critical thinking* means. If you do this in class, you may want to compare notes with other students.

Critical Thinking as Self-Defense

In most contexts today the term **critical** means censorious or faultfinding, but it comes to us from the Greek *kriticos* and Latin *criticus,* meaning able to discern or separate. It is this sense of critical that we have in mind—discerning or discriminating thought characterized by careful analysis and judgment. As student Denise Selleck described it: "Thinking critically is the ability to understand a concept fully, taking in different sides of an issue or idea while not being swayed by the propaganda or other fraudulent methods used to promote it." She recognizes the importance of an open mind and the element of self-defense implicit in critical thinking.

Today, in the information age, people have to know how to think, to think critically and creatively, if they are going to succeed. There are no certainties. We are surrounded by facts, all of which are open to interpretation. Such interpretation requires critical thought. And if our democracy is to endure, we all have a moral responsibility to engage in deliberate, critical thinking. How else can we make informed decisions about political candidates and issues?

In his novel *I Married a Communist,* Philip Roth describes a memorable high school English teacher who taught his students the liberating power of critical thinking. "Cri-ti-cal thinking," Mr. Ringold said, using his knuckles to rap out each of the syllables on his desk top—"there is the ultimate subversion."

Advertising and the media, with which we are confronted every day, require careful critical scrutiny if we are to protect ourselves from false claims, questionable judgments, and confusing or deceptive argument. We can be hard-pressed to distinguish information from promotion. Names of public buildings reflect their corporate sponsors. Sports stadiums reap lucrative financial rewards in exchange for assuming the names of large corporations, Minute Made Field in Houston, Cinergy Field in Cincinnati, Bank One in Arizona, for example. When we go to the movies, we can't tell which is a preview, which an ad for some unrelated product. School textbooks carry advertising as companies reach for young minds. The Public Broadcasting Service, which used to be the one source of advertising-free television, now carries as much advertising as some of its commercial rivals. Television infomercials push new products even as they masquerade as objective information. And, sandwiched in between the information we're seeking, the Internet bombards us with an increasing array of products and services for sale. We must be vigilant in our efforts to defend ourselves from those who would deliberately manipulate us for personal gain.

An Open Mind—Examining Your World View

Another definition of critical thinking that also captures the spirit we hope to foster in this book comes from Richard Paul of Sonoma State University: "the disposition to think clearly and accurately in order to be fair." He suggests the importance of developing an open mind, of listening attentively to the views of others.

It is, however, equally important to be aware of where our views come from. Cultures, subgroups within those cultures, and families within these groups tend to share what is called a **world view,** a set of assumptions about the world and the behavior of people in it. Without acknowledging that we hold such views, we may harbor prejudices about groups that cloud our thinking and restrict fair judgment. Many of these attitudes grow from the contexts of our lives that we take for granted—the opinions of parents and friends, our ethnic and religious backgrounds.

In the words of Professor Louis Menand, "Ideas are produced not by individuals, but by groups of individuals—ideas are social . . . ideas do not develop according to some inner logic of their own, but are entirely dependent, like germs on their human carriers and the environment." Knowledge and ideas are not absolutes but are subject to the time, place, and circumstances in which they are expressed. For instance, up until the twentieth century, women were considered incapable of making rational decisions on political issues and thus were denied the vote. Today, most cultures recognize that such a view was socially constructed, not inherently true. Henry Louis Gates, Jr., professor and director of the W. E. B. Du Bois Institute of Afro-American Research at Harvard, sees history as "a chronicle of formerly acceptable outrages":

> Once upon a time, perfectly decent folk took it for granted that watching two gladiators hack each other to death was just the thing to do on a summer afternoon, that making slaves of Africans was a good deal for all concerned. What were they thinking? You could say that posterity is a hanging judge, except that sooner or later capital punishment, too, will turn up on that chronicle of outrages.

Where does the weakness in Jennifer's defense lie?

Questioning our personal world view can be one of the most challenging steps in our growth as critical thinkers. In the following essay, newspaper columnist Jon Carroll points out that our world view, our opinions, can sometimes blind us to the truth.

The Problem with New Data

JON CARROLL

You may have heard that Dr. James Hansen, the man who first popularized   1
the notion that carbon dioxide levels and global warming were inextricably linked, has issued a new report saying that further studies have revealed that in fact other heat-trapping chemicals—methane, chlorofluorocarbons, particulate matter like coal soot, plus other smog-creating chemicals—are probably more responsible for the trend than carbon dioxide.

Any advance in scientific understanding is good news. Hansen's report   2
is particularly interesting because it is contrary to his previous position, indicating that he is able to separate his professional ego from his scientific conclusions and change his mind right out in public.

This is less usual than it should be. We are all afraid of being wrong, and   3
we will tend to cling to our opinions in the face of mounting evidence to the contrary. In ideal science, all opinions are merely way stations on the road to the truth; in real-world science, though, opinions are the basis of reputation and income, and the difference between the establishment view and the revealed truth is not easy to discern from the outside.

And there's another reason why Hansen's conclusions are good news—   4
it's a lot easier to control the production of these new culprits than it is the production of carbon dioxide, which is the unavoidable byproduct of the burning of all fossil fuels, as well as the gas that emerges from our mouths every time we exhale.

And yet, Hansen's report was greeted with considerable trepidation.   5
The results might be misinterpreted; big polluters might twist the data; Congress might have a fig leaf to cover its natural inclination to let big corporations do whatever they want

This is what happens when politics and science start to commingle. In   6
politics, opinions—they are called "positions" or "principles"—are the official yardstick of integrity. People who change their minds are considered to be weak, are said to waffle.

Someone who has staked out a tough position on carbon dioxide   7
would be seriously uninterested in data suggesting it's not really the problem. Someone who supported the Kyoto Protocol—which identified carbon dioxide as the principal culprit—would feel the urge to attack Hansen, who would be identified as a "former ally."

Following the facts wherever they lead is always dangerous in the polit-   8
ical arena.

In fact, Hansen has not changed his position on global warming at all.   9
He is still of the opinion that it forms a significant threat to the short-term
(less than 100 years) ecological health of the planet. But he has a nuanced
and evolving view of the causes.

"Nuanced" and "evolving" will, in the political world, buy you a cup of   10
coffee, provided you also have $2.

The urge to hang on tight knows no ideology. The gun lobby reflexively   11
brings up the slippery slope and the Second Amendment no matter what
the issue, making something like trigger locks as controversial as universal
confiscation of firearms.

Multiculturalists reflexively support bilingual education, despite new   12
studies suggesting that kids from different cultures learn better when a single language is the classroom standard.

Look into the heart of your opinions: What if early detection of breast   13
cancer had no real effect on mortality rates? What if secondhand smoke
turned out to be no health risk at all? What if free condoms for every child
lowered disease rates by 50 percent? What if air bags were bad, or good, or
whatever is the opposite of what you currently believe they are?

It's the brain lock issue. We want to believe something because it fits   14
with the other things we believe, because the people we know believe it,
because the people who believe the other things are loathsome.

Alas, the universe of facts is not a democracy. If it were, I'd vote for fried   15
pork rinds as a health food.

EXERCISE 1C

Examining Your World View

1. Professor Henry Louis Gates lists gladiators and slavery as two of the
   "acceptable outrages" that history chronicles. We added denying
   women the vote. As a class, add to this list.

2. Look closely at these "outrages"—gladiators, slavery, women being denied the vote, and others generated by your responses to question 1
   above. In each case, ask which group held this view and what they had
   to gain from supporting this belief?

3. Gates predicts that one day capital punishment will be viewed as a "formerly acceptable outrage." Here's a chance to "deconstruct" a socially
   constructed belief, to examine the roots of your own beliefs. As Jon Carroll says, "Look into the heart of your opinions." Write a paragraph stating your position on capital punishment and include the views held by
   your family, friends, and religion (if you belong to a religious group).
   Then compare paragraphs with a small group of your classmates and,
   with their help, start to create a description of your own world view. This
   will not be an easy task, but don't be discouraged or feel threatened.

Putting such views into writing or even formulating what you think can be a challenge. There is no right or wrong answer here—just a critical exploration of your thoughts discussed with your peers. During this discussion, keep the following questions in mind:

Do you automatically dismiss positions opposed to your own? Are you guilty of what Jon Carroll calls "brain lock"?

Do you take your own beliefs for granted without recognizing the need for support?

Do you deny that your beliefs could change?

Do you accept public information without question?

Do you recognize that some assumptions based on your world view need to be critically evaluated?

Media Literacy

Even news reporting in reputable newspapers requires intelligent evaluation. Headlines and lead paragraphs can be misleading or emphasize only one element in a complex story. Like individuals, all forms of media reflect a world view. Newspapers, magazines, television programs, scholarly articles, books, and movies express a point of view even if it's not immediately apparent. Media watch organizations, whose goal it is to expose bias, have in fact their own bias or world view.

A recent segment of Public Television's *News Hour* focused on media coverage of the Middle East conflict. Included in the discussion were representatives from CNN, the *Boston Globe,* and two media watch groups. The representative from one of these watch groups claimed that "the media has tended to airbrush away Palestinian extremism," that certain Palestinians are portrayed as being moderate when they're not. The representative of the other media watch group claimed that the media was remiss in not criticizing "Israel's brutal occupation" of Palestine. Their world views are obviously different.

Many journalists faced with this kind of criticism struggle to be fair. The editor from the *Boston Globe* focused on the challenge of choosing unbiased language to describe the conflict: "The term 'occupied territories' is a matter of controversy. Some would rather say 'disputed land.' Some people will talk about an 'incursion' into the Palestinian territories. Palestinians tend to prefer the word 'invasion.'"

Or the media may make an explicit decision about what it will or will not cover, as it did in the aftermath of September 11 when it decided not to show film of victims jumping from the World Trade Center. In the case of the Middle East conflict, a CNN executive made explicit a policy of not giving suicide bombers and their families the same amount of coverage they will give to the victims of terrorism "because there's no moral equivalence between the perpetrators of mass murder and the victims of mass murder."

As a reader and researcher, you must examine your sources for bias and its impact on the information you're seeking. If you're writing a paper on global warming, it's important to know that magazines published by Greenpeace and the Sierra Club, for example, support all environmental protections and thus emphasize the dangers of global warming. The American Enterprise Institute or a conservative magazine such as the *National Review* may be skeptical about the impact of global warming. (See "Say Goodbye to SUVs," by Rich Lowrey, the editor of the *National Review,* in Chapter 6.) Thus, in gathering information for your papers, you must carefully navigate between conflicting interests in order to find reliable information. Ask teachers and librarians about the bias of a particular source.

EXERCISE 1D

Scrutinizing the Media

Read these two excerpts from different papers, the *New York Times* and the *San Francisco Chronicle,* reporting on the same Supreme Court decision.

High Court Upholds Buffer Zone of 15 Feet at Abortion Clinics

LINDA GREENHOUSE

Washington, Feb. 19—The Supreme Court today upheld a lower court's order keeping demonstrators at least 15 feet away from the doorways and driveways of clinics in upstate New York that were the targets of blockages and boisterous protests in the early 1990s. The decision reaffirmed the Court's broadly protective approach toward maintaining access for patients entering abortion clinics. . . .

On the same date, the *San Francisco Chronicle,* relying on the *Los Angeles Times,* reported:

Abortion Foes Entitled to Confront Patients
Supreme Court Says It's Free Speech

DAVID G. SAVAGE
Los Angeles Times

Washington—Abortion protesters have a free-speech right to confront pregnant women on the sidewalks outside clinics and to urge them vehemently not to go ahead with the procedure, the Supreme Court ruled yesterday.

The 8–1 decision calls into doubt a wave of new city ordinances and judges' orders that have barred persistent protesters from confronting and harassing doctors, nurses and patients outside clinics. . . .

1. How are the two articles different?

2. What conclusions might you draw about the writers who presented the two differing slants on the abortion clinic ruling quoted above?

3. Look for a single news story that is reported in different ways. You may compare two different print versions of a story from the same date, as we illustrate, or choose two or more TV news broadcasts on the same evening and note differences in emphasis and language. Network news programs may differ from those on cable television or Public Broadcasting Service. Quote from print stories or summarize the TV programs, and describe how different sources present the same facts.

AUDIENCE AND PURPOSE

A major distinction between writing outside the classroom and writing for a class lies in the audience to whom we write, what novelist and essayist Virginia Woolf referred to as "the face beneath the page." Job-related writing tasks, for example, include a designated audience and a real purpose. An employee may write to a superior requesting a raise or to another company proposing a cooperative venture. Readers of a newspaper often express their opinions in persuasive letters to the editor, and many a college student has depended on familiarity with the audience and careful manipulation of circumstance to explain a poor grade to parents. But in a class, students are asked to write papers for the teacher to critique and grade, usually with no specified purpose beyond successfully completing an assignment. Teachers cannot remove themselves from the role of ultimate audience, but for most of the major writing assignments in this text we have suggested an additional audience to lend some authenticity to each project and to guide you in your writing choices.

Although different academic disciplines require variations in format, all good writing of an explanatory or persuasive nature is built on a balance between three essential elements: **knowledge of the subject or argument,** an identified **audience,** and a clearly defined **purpose.** The task of thinking through an argument, its audience, and purpose introduces a significant critical thinking component to an assignment. Only when you take a conscious rhetorical stance toward your writing can you have an appropriate voice and give power to what you write. The goal for you, therefore, is to define your subject or argument, identify your audience, determine your purpose in writing to this particular audience, and thus establish a tone that fits the writing task.

For example, suppose you have found that the college preparation provided by your high school was clearly inadequate. You have decided to take steps to remedy the situation. You will have to write letters to several different people explaining your concerns, citing supporting examples, and suggesting possible solutions. You know the issues and your purpose is clear: explaining a problem and calling for action. But the tone of your letters will vary according to your audience. The language you choose and the emphasis of your argument will be different when you direct your argument to a classmate for support; to your high school principal and teachers expressing your concerns; and to local, state, and national political representatives asking for help in the improvement of secondary education. For more on the relationship between writer and audience, see the section on *Rogerian Strategy* in Chapter 4.

WRITING ASSIGNMENT 1

Considering Your Audience and Purpose

Choose any public issue that disturbs you—be it small or large, campus, community, or cosmic—and write *two* short papers (one-and-a-half to two pages *each*), expressing your concern. Before you start this assignment, look ahead in this chapter to the suggestions under "Writing as a Process" and follow the stages outlined there.

1. In the first version, direct your writing to someone connected to, perhaps responsible for, the problem you are concerned about. Your purpose here is to communicate your concern or displeasure and possibly persuade the person responsible to take appropriate action.

2. In the second version, address an individual who is in no way connected to the problem you are disturbed about. Your purpose here is to explain the situation and to inform your reader of something he may know nothing about and is not necessarily in a position to change. This means you must include more background detail than was necessary in your first paper.

Label the two papers at the top (*1*) and (*2*) and clearly identify each audience.

WRITING AS A PROCESS

What is written without effort is in general read without pleasure.

—SAMUEL JOHNSON

Where do you begin when faced with a writing assignment? Many students turn to the five-paragraph essay format—introduction, three supporting paragraphs, and conclusion—and choose material that will fit easily into this preconceived mold. Writers rely on this formula because they fear that without it they will produce an incoherent essay. They assume that if they follow it, their writing will at least be organized. Even inexperienced writers must learn to let go of this "safety net" because although it may save them from anxiety and a disorganized essay, it can also determine the content of the essay; if an idea does not fit easily into the mold, the writer must discard it. This rigid structure prevents writers from exploring their topic, from following thoughts that may lead to interesting insights, and from allowing the material, the content, to find the shape that best suits it.

The most common misconception that student writers have is that good writers sit at their desks and produce in one sitting a polished, mechanically correct, cohesive piece of writing. If students are unable to do this, they conclude that they cannot write and approach all writing tasks with dread. As a first step toward improving their writing, students must discard this myth and replace it with a realistic picture of how writers write. Hemingway, in Paris writing his first collection of short stories, *In Our Time,* spent whole mornings on single paragraphs. French novelist Gustave Flaubert, who wrote *Madame Bovary,* would spend a day finding *le mot juste,* the right word. While no one expects students, whose goal it is to produce a competent essay or report rather than a literary masterpiece, to spend this kind of time on their writing, students must realize that writing is a complex intellectual act, that it involves many separate tasks, and that the mind is simply not able to handle all of these tasks at once. As writer Henry Miller saw it, "Writing, like life itself, is a voyage of discovery." Let's look at the distinct tasks involved in the act of writing a paper on this voyage:

Generating ideas

Focusing a topic

Establishing a thesis

Organizing the essay

Organizing paragraphs

Providing transitions between sentences and paragraphs

Polishing sentences for fluency

Choosing appropriate diction (word choice)

Correcting grammar, usage, spelling, and punctuation

Each of these tasks could, of course, be broken down further. What is the solution to this problem, this mental overload that writing forces on us? The answer is that it must be done in stages.

Writing is a **process** that breaks down into roughly three stages—**creating, shaping,** and **correcting.** A common error students make is to focus their energy on what should be the last stage (correcting) at the beginning, when the focus should be on the creative stage of the writing process. The effect of this misplaced attention is to inhibit creative thinking. It is essential that the writer give ample time to the first stage, to generating ideas, to following impulsive thoughts even if they may initially appear unrelated or irrelevant. At this stage a writer must allow himself to experience confusion, to be comfortable with chaos; he must learn to trust the writing process, to realize that out of this chaos a logical train of thought will gradually emerge. Most important of all, writers must learn to suspend all criticism as they explore their topic and their thinking.

Strategies for Generating Ideas

Two concrete methods for beginning this exploration of your topic are brainstorming and freewriting, one or both of which you may already be familiar with.

To **brainstorm,** simply put the topic of the writing assignment at the top of a blank piece of paper or your screen. Then jot down words or phrases that come to mind as you think about this topic—as many words as possible even if you are not sure they relate directly. After brainstorming, look at your list: Circle ideas that you want to develop, draw lines through those that are decidedly unrelated or uninteresting, and draw arrows or make lists of ideas that are connected to one another. At this point you should be able to go to the next stage, organizing your essay either by writing an outline or simply by listing main points that you want to develop into paragraphs. Brainstorming is particularly effective with two or more people.

In **freewriting,** you begin by writing your topic on a blank sheet, but instead of jotting down words and phrases, you write continuously, using sentences. These sentences do not have to be mechanically correct, nor do they have to be connected. The only rule of freewriting is that you may not stop writing; you may not put down your pen or leave the keyboard for a set length of time. After freewriting for five to ten minutes if writing by hand, or longer if using a computer, read over your freewriting, circling ideas that you find interesting or insightful. Now you may do another freewriting on the idea or ideas you have circled, or you may try to formulate a thesis or list ideas you want to develop.

Both of these methods have two things in common. They are relatively painless ways to begin the writing process, and they allow you to circumvent your own worst enemy, self-criticism, the voice that says, "That's not right," "That's not what I mean," "This doesn't make sense." Critical evaluation of your writing is necessary but self-defeating if you are critical at the beginning. In addition, freewriting may offer surprising access to ideas you never knew you had.

If your paper requires research, you will want to start reading relevant journals, books, and Web sites. You may have started this process when searching for a topic. As you read you will need to take notes either on note cards, in a reading journal, or on a laptop computer where you can store them until you are ready to print them out. No matter the source, be sure to record the data necessary for documentation (see Chapter 9). We suggest you try brainstorming and freewriting on writing assignments throughout this text.

The First Draft

After exploring a topic in this way and examining data if you have done research, you will have a sense of what you want to say and will be ready for a first draft. When a paper requires research, consult Chapter 9 both before you start the process and again later when you are ready for the "polishing" stage discussed below.

Successful writer Anne Lamott, in her book about writing, *Bird by Bird: Some Instructions on Writing and Life,* discusses the role of first drafts. Her advice grew out of her own experience as a writer and from writing classes she has taught. The title refers to a family story in which her brother, when 10 years old, was overwhelmed by a school report on birds that had been assigned three months earlier and was now due. Their father, a professional writer, put his arm around his almost weeping son and counseled, "Bird by bird, buddy. Just take it bird by bird." Good advice for writing and for life. See if you can start treating your first drafts as what Lamott calls "the child's draft" in the following excerpt from her book.

The Child's Draft

Now, practically even better news than that of short assignments is the idea of shitty first drafts. All good writers write them. This is how they end up with good second drafts and terrific third drafts. People tend to look at successful writers, writers who are getting their books published and maybe even doing well financially, and think that they sit down at their desks every morning feeling like a million dollars, feeling great about who they are and how much talent they have and what a great story they have to tell; that they take in a few deep breaths, push back their sleeves, roll their necks a few times to get all the cricks out, and dive in, typing fully formed passages as fast as a court reporter. But this is just the fantasy of the uninitiated. I know some very great writers, writers you love who write beautifully and have made a great deal of money, and not *one* of them sits down routinely feeling wildly enthusiastic and confident. Not one of them writes elegant first drafts. All right, one of them does, but we do not like her very much. We do not think that she has a rich inner life.

Very few writers really know what they are doing until they've done it. Nor do they go about their business feeling dewy and thrilled. They do not type a few stiff warm-up sentences and then find themselves bounding along like huskies across the snow. One writer I know tells me that he sits down every morning and says to himself nicely, "It's not like you don't have a choice, because you do—you can either type or kill yourself." We all often feel like we are pulling teeth, even those writers whose prose ends up being the most natural and fluid. The right words and sentences just do not come pouring out like ticker tape most of the time. . . .

For me and most of the other writers I know, writing is not rapturous. In fact, the only way I can get anything written at all is to write really, really shitty first drafts.

The first draft is the child's draft, where you let it all pour out and then let it romp all over the place, knowing that no one is going to see it and that you can shape it later. You just let this childlike part of you channel whatever voices and visions come through and onto the page. If one of the characters wants to say, "Well, so what, Mr. Poopy Pants?," you let her. No one is going to see it. If the kid wants to get into really sentimental, weepy, emotional territory, you let him. Just get it all down on paper, because there may be something great in those six crazy pages that you would never have gotten to by more rational, grown-up means. There may be something in the very last line of the very last paragraph on page six that you just love, that is so beautiful or wild that you now know what you're supposed to be writing about, more or less, or in what direction you might go—but there was no way to get to this without first getting through the first five and a half pages.

The Time to Be Critical

In agreement with Anne Lamott, teacher and writer Donald Murray, in an essay on revision entitled "The Maker's Eye," points out a key difference between student writers and professional writers:

When students complete a first draft, they consider the job of writing done—and their teachers too often agree. When professional writers complete a first draft, they usually feel that they are at the start of the writing process. When a draft is completed, the job of writing can begin.

The time to be critical arrives when you have a complete draft. Now is the time to read with a critical mind, trusting your instinct that if a word, a sentence, or a passage seems unclear or awkward to you, your reader will most likely stumble over the same word, sentence, or passage. You are ready to re-shape your first draft, adding and deleting ideas, refining your thesis, polishing sentences for fluency, and finally writing another draft. Writer Zora Neale Hurston described the process as "rubbing your paragraphs with a soft cloth."

Hurston didn't have the advantage of a word processor with which to move words, sentences, and paragraphs around freely. Sometimes the writing of the first draft will tell you when you need to do a little more research, expand your explanation of a point, or check some of your facts to be sure of your evidence. Computers make it relatively easy to revise your work and make repeated drafts. Just remember to save your work as you go.

Finally, you will be ready to check your spelling (in the dictionary or with a computer spellchecker) and your punctuation (in an English handbook; to date, computer grammar checkers have been disappointing) and to read your essay aloud to yourself or to a friend, always ready to write another draft if it becomes necessary.

Every stage in the writing process is important. To slight one is to limit the success of the final product. There are exceptions of course. Some writers are able to compress some of these steps, to generate and organize ideas in their minds before ever putting pen to paper. But for most of us, successful writing results from an extended writing process that is continually recursive.

> **A caution:** The danger in the way we have described the writing process is that we make it seem as though it progresses in three neat steps, that it proceeds in a linear fashion from prewriting to writing to rewriting and correction. In fact, this process is messy. You may be editing the final draft when you decide to add a completely new paragraph, an idea that didn't exist in any of the previous drafts. Nevertheless, if you realize that writing involves many separate tasks, that it is chaotic and unpredictable, you will not be defeated before you begin by criticizing yourself for having to do what all writers do—struggle to find your way, to express your thoughts so that you and your reader understand them.

One Writer's Process

Let us add to Lamott's advice and our suggestions a description of the writing process that produced this section of Chapter 1.

Day 1:

I spent two hours at the computer writing on the topic, "writing as a process." During this **freewriting,** my goal was to say everything I could think of on this subject that was important for students to know. Most of the paragraphs were focused on one point, but there were no transitions between sentences and paragraphs, and most of the sentences were only an approximation of the ideas I was trying to express. As I typed, I **jotted down ideas** which I wanted to include but which at the moment were interrupting the idea I was currently working on. I gave no thought to punctuation or spelling. Getting ideas on paper was my top priority.

Day 2:

I printed a copy of the three pages of freewriting I had done the previous day and spent three hours revising: eliminating, adding, and moving passages; providing transitions; and rephrasing most of the sentences.

Day 3:

I spent one hour polishing my sentences but made no major additions or deletions in the content.

Day 4:

I spent one last hour on a final review of my sentences, revising only a few of them. I checked my spelling with the help of a computer program, which indeed turned up several misspellings. I also read carefully for homonyms—which no spellcheck program can catch. For example: *there* instead of *their, its* instead of *it's,* or *lose* instead of *loose.* Throughout this book, as you work on each writing assignment, you'll find suggestions for the essential process of **revision,** especially in Chapter 8.

As you can see, it took a total of seven hours to write three single-spaced, typed pages that will take most readers ten minutes to read. And still I was not finished. The next step was to give this draft to my co-author, who made further revisions. In Chapter 8, you will find an entire writing assignment devoted to revising one of the essays you considered finished. As Donald Murray notes in his essay on revision, "Most readers underestimate the amount of rewriting it usually takes to produce spontaneous reading." But we can take heart from novelist Kurt Vonnegut: "This is what I find most encouraging about the writing trades: They allow mediocre people who are patient and industrious to revise their stupidity, to edit themselves into something like intelligence."

Reason, Intuition, Imagination, and Metaphor

The heart has its reasons which reason knows nothing of.

—BLAISE PASCAL

While good critical thinking depends on reason and embraces scientific methods, it can also include intuition, imagination, and creativity as well as logic.

Our theory of critical thinking welcomes originality, encourages personal opinion, embraces creative thinking, and considers paradox and ambiguity to be central to thinking and writing well. Playwright Tony Kushner learned from his Columbia University Shakespeare professor that "everything in Shakespeare was paradoxical and contradictory." From this he began "to understand something about life, . . . that two opposites can exist simultaneously." He embraced the notion that epic theatre should present contradictions and thus encourage active critical thought.

The French philosopher Blaise Pascal, quoted above, declared that there were two extravagances: "to exclude reason and to admit only reason." Contemporary biologist Richard Dawkins, supporting this view, claims that scientists must also be poets and thinks that poets are well served by a knowledge of science. Poet John Ciardi joked about reason and the natural world:

Who could believe an ant in theory,
A giraffe in blueprint?
Ten thousand doctors of what's possible
Could reason half the jungle out of being.

Sometimes a **metaphor** (a figure of speech that helps us understand one thing in terms of another) can carry, through images and associations, an understanding beyond what explicit reasoning can convey. Seeing comparisons, exploring relationships, is fundamental to successful critical thinking.

In their book *Metaphors We Live By*, linguists George Lakoff and Mark Johnson point out how deeply dependent on metaphor we are when we think and speak, citing the relationship between the way we use the term *argument* and the metaphors of war associated with it. Here are a few of their examples.

He *attacked* every weak point in my argument.
He *shot down* all of my arguments.
His criticisms were *right on target*.

Politicians often turn to war metaphors to strengthen their arguments. A recent episode in the U.S. Senate led to attack metaphors. A "battle" developed between the Republicans and Democrats. They had a "field day" arguing over what some called the "nuclear option," and then compromising in what Senator Orrin Hatch called "a truce, not a treaty" but others saw as only a brief "cease fire." The images are clear.

Advertising frequently relies on metaphor to deliver its message. Look at the ad below and note all the words which support the war metaphor. The advertising industry knows the power of such metaphors, and the medical profession casts many of its approaches to disease in the same language. Strong metaphors create images often more powerful than simple presentation of facts.

CANCER.

IT'S A WAR.

THAT'S WHY WE'RE DEVELOPING 316 NEW WEAPONS.

America's pharmaceutical companies are developing 316 new medicines to fight cancer—the second leading cause of death in the United States. Gene therapies, "magic bullet" antibodies, and light-activated medicines are all new weapons in the high-tech, high-stakes war against cancer. Pharmaceutical company researchers have already discovered medicines that are allowing more and more cancer survivors to say, "I won the battle." We hope one day we can all say, "We won the war."

America's Pharmaceutical Companies

Leading the way in the search for cures

www.searchforcures.org

In the following poem, Richard Wilbur uses metaphor to describe his daughter's struggle to produce a story.

THE WRITER

In her room at the prow of the house
Where light breaks, and the windows are tossed with linden,
My daughter is writing a story.

I pause in the stairwell, hearing
From her shut door a commotion of typewriter-keys
Like a chain hauled over a gunwale.

Young as she is, the stuff
Of her life is a great cargo, and some of it heavy:
I wish her a lucky passage.

But now it is she who pauses,
As if to reject my thought and its easy figure.
A stillness greatens, in which

The whole house seems to be thinking,
And then she is at it again with a bunched clamor
Of strokes, and again is silent.

I remember the dazed starling
Which was trapped in that very room, two years ago;
How we stole in, lifted a sash

And retreated, not to affright it;
And how for a helpless hour, through the crack of the door,
We watched the sleek, wild, dark

And iridescent creature
Batter against the brilliance, drop like a glove
To the hard floor, or the desk-top,

And wait then, humped and bloody,
For the wits to try it again; and how our spirits
Rose when, suddenly sure,

It lifted off from a chair-back,
Beating a smooth course for the right window
And clearing the sill of the world.

It is always a matter, my darling,
Of life or death, as I had forgotten. I wish
What I wished you before, but harder.

EXERCISE 1E

Understanding Figurative Language

Consider this poem for a few minutes. To what two things does Wilbur compare the writing process? What do these images say about his view of the writing process?

Metaphors can provide a vivid means of probing and revealing ideas. The creative thinking we do when we compare one thing to another can lead to new understanding. When we think creatively about our writing process, we are likely to *see* our writing in fresh and instructive ways.

"I was on the cutting edge. I pushed the envelope. I did the heavy lifting. I was the rainmaker. Then I ran out of metaphors."

WRITING ASSIGNMENT 2

Your Writing Process

Write an essay in which you discuss your writing experiences and yourself as a writer. Describe in some detail your writing process and what you consider your strengths and weaknesses as a writer. Identify and explain a metaphor that describes your own writing process. Conclude with your thoughts about the value of writing well.

Begin this assignment by brainstorming or freewriting, then move on to a first draft. Delay organizing, revising sentences, and correcting errors until your first draft is complete.

Audience

Your primary audience for this assignment is your instructor, but you will also be an audience as you write your way to an understanding of yourself as a writer.

Purpose

To inform your instructor about your writing experiences and to gain insight into your particular writing process.

HE OR SHE?

You will notice that in our references to a writer or a student in this text, we use both female and male designations. This reflects not arbitrary choice but one of the ways writers today resolve the problem posed by the lack of a gender-neutral pronoun for the third person singular. This deficiency in our language reflects more than a simple inconvenience. The way we use language—the choices we make, the emphasis we place—suggests a broad range of personal and community attitudes, a world view, conscious and subliminal. A society described only in terms of masculine references assumes a world dominated by men. It is not surprising that as women began to share the public worlds of business, politics, medicine, art, and sport, the universal *he, him, his,* without the balance of *she, her, hers,* presented a bruising contradiction and a linguistic dilemma for writers and public speakers. Women were no longer willing to seem invisible.

Attempts to invent a new singular pronoun comparable to the helpful plural "they" to solve this problem have so far failed. In the meantime we are left with a number of choices. We must choose carefully on the basis of audience, purpose, circumstance, context, and, ultimately, personal inclination, all the time recognizing the implications of our choice.

Often we can use a plural noun to which the all-purpose plural pronouns—they, their, them—refer:

> **Writers** need to be aware of **their** audience when choosing language.

But when the noun we are referring to is singular, we have various choices:

> **Each** writer must consider the audience when making revisions.

> First, **he or she** must decide how much background information the particular audience will need.

> First, **he** must decide how much background information the particular audience will need. [This represents the traditional use of "he" as a referent for both males and females.]

First, *she* must decide how much background information the particular audience will need. [This choice redresses centuries of exclusion.]

Or we may sometimes drop the pronoun:

Each writer must consider the audience when revising a paper. [A simplification of ". . . when revising his/her paper."]

Many readers object to the awkwardness that multiple pronouns create in the flow of a sentence. But others are offended by the implicit sexism of relying exclusively on the third person masculine pronoun [*he, him, his*].

WHAT YOU CAN EXPECT FROM THIS BOOK

More Than One Approach

We explore a variety of strategies for expanding both writing and thinking skills, emphasizing the symbiotic relationship between them. We propose no formulas, no quick solutions. The writing assignments throughout this book aim to avoid rigid adherence to form. Contrary to the advice of many writing texts, assignments in real life are not limited to prescribed numbers of paragraphs or a required sequence of parts. Essays or reports, whether explanatory or persuasive, should be designed to communicate a writer's ideas in such a way that the writer's purpose is clear and logical and satisfies the needs of a particular audience or discipline.

Collaboration

With your instructor, you can work out collaborative approaches to many exercises and writing assignments. You will find that the more opportunities you have to work with classmates, the clearer your thinking is likely to become, and the more likely it will be that the assignments reflect the writing and problem solving you will encounter in the working world. Writing in the workplace more often than not requires collaboration with others. (This text, written by two authors, represents an example of such a collaboration.)

Sharpening Sentence Skills and Increasing Coherence

Throughout many of the chapters, you will find practice in sentence-building skills, simple review for some of you, new strategies for others. Ideas tend to travel in sentences, and the greater the fluency of your sentences, the better equipped you will be to express complex reasoning in cohesive, logical prose.

This is not a handbook of grammar and usage, but rather a carefully sequenced selection of **rhetorical strategies** selected to complement particular topics and issues. The logical relationships between ideas in a sentence and techniques for creating coherence come in Chapters 3, 4, and 8. These sentence skills may also be addressed on an individual basis as the need arises, not necessarily in the sequence given.

ENJOYING THE CHALLENGE OF THINKING AND WRITING

In his poem *The Four Quartets,* T. S. Eliot writes of the "intolerable wrestle / With words and meaning." But before you conclude that this whole enterprise is to be a bleak struggle, let us assure you that our goal is quite the contrary. Systematic thinking can be an adventure. Polishing your prose to convey your ideas precisely and logically can be enormously satisfying. Writer Isaac Asimov expresses such an outlook well:

> Thinking is the activity I love best, and writing to me is simply thinking through my fingers.

Our expectations are broad and flexible. What we ask is that you reflect on your ideas, support your opinions, and practice writing about them with care. We hope to foster fair and independent thinking, a capacity for empathy, and the ability to advocate your own ideas logically and fluently.

SUMMARY

This book emphasizes the relationship between thinking clearly and writing well and stresses the importance of expressing ourselves persuasively while thinking critically about what we read, view, and hear. As we think critically, we need to understand the world view of others and recognize our own world view.

When writing, we need to think about the **audience** and the **purpose** for which we are writing. For an essay to be successful, we need to follow a sequential writing process that avoids formulaic structure and doesn't rush directly to a finished draft. While our main concern is with analytical thinking and argument, we also embrace creative thought and the imagination.

KEY TERMS

Brainstorming   unrestrained, spontaneous generation of ideas.

Critical thinking   discerning or discriminating thought characterized by fairness, open-mindedness.

Freewriting   unrestrained, spontaneous, continuous generation of complete sentences for a set length of time.

Metaphor   figure of speech that imaginatively implies a comparison between one object and another.

World view   a set of assumptions about the world and the behavior of people in it.

CHAPTER 2

Inference—Critical Thought

Question

What do you infer from this cartoon?

"I knew the woodpeckers were a mistake."

Answer

A pair of woodpeckers pecked holes in Noah's Ark, and as a result, the boat is sinking. Though we do not see the woodpeckers, we know they are a pair as the pairs of giraffes, lions, horses, and other animals tell us whose boat this is. The cartoon's caption combined with the image of the sinking boat lead us to the conclusion that the woodpeckers are the culprits. We do not see them in action, but on the basis of the **evidence**, we make an **inference.**

WHAT IS AN INFERENCE?

An inference is a conclusion about the unknown made on the basis of the known. We see a car beside us on the freeway with several new and old dents; we infer that the driver must be a bad one. A close friend hasn't called in several weeks and doesn't return our calls when we leave messages; we infer that she is angry with us. Much of our thinking, whether about casual observations or personal relationships, involves making inferences. Indeed, entire careers are based on the ability to make logical inferences. In *Snow Falling on Cedars*, a novel by David Guterson, a coroner describes his job:

> It's my job to infer. Look, if a night watchman is struck over the head with a crowbar during the course of a robbery, the wounds you're going to see in his head will look like they were made with a crowbar. If they were made by a ball-peen hammer you can see that, too—a ball-peen leaves behind a crescent-shaped injury, a crowbar leaves, well, linear wounds with V-shaped ends. You get hit with a pistol butt, that's one thing; somebody hits you with a bottle, that's another. You fall off a motorcycle at 40 miles an hour and hit your head on gravel, the gravel will leave behind patterned abrasions that don't look like anything else. So yes, I infer from the deceased's wound that something narrow and flat caused his injury. To infer—it's what coroners do.

Such reasoning is the basis for the popular television series, *CSI: Crime Scene Investigation*, in which a team of investigators use cutting edge scientific tools to examine the evidence, make logical inferences and catch the killer. Critical thinking has always been an essential part of a good mystery.

How Reliable Is an Inference?

The reliability of inferences covers an enormous range. Some inferences are credible, but inferences based on minimal evidence or on evidence that may support many different interpretations should be treated with skepticism. In fact, the strength of an inference can be tested by the number of different explanations we can draw from the same set of facts. The greater the number of possible interpretations, the less reliable the inference.

In the cartoon, given the woodpeckers and the sinking boat, we can arrive at one inference only: the birds made holes in the boat. But the inferences drawn in the other two cases are less reliable. The driver of the dented car may not be the owner: She may have borrowed the car from a friend, or she may own the car but have recently bought it "as is." Our friend may not have called us for a number of reasons: a heavy work schedule, three term papers, a family crisis. She may not have received our messages. These alternate explanations weaken the reliability of the original inferences. Clearly, the more evidence we have to support our inferences and the fewer interpretations possible, the more we can trust their accuracy.

THE LANGUAGE OF INFERENCE

The verbs to infer and to imply are often confused, but they can be readily distinguished:

to imply: To suggest, indicate indirectly, hint, intimate; what a writer, speaker, action, or object conveys.

to infer: To arrive at a conclusion by reasoning from facts or evidence; what a reader, listener, or observer determines or concludes.

A writer, speaker, action, or object **implies** something, and readers, listeners, or observers **infer** what that something is. A final distinction: Only *people* (and animals) can make inferences; *anything* can imply meaning.

EXERCISE 2A

Interpreting a Cartoon

Quickly, determine the message the following cartoon implies. What inferences do you draw from the evidence given? After writing a short response, compare your interpretation with those of others in the class. Are they the same?

WHAT IS A FACT?

You're neither right nor wrong because others agree with you. You're right because your facts and reasoning are right.
—INVESTOR AND COLUMBIA PROFESSOR BEN GRAHAM TO CEO WARREN BUFFET

We make inferences based on our own observations or on the observations of others as they are presented to us through speech or print. These observations often consist of **facts, information that can be verified.** The boat is sinking. We see dents in the car. You have not spoken to your friend in several weeks. "A crowbar leaves linear wounds with V-shaped ends." Our own observations attest to the truth of these claims. But often we are dependent on others' observations about people, places, and events that we cannot directly observe. Take, for example, the claim that in Boston, on September 11, 2001, Mohamed Atta boarded a flight that flew into the World Trade Center. Few of us observed this action firsthand, but those who did reported it, and we trust the veracity of their reports. Books, newspapers, magazines, and television programs are filled with reports—facts—giving us information about the world that we are unable to gain from direct observation. If we doubt the truth of these claims, we usually can turn to other sources to verify or discredit them. As former United States Senator Daniel Patrick Moynihan stated, "Everyone is entitled to his own opinion, but not his own facts."

Facts and Journalism

In "The Facts of Media Life," Pulitzer prize winning journalist and former *New York Times* executive editor Max Frankel comments on the growing number of journalists, some of them well known, who have forgotten that verifiable facts are the foundation of good journalism.

The Facts of Media Life

In journalism, the highest truth is truth. Period.

The roster of fallen journalists grows apace: Stephen Glass, Mike Barnicle,   1
Patricia Smith, James Hirsch, a whole team of CNN investigators. But the
year's toll is proof not that many reporters often lie; it bespeaks a heroic battle by the news media to preserve the meaning of fact and the sanctity of
quotation marks. Reporters have been losing their jobs for committing fiction, a crime that is no crime at all in too many other media venues, notably
film and television docudramas.

While news teams root out the tellers of tall tales, the rest of our culture   2
argues that a good yarn justifies cutting corners, imagining dialogue, in-
venting characters and otherwise torturing truth.

What's wrong with a little mendacity—so goes the theory—to give a   3
tale velocity?

It is unforgivably wrong to give fanciful stories the luster of fact, or to   4
use facts to let fictions parade as truths.

Happily, journalism's infantry slogs on, struggling to distinguish fact   5
from fiction. It wants to preserve the thrills of reality and believes that readers deserve the honesty implicit in Frank McCourt's refusal to put quotation
marks around the reconstructed dialogue in his memoir of an Irish childhood, "Angela's Ashes."

It is a noble but uphill struggle. Admired intellectuals like Joyce Carol   6
Oates have scoffed at the distinction, observing that all language tends by
its nature to distort experience and that writing, being an art, "means artifice." But see how much she, too, values separating fact from fiction: Oates
defeats her own defense of artifice with the supporting observation that
Thoreau compressed two years into one in "Walden" and "lived a historical
life very different from the . . . monastic life he presents in his book." How
could she ever know in a world without fact?

Facts, unlike literature, do not promise truth. They only record what has   7
been seen and heard somehow, by someone, subject to all the frailties and
biases of their observers and interpreters. Yet they must be defended, particularly in a society that values freedom, because by definition, facts can be
challenged, tested, cross-examined. Wrong facts and the truths derived
from them are always correctable—with more facts. Fictional facts are forever counterfeit.

A film, *Shattered Glass*, has been made about Stephen Glass, one of the
"fallen journalists" identified by Frankel. The film depicts the rise and fall of
this *New Republic* reporter who also contributed stories to *Rolling Stone*. And
the list of "fallen journalists" continues to grow with the addition of Jayson
Blair of the *New York Times*, who filed dispatches from various locations when
he was actually in New York. He also fabricated comments and scenes as well
as taking material from other newspapers and wire services. Needless to say,
Blair lost his job as did one of his editors, and the reputation of our country's
most prestigious newspaper was damaged.

EXERCISE 2B

Questions for Discussion

1. What does Frankel mean by "the sanctity of quotation marks"? For
   more on this issue, see "plagiarism" in Chapter 9.

2. Why did author Frank McCourt refuse to put quotation marks around
   the dialogue in his childhood memoir, *Angela's Ashes*?

WHAT IS A JUDGMENT?

When we infer that the woodpeckers are sinking the boat, we laugh but are unlikely to express approval or disapproval. On the other hand, when we infer that the woman in the car in front of us is a poor driver, we express disapproval of her driving skills; we make a **judgment,** in this case a statement of disapproval. Or, when we infer from a friend's volunteer work with the homeless that she is an admirable person, we express our approval, that is, make a favorable judgment. **A judgment is also an inference, but although many inferences are free of positive or negative connotation, such as "I think it's going to rain," a judgment always expresses the writer's or speaker's approval or disapproval.**

Certain judgments are taken for granted, become part of a culture's shared belief system, and are unlikely to be challenged under most circumstances. For example, most of us would accept the following statements: "Taking the property of others is wrong" or "People who physically abuse children should be punished." But many judgments are not universally accepted without considerable well-reasoned support or may be rejected regardless of additional support and cogent reasoning. Frequently, a judgment is further complicated by potentially ambiguous language and even punctuation. Take, for example, the highly controversial wording of the Second Amendment to the Constitution:

Amendment II
A well-regulated militia, being necessary to the security of a free State, the right of the people to keep and bear arms, shall not be infringed.

Those in favor of gun control interpret this to mean that only "a well-regulated militia," not every individual, is guaranteed the right to bear arms. "Well-regulated" implies an official militia, not a private one free of government regulations. But those against gun control believe that the Second Amendment guarantees "the people," meaning all individuals, the right to bear arms. This ongoing controversy continues to defy resolution.

EXERCISE 2C

Distinguishing Between Facts, Inferences, and Judgments

A. Determine whether the following statements are facts (reports), inferences, or judgments and explain your reasoning. Note that some may include more than one, and some may be open to interpretation.

> *Example:* I heard on the morning news that the city subway system has ground to a halt this morning; many students will arrive late for class.

"I heard on the morning news that the city subway system has ground to a halt this morning."[**Fact:** I did hear it and the information can be verified.]

"Many students will arrive late for class." [**Inference:** This is a conclusion drawn from the information about the breakdown of the subway.]

1. The United States invaded Iraq in the spring of 2003.
2. Material on the Internet should not be censored by government or any other organization.
3. For sale: lovely three-bedroom house in forest setting, easy commute, a bargain at $475,000.
4. Forty-one percent of Californians who die are cremated—almost twice the national average of 21 percent.
5. Winslow Homer didn't begin to paint seriously until 1862.
6. Eric has a drinking problem.
7. Critic Ben Brantley called the latest production of Shakespeare's *As You Like It* "exhilarating."
8. After I took those vitamin pills recommended by the coach, I scored a touchdown. Those pills sure did the trick.

B. In this excerpt taken from a newspaper article, carefully distinguish those statements that are factual from those that are not.

On Wednesday, March 9, a Los Angeles court dismissed charges against two physicians who allowed a terminally ill patient to die.[1] For generations organized medicine has focused on saving lives, no matter what the price in emotional trauma, physical pain, or economic cost, because we are a death denying society.[2] But keeping people alive in the face of a painful death should not be inevitable, as Drs. White and Rosenbaum maintained when they shut off artifical life-support for their bain damaged patient at the urging of his family.[3] Although doctors and nurses should remain bound by some rules of law and ethics, they should be able to treat their patients in the most humane way possible as long as they have the informed consent of the patient or of his/her family if the patient can't give it.[4] Thus doctors should not be penalized for allowing a terminally ill patient's life to end mercifully, especially if the patient is clearly "brain dead."[5] The definition of "brain dead"remains a controversial issue but not one which should halt humane medical decisions.[6]

Overall, do you consider this article to be based on fact or judgment?

In what section of the newspaper would you expect to find this article?

EXERCISE 2D

Drawing Logical Inferences

Draw inferences from the following statistics and evaluate the relative reliability of your inferences.

NUMBERS

 $725 million Total fines the Justice Department levied on two of the world's largest drug companies for fixing vitamin prices

$1.4 billion Other antitrust fines collected by Justice since 1997

$95 million Annual budget for Justice's antitrust division

 $28.5 million Box-office receipts on the opening day of *Star Wars: Episode I*

$300 million Estimated cost to the economy of people's skipping work to see the movie

----

77% Proportion of parents surveyed who say they would like to use a V-chip to block TV programs, if they had one

2 Number of nationwide electronics chain stores that stopped selling V-chip decoder boxes, for lack of interest

----

 3% Teenage girls in Fiji with eating disorders in 1995, before TV arrived

15% Fijian girls with eating disorders three years after the islands got TV

Sources: Washington *Post*, CNN, AP, L.A. *Times*, Kaiser Foundation

BOB HAMBLY FOR TIME

EXERCISE 2E

Solving Riddles, Reading Poetry

Use your inferential skills to solve these riddles by English poet John Cotton:

1.
Insubstantial I can fill lives,
Cathedrals, worlds.
I can haunt islands,
Raise passions
Or calm the madness of kings.
I've even fed the affectionate.
I can't be touched or seen,
But I can be noted.

2.
We are a crystal zoo,
Wielders of fortunes,
The top of our professions.
Like hard silver nails
Hammered into the dark
We make charts for mariners.

3.
I reveal your secrets.
I am your morning enemy,
Though I give reassurance of presence.
I can be magic,
or the judge in beauty contests.
Count Dracula has no use for me.
When you leave
I am left to my own reflections.

4.
My tensions and pressures
Are precise if transitory.
Iridescent, I can float
And catch small rainbows.
Beauties luxuriate in me.
I can inhabit ovens
Or sparkle in bottles.
I am filled with that
Which surrounds me.

5.
Containing nothing
I can bind people forever,
Or just hold a finger.
Without end or beginning

I go on to appear in fields,
Ensnare enemies,
Or in another guise
Carry in the air
Messages from tower to tower.

6.
Silent I invade cities,
Blur edges, confuse travelers,
My thumb smudging the light.
I drift from rivers
To loiter in the early morning fields,
Until Constable Sun
Moves me on.
—JOHN COTTON, *THE TOTLEIGH RIDDLES, TIMES LITERARY SUPPLEMENT*

Now apply the same skills to these two poems by Sylvia Plath (1933–1963). What does each describe?

7.
I am silver and exact. I have no preconceptions.
Whatever I see I swallow immediately
Just as it is, unmisted by love or dislike.
I am not cruel, only truthful—
The eye of a little god, four-cornered.
Most of the time I meditate on the opposite wall.
It is pink, with speckles. I have looked at it so long
I think it is a part of my heart. But it flickers.
Faces and darkness separate us over and over.
Now I am a lake. A woman bends over me,
Searching my reaches for what she really is.
Then she turns to those liars, the candles or the moon.
I see her back, and reflect it faithfully.
She rewards me with tears and an agitation of hands.
I am important to her. She comes and goes.
Each morning it is her face that replaces the darkness.
In me she has drowned a young girl, and in me an old woman
Rises toward her day after day, like a terrible fish.

8.
I'm a riddle in nine syllables,
An elephant, a ponderous house,
A melon strolling on two tendrils.
O red fruit, ivory, fine timbers.
This loaf's big with its yeasty rising.
Money's new-minted in this fat purse.
I'm a means, a stage, a cow in calf.
I've eaten a bag of green apples,
Boarded the train there's no getting off.

Turn your inference skills to this more serious poem by Philip Levine. What question did the boy have? What answer does the man find?

ON ME!

In the next room his brothers are asleep,
the two still in school. They just can't wait
to grow up and be men, to make money.
Last night at dinner they sat across from him,
their brother, a man, but a man with nothing,
without money or the prospect of money.
He never pays, never tosses a bill
down on the bar so he can say, "On me!"
At four in the morning when he can't sleep,
he rehearses the stale phrase to himself
with a delicate motion of the wrist
that lets the bill float down. He can't pace
for fear of waking his mom who sleeps
alone downstairs in the old storage room
off the kitchen. When he was a kid, twelve
or fourteen, like his brothers, he never knew
why boys no older than he did the things
they did, the robberies, gang fights, ODs,
rapes, he never understood his father's wordless
rages that would explode in punches
and kicks, bottles, plates, glasses hurled
across the kitchen. The next morning would be
so quiet that from his room upstairs
he'd hear the broom-straws scratching the floor
as his mother swept up the debris and hear
her humming to herself. Now it's so clear,
so obvious he wonders why it took
so long for him to get it and to come of age.

ACHIEVING A BALANCE BETWEEN INFERENCE AND FACTS

We need to distinguish inferences, facts, and judgments from one another to evaluate as fairly as possible the events in our world. Whether these events are personal or global, we need to be able to distinguish between facts, verifiable information that we can rely on, and inferences and judgments, which may or may not be reliable.

We also need to evaluate the reliability of our own inferences. Are there other interpretations of the facts? Have we considered all other possible interpretations?

Do we need more information before drawing a conclusion? These are useful thinking skills that we need to practice, but how do these skills relate to writing? To answer that question, read the following paragraph and distinguish between statements of fact and inference.

> A white player's life in the National Basketball Association is a reverse-image experience all but unique in American culture. Although fewer than 13 percent of United States citizens are African-American, about 80 percent of the N.B.A.'s players are. Of the 357 players on N.B.A. rosters, 290 were African-American, including several of mixed descent. Every one of the league's 20 leading scorers was black, and all but 2 of its leading rebounders. Not one N.B.A. team has as many whites as blacks.
> —ADAPTED FROM "THE LONELINESS OF BEING WHITE" BY BRUCE SCHOENFELD

This paragraph contains one inference while the remaining statements are factual, capable of verification. Notice that the facts support and convince us of the inference.

INFERENCE	FACTS
A white player's life in the National Basketball Association is a reverse-image experience all but unique in American culture.	Although fewer than 13 percent of United States citizens are African-American, about 80 percent of the N.B.A.'s players are.
	Of the 357 players on N.B.A. rosters, 290 were African-American, including several of mixed descent.
	Every one of the league's 20 leading scorers was black, and all but 2 of its 20 leading rebounders.
	Not one N.B.A. team has as many whites as blacks.

Facts Only

> Now, what I want is Facts. Teach these boys and girls nothing but Facts. Facts alone are wanted in life. Plant nothing else, and root out everything else. You can only form the minds of reasoning animals upon Facts: nothing else will ever be of any service to them. This is the principle on which I bring up my own children, and this is the principle on which I bring up these children. Stick to Facts, sir!

So says Thomas Gradgrind in Charles Dickens' novel *Hard Times,* an indictment against Victorian industrial society. Dickens knew that facts alone do not make for a good education nor for good writing and thus gave that speech to an unsympathetic character. Expository writing frequently consists of a blend of inference and fact, with the one supporting the other. If you were to write a paper consisting only of facts, it would be of no interest to the reader because reading facts that lead nowhere, that fail to support a conclusion, is like reading the telephone book. Jeff Jarvis, a book reviewer for the *New York Times Book Review,* comments on the dangers of this kind of writing:

> Objectivity, in some quarters, means just the facts, ma'am—names, dates, and quotations dumped from a notebook onto the page. But facts alone, without perspective, do not tell a story. Facts alone, without a conclusion to hold them together, seem unglued. Facts alone force writers to use awkward transitions, unbending formats or simple chronologies to fend off disorganization.

A facts-only approach can also have serious consequences in our schools' textbooks. A recent report on public education cites such facts-only textbooks as one of the causes of students' lack of interest and poor achievement.

> Elementary school children are stuck with insipid books that "belabor what is obvious" even to first graders. At the high school level, history—or "social studies"—texts are crammed with facts but omit human motivations or any sense of what events really meant.

Keep the danger of a facts-only approach in mind when you are assigned a research paper. Do not assume that teachers are looking exclusively for well-documented facts; they also want to see what you make of the data, what conclusions you draw, what criticisms and recommendations you offer. Do not fall into the trap of one eager young college freshman, Charles Renfrew, who, proud of his photographic memory, expected high praise from a distinguished philosophy professor for a paper on Descartes. He suffered disappointment but learned a lasting lesson when he read the comment: "Too much Descartes, not enough Renfrew." A photographic memory for factual information can be an asset, but your own inferences and judgments fully explained are also important. Don't leave your readers asking "so what?" when they finish your paper. Tell them.

Selecting Facts

Equally important when considering the facts you use in your papers is your selection of which facts to include and which to omit. When we omit relevant facts, we may be reflecting personal, political, or cultural biases and in the process distorting "reality." The omission of certain facts from accounts of historical events can have serious consequences, in small ways and large. African American writer Audre Lorde, in her book *Zami: A New Spelling of My Name,* illustrates this point eloquently:

> I had spent four years at Hunter High School, with the most academically advanced and intellectually accurate education available for "preparing young women for college and career." I had been taught by some of the most highly considered historians in the country. Yet, I had never once heard the name mentioned of the first man to fall in the American revolution [Crispus Attucks], nor even been told that he was a Negro. What did that mean about the history I had learned?

Lorde is illustrating what others in recent decades have noted. For example, Harvey Wasserman's *History of the United States* and Frances Fitzgerald's *America Revised: History Schoolbooks in the Twentieth Century* explore the ways in which historians, through a systematic selection process, have distorted history. (Some would say Wasserman also distorts history in his efforts to right past wrongs.)

Inferences Only

It is possible to err in another direction as well; a paper consisting only of inferences and judgments would bore and antagonize readers as they search for the basis of our claims, the facts to support our opinions. In his recent biography of William Shakespeare, *Will in the World*, noted scholar Stephen Greenblatt irritated some Shakespeare authorities and other readers by drawing on a sketchy collection of facts to reconstruct the life of the great playwright about whom little is known. Greenblatt tells a good story, but are his inferences supported by the facts?

For example, in trying to create a childhood love of the theatre for Shakespeare, Greenblatt cites the surviving record of another man of Shakespeare's time, Willis, who, at a young age, went with his father to the theatre in Gloucester, where the boy stood "between his [father's] legs." Greenblatt adds to this testament the fact that Shakespeare's father, the mayor of Stratford, thirty miles from Gloucester, hired players when his son would have been five, and concludes that Shakespeare, too, must have gone as a child to the theatre. "When the bailiff [or mayor] walked into the hall, everyone would have greeted him. . . . His son, intelligent, quick, and sensitive, would have stood between his father's legs. For the first time in his life William Shakespeare watched a play." Notice the shift from the qualifier "would" to direct assertion. But are the facts sufficient to support his inference? One critic would certainly answer in the negative. Oxford professor Richard Jenkyns ridicules Greenblatt's reasoning: "Some people have birthmarks, and so Shakespeare may have had one."

READING CRITICALLY

Finally, distinguishing between facts, inferences, and judgments and evaluating their reliability allow us to analyze information, to read critically as writers, as consumers, as voters. Whether it is an article we find on the Internet, an auto salesperson, or a political candidate, we need to be able to separate facts from judgments and to ask that the judgments offered be supported by the facts. If we read or listen without these distinctions in mind, we are susceptible to false claims and invalid arguments, often with serious consequences for us as individuals and for society as a whole.

EXERCISE 2F

Thinking Critically About Your Own Thinking

Write a paragraph or two about a recent inference you've made. Include what facts the inference was based on and why you made it. Discuss with your classmates whether the inference was logical given the facts that led to it, whether others might have made a different inference from the same data, and why they might have done so.

WRITING ASSIGNMENT 3

Reconstructing the Lost Tribe

"When we first started seeing each other, we would always use the same word for snow."

The cartoon above refers to the fact Eskimos have many words for snow, their vocabulary reflecting their environment. Similarly, the Hmong of Laos have many words for mountains—their shapes, slopes, and elevations—to describe their environment. As anthropologist Clyde Kluckhohn points out, "Every language is a special way of looking at the world and interpreting experience. Concealed in the structure of language are a whole set of unconscious assumptions about the world and the life in it." Simply put, a language reflects its culture.

With that idea in mind, imagine that a previously unknown civilization has been discovered and that linguistic anthropologists, after observing the civilization for a while, have delineated the following characteristics about the society's language:

> Three words for terrain, designating "absolutely flat," "rolling," and "slightly hilly."

> No word for ocean.

Dozens of terms for grains, including eight for wheat alone.

Several words for children, some of which translate as "wise small one," "innocent leader," and "little stargazer."

Seven terms to describe the stages of life up to puberty, only one term to describe life from puberty to death.

The word for sex translates as "to plant a wise one."

Terms for woman are synonymous with "wife and mother."

Terms for man are synonymous with "husband and father."

Twenty words for book.

No words for violent conflict or war.

Nine words for artist.

Terms for praise translate as "peacemaker" and "conciliator."

Words designating cow, pig, calf, and sheep but no terms for beef, pork, veal, leather, or mutton.

Several words for precipitation, most translating as "rain," only one meaning "snow."

Several words for leader but all are plural.

Four words meaning theatre.

The Topic

Write an essay in which you characterize the society that uses this language. (Consider giving a name to this tribe to help focus your sentences.)

As you analyze the characteristics of the language, you will be reconstructing a culture. Obviously, because the data are limited, you will have to make a few educated guesses and qualify conclusions carefully. ("Perhaps," "possibly," "one might conclude," "the evidence suggests," and similar hedges will be useful.)

The Approach

Examine and group the data; look for patterns.

Draw inferences, depending only on the data given.

Cite evidence to support these inferences—be sure to base all your conclusions on the linguistic evidence provided. Do not draw inferences that you don't support with specific examples. **Be sure to use all the data.** Explain your line of reasoning—how and why the data lead to the inferences you have made.

Don't simply write a narration or description based on the information. A narrative or story will only imply the conclusions you have arrived at from examining the data. This can be enjoyable to write and entertaining to read and certainly requires critical thinking, as does all good fiction. But your purpose here is to explain why you have made the inferences you have and to back up your inferences with facts drawn from the language list.

The Structure

The **opening section** of any essay must provide readers with the necessary **background information** so that they can understand what you are doing and what you are going to say. In this case: What information do you have? How have you come by this information? What are you going to attempt to do with this information? What principle concerning language and society are you going to base your conclusions on?

Each **supporting paragraph** should deal with one distinct aspect of the civilization. Arrange the paragraphs so you can move smoothly from one paragraph to the next.

Some possibilities for the **conclusion** of the essay: What general conclusion(s) can you come to about this society based on the more specific conclusions you have presented in the supporting paragraphs? Is there any overall point you want to make about this society?

OR

What do you find admirable about this society? Do you have any criticisms of the society?

OR

Do you have any questions about the society?

Of course, the conclusion can deal with more than one of these possibilities.

Audience and Purpose

You have a wide range of possibilities here; we leave the choice to you. Your paper may assume the form of a report, scholarly or simply informative, directed to any audience you choose. It may be a letter to a personal friend or fictional colleague. It may be a traditional essay for an audience unfamiliar with the assignment, explaining what the language tells us about the people who use or used it. **What is crucial for success is that you, as the reporter-writer, assume that *you have not seen this tribe and have no firsthand evidence of it. You will also assume that your reader does not have a copy of this assignment;* it is up to you to cite all the specific evidence (the terms given in the list) to justify your inferences.**

MAKING INFERENCES—ANALYZING IMAGES

When you support a judgment with factual evidence and reasoning, you are mounting an argument, as we explain in more detail in Chapter 3. But it is also possible to persuade with **visual images.** Increasingly, we live in a world of intense visual stimulation. Television, computers, printed media, billboards—we are surrounded by pictorial impressions designed to persuade, telling us what to buy, what to think, how to vote. Pictures in the news, entertainment visuals, advertising, all play significant roles in our culture. Thus it is important that we train ourselves in media literacy—to interpret visual images in much the same way that we develop our skills in making inferences as we read printed texts.

In the cartoons you looked at earlier in this chapter, we discussed the ways in which the illustrator led you to make inferences, to reach a conclusion that was implied by the picture. In a similar way, a news photo on the front page of a newspaper may suggest a particular way to interpret an event or view a political figure. Photos of war scenes often carry an antiwar message or promote one side in the conflict over another. Pictures of starving children may plead for humanitarian aid. An unflattering photo of a political candidate may be chosen to discourage voters.

In advertising, the visual image often provides the evidence leading to an inference which carries a judgment: a product is better than others of its kind. The judgment is sometimes obvious, sometimes implicit. This holds true whether you're reading a magazine, noting a billboard as you drive, or viewing commercials on television or a Web page. Figuring out the underlying suggestive messages of a product can be fun as well as instructive.

When you see an image of a luxury car speeding up a steep mountain road surrounded by gorgeous scenery, it doesn't take you long to realize that the auto company is suggesting you should buy their model because it is powerful and beautiful and will take you to dramatic places at a thrilling speed. Most of us drive cars. Most of us would willingly be transported to such a world.

When a beer commercial excites your interest with glamorous models having fun and scarcely mentions the brand, the argument is more subtly suggestive. Some ads are so subtle that you are left wondering what the product is or exactly how the image relates to the product. The hope here is usually that the inference is subliminal, below the viewer's conscious reasoning, the argument indirect. But with careful analysis, you can evaluate the visual clues and infer the message. A number of companies refused our requests to use their ads in this text. Can you figure out why? We appreciate those who cooperated and wonder why others wouldn't rejoice over multiple copies of free advertising.

In the following ad, note how the product name, Pirelli (tires made in Italy), is reduced to a small corner. It is the image that carries the message. Even if you don't recognize the geography of Rio de Janeiro with its harbor and wide bay, or Brazil's famous soccer player, Ronaldo, standing in for the statue of Christ the Redeemer, which presides on the mountain top above the city, you can see a figure of tremendous power filling the foreground, towering over an impressive landscape. With arms outspread, he suggests control of this landscape, a godlike figure dominating the world, as reassuring as he is powerful. The picture itself is arresting, catching a reader's attention even before he has a chance to read the caption. Were you able to see the picture in color, you would recognize a mystical light emanating from the figure, the whole scene bathed in a warm reddish glow. The image is one of inspiration—inspiring both power and control, underscoring the combination of power and control any driver would want in a tire.

POWER IS NOTHING WITHOUT CONTROL.

EXERCISE 2G

Making Inferences About Visual Images

1. In a paragraph or two put your inferential skills to work by analyzing the following two advertisements. For each ad, fully explain exactly how the advertisers are using the visual images to make their arguments and sell their products. Do you find the ads effective? Why or why not?

2. Find a magazine or Web page ad that persuades with visual images and write an analysis of it. Attach the ad or a copy of it to your response. You may have a chance in class to try out your choice on classmates and see if they reach the same conclusion you do. If they don't, what does it say about the effectiveness of the ad?

3. Select a news photo that implies a judgment of an event or a prominent political or sports figure in a current newspaper or news magazine. Write a paragraph in which you discuss the editor's choice of photo. What is he implying with this choice?

He's relaxed. He's insured by Chubb.™

< CHUBB COMMERCIAL INSURANCE

< CHUBB SPECIALTY INSURANCE

< CHUBB PERSONAL INSURANCE

Worth magazine called Chubb "the gold standard for property-casualty insurance... Chubb's best feature is a three-decade history of swiftly paying claims that other companies might balk at."

Chubb refers to the insurers of the Chubb Group of Insurance Companies.
Actual coverage is subject to the language of the policies as issued. Chubb, Box 1615, Warren, NJ 07061 1615
2003 Chubb & Son, a division of Federal Insurance Company. All rights reserved.

For more information, consult your independent agent, or visit us at www.chubb.com and click on "Find an agent."

MAKING INFERENCES—
WRITING ABOUT FICTION

Many students are intimidated by assignments that require them to write about a poem, play, short story, or novel. What can they say about a piece of literature? Isn't there a right answer known to the author and the teacher but not to them?

Fiction is implicit; it does not explain explicitly. Writers of fiction—through character, plot, setting, theme, point of view, symbolism, irony, and imagery—imply meaning. Fiction is oblique. The work implies meaning; you infer what that meaning is. As you can see, interpreting literature requires critical thinking; it asks you to make inferences about the meaning of the work and to support these inferences with details from it as you have done with cartoons, statistics, poems, and ads earlier in this chapter.

Reading is the making of meaning, and the meaning we make depends on who we are. Our sex, age, ethnicity, culture, and experience all influence our reading. Given the multiple interpretations possible, there is not a single right answer but only well-supported inferences that add up to a logical interpretation.

A final point: A critical essay is not a continuation of class discussion but a formal piece of writing that can stand on its own apart from the class. To accomplish this, you may think of your audience as one who is not familiar with the work you are writing about. This does not require you to retell every detail of the piece, but it ensures that you include the relevant details, the facts, on which your inferences are based rather than assume your reader knows them.

The next two assignments will give you ample opportunity to practice the skill of reading closely and thinking critically while making and supporting inferences about literature. The two stories on which the assignments are based are both quite short, so regardless of the one chosen by your instructor, you may want to read both and see how you do.

EXERCISE 2H

Making Inferences About Fiction

Read *Grace Period* by Will Baker and then explain the meaning of the title. Support your answer, your judgment, with facts, details taken from the story.

Grace Period

WILL BAKER

You notice first a difference in the quality of space. The sunlight is still   1
golden through the dust hanging in the driveway, where your wife pulled out a few minutes ago in the Celica on a run to the mailbox, and the sky is still a regular blue, but it feels as if for an instant everything stretched just slightly, a few millimeters, then contracted again.

You shut off the electric hedge trimmers, thinking maybe vibration is af-   2
fecting your inner ear. Then you are aware that the dog is whining from under the porch. On the other hand you don't hear a single bird song. A semi
shifts down with a long backrap of exhaust on the state highway a quarter
mile away. A few inches above one horizon an invisible jet is drawing a thin
white line across the sky.

You are about to turn the trimmers on again when you have the star-   3
tling sense that the earth under your feet has taken on a charge. It is not
quite a trembling, but something like the deep throb of a very large dy-
namo at a great distance. Simultaneously there is a fluctuation of light, a
tiny pulse, coming from behind the hills. In a moment another, and then
another. Again and more strongly you have the absurd sense that everything inflates for a moment, then shrinks.

Your heart strikes you in the chest then, and you think instantly   4
aneurysm! You are 135 over 80, and should have had a checkup two
months ago. But no, the dog is howling now, and he's not alone. The
neighbors' black lab is also in full cry, and in the distance a dozen others
have begun yammering.

You stride into the house, not hurrying but not dawdling either, and   5
punch in the number of a friend who lives in the city on the other side of
the hills, the county seat. After the tone dance a long pause, then a busy
signal. You consider for a moment, then dial the local volunteer fire chief,
whom you know. Also busy.

Stretching the twenty-foot cord, you peer out the window. This time the   6
pulse is unmistakable, a definite brightening of the sky to the west, and
along with it a timber somewhere in the house creaks. You punch the Sheriff.
Busy. Highway Patrol. Busy. 911. Busy. A recorded voice erupts, strident and
edged with static, telling you all circuits are busy.

You look outside again and now there is a faint shimmering in the air.   7
On the windowsill outside, against the glass, a few flakes of ash have settled.
KVTX. Busy. The *Courier*. Busy. On some inexplicable frantic whim you dial
out of state, to your father-in-law (Where is your wife, she should have the
mail by now?) who happens to be a professor of geology on a distinguished
faculty. The ringing signal this time. Once. Twice. Three times. A click.

"Physical plant."   8

Doctor Abendsachs, you babble, you wanted Doctor Abendsachs.   9

"This is physical plant, buddy. We can't connect you here."   10

What's going on, you shout, what is happening with the atmosphere—   11

He doesn't know. They are in a windowless basement. Everything fine   12
there. It's lunchtime and they are making up the weekly football pool.

It is snowing lightly now outside, on the driveway and lawn and   13
garage. You can see your clippers propped pathetically against the hedge.
Once more, at top speed, you punch your father-in-law's number. Again a
ringing. A click.

This time a recording tells you that all operators are busy and your call   14
will be answered by the first available. The voice track ends and a burst of

music begins. It is a large studio orchestra, heavy on violins, playing a version of "Hard Day's Night." At the point where the lyrics would be "sleeping like a log" the sound skips, wobbles, and skips again as if an old-fashioned needle has been bumped from a record groove.

You look out the window once more, as the house begins to shudder, and   15
see that it is growing brighter and brighter and brighter.

WRITING ASSIGNMENT 4

Interpreting Fiction

Read the short story, "Hostess," by Donald Mangum, and write an essay based on the inferences you make about the narrator. Include the facts on which these inferences are based and an explanation of why you made such inferences.

Audience

Someone who has not read the story.

Purpose

To read closely and characterize the hostess—what kind of woman is she?

Hostess

DONALD MANGUM

My husband was promoted to crew chief, and with the raise we moved into   1
a double-wide, just up the drive. Half the park came to the house-warming. Well, Meg drank herself to tears and holed up on the toilet, poor thing. "Meg? Hon?" I said from the hall. "You going to live?" She groaned some-thing. It was seeing R.L. with that tramp down in 18 that made her do this to herself. Now there was a whole line of beer drinkers doing the rain dance out in the hall, this being a single-bath unit. I was the hostess, and I had to do something. "Sweetheart," I said, knocking. "I'm going to put you a bowl on the floor in the utility room." The rest of the trailer was carpeted.

Dale, my husband, was in the kitchen with an egg in his hand, squeezing   2
it for all he was worth. Veins stuck out everywhere on his arm. Paul and Eric were laughing. "What's going on in here?" I said.

Dale stopped squeezing and breathed. "I got to admit," he said, "I never   3
knew that about eggs." I could have kicked him when he handed Paul five dollars. I found the bowl I was after, plus a blanket, and took care of Meg.

Then Hank and Boyce almost got into a fight over a remark Hank made   4
about somebody named Linda. They had already squared off outside when it came out that Hank was talking about a Linda *Stillman,* when Boyce thought he meant a Linda *Faye.* Well, by that time everybody was ready for something, so the guys agreed to arm-wrestle. Hank won, but only because Boyce started laughing when Kathy Sueanne sat in Jason's supper and Jason

got madder than Kathy Sueanne did because there wasn't any more potato salad left.

You won't believe who showed up then. R.L.! Said he was looking for 5
Meg. "You think she wants to see you, R.L.?" I said. "After what you did to her with that trash Elaine?" So he said he'd only kissed Elaine a couple of times. "Or not even that," he said. "She was the one kissed *me*."

"You know what you can kiss," I said. He stood there looking like some 6
dog you'd just hauled off and kicked for no good reason. "Well, come on," I said, taking him by the shirt. I led him to the utility room to show him the condition he'd driven his darling to. I'm here to say, when R.L. saw that precious thing curled up in front of the hot-water heater he sank to his knees in shame. I just closed the door.

Back in the den, there was this Australian kangaroo giving birth on the 7
television. The little baby kangaroo, which looked sort of like an anchovy with legs, had just made it out of its mama and was crawling around looking for her pouch. The man on the show said it had about ten minutes to get in there and find a teat or it would die. He said a lot of them don't make it. I got so wrought up watching that trembly little fellow that I started cheering him on. So did everyone else. Well, to everyone's relief, the little thing made it. Then Gus wanted to know why everyone over there always called each other Mike. Nobody had any idea.

Eric ate a whole bunch of dried cat food before figuring out what it was 8
and that somebody had put it in the party dish as a joke. He tried to act like it didn't bother him, but he didn't stay too long after that. Melinda went out to her car for cigarettes, and a yellow jacket stung her behind the knee, so when she came in howling, Rod slapped this wad of chewing tobacco on the spot to draw out the poison, which made her howl even louder, till I washed it off and applied meat tenderizer and let her go lie in the guest bed for a while.

That's when something strange happened. The phone started ringing, 9
and I ran back to get it in Dale's and my bedroom, which was the closest to quiet in the trailer. I answered and just got this hollow sound at first, like you get with a bad connection over long-distance.

There was a mumble, then a woman's voice said, "She's gone." I didn't 10
recognize the voice, but I was sure what "gone" meant by the way she said it. It meant someone had died. Then she said—and she almost screamed it—"Someone should have been here. Why weren't you and Clarence here?"

Now, I don't know a soul in this world named Clarence, and this was 11
clearly a case of the wrong number. "Ma'am," I said as gently as I knew how.

"You'll have to talk louder," she said. "I can hardly hear you." 12

I curled my hand around my lips and the mouthpiece and said, 13
"Ma'am, you have dialed the wrong number."

"Oh, God, I'm sorry," she said. "Oh dear God." And here is the strange 14
thing. The woman did not hang up. She just kept saying, "Dear God" and crying.

I sat there listening to that woman and to all the happy noise coming   15
from everywhere in the trailer and through the window from outside, and
when she finally brought it down to a sniffle I said, "Honey, who was it that
passed away?"

"My sister," she said. "My sister, Beatrice." And it was like saying the   16
name started her to sobbing again.

"And none of your people are there?" I said.   17

"Just me," she said.   18

"Sweetheart, you listen to me," I said, trying to close the window for   19
more quiet. Sweet Christ, I thought. Dear sweet Christ in Heaven. "Are you
listening, angel? You should not be alone right now. You understand what
I'm telling you?" I said, "Now, I am right here."

EXERCISE 21

Analyzing a Film

As a final exercise in making and supporting inferences, rent the John Sayles
film *Limbo*. The conclusion of the movie is open to interpretation; members of
the audience are left to decide for themselves if the three individuals stranded
on the island are rescued or murdered. What do you think? Write a short paper
explaining your answer, citing as evidence specific details from the movie.

SUMMARY

In order to interpret the world around us and write effectively about it,
we need to be able to distinguish **facts, inferences,** and **judgments**
from one another and to evaluate the reliability of our inferences.

In written exposition and argument, and in the interpretation of visual images, literature, and film, it is important to achieve a balance
between fact and inference, to support our inferences with facts and
reasoning.

KEY TERMS

Facts   information that can be verified.

Inference   a conclusion about something we don't know based on what we
do know.

Judgment   an inference that expresses either approval or disapproval.

CHAPTER 3

The Structure of Argument

You always hurt the one you love!

In logic, an argument is not a fight but a rational piece of discourse, written or spoken, that attempts to persuade the reader or listener to believe something. For instance, we can attempt to persuade others to believe that cutting old timber will harm the environment or that a vote for a particular candidate will ensure a better city government. Though many arguments are concerned with political issues, arguments are not limited to such topics. We can argue about books, movies, athletic teams, and cars, as well as about abstractions found in philosophical and political issues. Whenever we want to convince someone else of the "rightness" of our position by offering reasons for that position, we are presenting an argument.

What is the difference between an argument and an opinion? When we offer our own views on an issue we are expressing an **opinion.** We all have them. We all should have them. But we should also recognize the difference between voicing an opinion and developing an argument. Someone might insist that using animals for medical research is wrong; a research physician might respond that this attitude is misguided. Both are expressing opinions. If they both stick to their guns but refuse to elaborate on their positions, then each may simply dismiss the opponent's statement as "mere opinion," as nothing more than an emotional reaction. If, on the other hand, they start to offer reasons in support of their opinions, then they have moved the discussion to an argument. The critic might add that animals suffer pain in much the same way that humans do, and thus experiments inflict cruel suffering on the animals. The physician might respond that modern techniques have greatly reduced animal suffering and that such experiments are necessary for medical breakthroughs. They are now offering support for their opinions. Don't be afraid of your opinions. Just be prepared to defend them with good reasoning. Think of opinions as starting points for arguments.

PREMISES AND CONCLUSIONS

The structure of all arguments, no matter what the subject, consists of two components: **premises** and **conclusions.** The **conclusion** is the key assertion that the other assertions support. These other assertions are the **premises,** reasons that support the conclusion. For example:

> Because state lotteries generate much-needed funds for public education, North Carolina should adopt its own lottery.

In this example, the conclusion—that North Carolina should adopt a state lottery—is supported by one premise: that state lotteries generate much-needed funds for public education.

For a group of assertions to be an argument, the passage must contain both these elements—**a conclusion and at least one premise.**

Now look at the same argument with an additional premise added:

> Because state lotteries generate much-needed funds for public education and because our neighboring states have lotteries which attract money from our state, North Carolina should adopt its own lottery.

Which argument do you think is stronger?

Now look at the following letter to the editor of a news magazine:

I was horrified to read "Corporate Mind Control" and learn that some companies are training employees in New Age thinking, which is a blend of the occult, Eastern religions, and a smattering of Christianity. What they're dealing with is dangerous—Krone Training will be disastrous to the company and the employee.

This writer thinks that she has written an argument against Krone Training, but her letter consists of a conclusion only, which is in essence that Krone Training is not a good idea. Because she fails to include any premises in support of her conclusion, she fails to present an argument and fails to convince anyone who did not already share her belief that Krone Training is "dangerous" and "disastrous." A conclusion repeated in different words may look like an argument but shouldn't deceive a careful reader. (See Chapter 6 for more on fallacious, or deceptive, arguments.) Can you formulate a premise that would transform the letter into an argument?

DISTINGUISHING BETWEEN PREMISES AND CONCLUSIONS

In order to evaluate the strength of an argument, we need to understand its structure, to distinguish between its premises and conclusion. **Joining words**—conjunctions and transitional words and phrases—indicate logical relationships between ideas and therefore often help us to make this distinction. Notice the radical change in meaning that results from the reversal of two clauses joined by the conjunction "because":

I didn't drink because I had problems. I had problems because I drank.

—BARNABY CONRAD

The use of joining words in argument is especially important because they indicate which assertions are being offered as premises and which are offered as conclusions. For example:

Instead of building another bridge across the bay to alleviate traffic congestion, we should develop a ferry system **because** such a system would decrease air pollution as well as traffic congestion.

A ferry system would decrease air pollution as well as traffic congestion, **so** we should develop a ferry system rather than build another bridge.

In the first example, "because" indicates a premise, a reason in support of the conclusion that creating a ferry system makes more sense than building a bridge. In the second example, "so" indicates the conclusion. Both statements present essentially the same argument; the difference between the two sentences is rhetorical—a matter of style, not substance.

"Because" and "since" frequently introduce premises. "So," "therefore," "thus," "hence," and "consequently" often introduce conclusions.

> *conclusion* because *premise*
>
> *premise* therefore *conclusion*
>
> *Note:* "and" often connects premises.

STANDARD FORM

With the help of joining words and transitional phrases, we can analyze the structure of an argument and then put it into **standard form.** An argument in standard form is an argument reduced to its essence: its premises and conclusion. In other words, it is an outline of the argument. In the previous argument on state lotteries, each premise is indicated by the "because" that introduces it, the conclusion then following from these two premises. In standard form, the argument looks like this:

Premise 1   State lotteries generate much-needed funds for public education.

Premise 2   Neighboring states have lotteries which attract money from our state.

∴ North Carolina should adopt its own lottery.

Note: ∴ is a symbol in logic meaning "therefore."

Read this argument about college grading policies taken from a *New York Times* editorial by Clifford Adelman, a senior research analyst with the Department of Education.

> If there are 50 ways to leave your lover, there are almost as many ways to walk away from a college course without penalty. What are prospective employers to make of the following "grades" that I have seen on transcripts: W, WP, WI, WX, WM, WW, K, L, Q, X and Z. What does "Z" mean? "The student 'zeed out,' " one registrar told me. At another institution, I was told that it stood for "zapped." Despite the zap, I was informed, there was no penalty.
>
> But there is a penalty. The time students lose by withdrawing is time they must recoup. All they have done is increase the cost of school to themselves, their families and, if at a public institution, to taxpayers.

This increasing volume of withdrawals and repeats does not bode well for students' future behavior in the workplace, where repeating tasks is costly. Many employers agree that work habits and time-management skills are as important as the knowledge new employees bring. It wouldn't take much for schools to change their grading policies so that students would have to finish what they start.

Though this argument is three paragraphs long, in standard form it can be reduced to four sentences:

Premise 1   The time students lose by withdrawing is time they must recoup.

Premise 2   They increase the cost of school to themselves, their families, and, if at a public institution, to taxpayers.

Premise 3   Work habits and time-management skills are as important as the knowledge new employees bring to the workplace.

∴ Schools should change their grading policies so that students would have to finish what they start.

The first paragraph provides the reader with necessary background information because the writer can't assume that his readers will know the specifics of current college grading policies. The second paragraph contains two of his three premises, while the final paragraph contains his third premise (and development of that premise) and his conclusion.

The conclusion of this argument—that schools should change their grading policy—is an inference, a judgment. Indeed, all conclusions are inferences. If they were facts we would not need to supply premises to support them; we would simply verify them by checking the source. In this argument, the first two premises are factual and the third is an inference, one that, on the basis of experience, most of us would be inclined to accept.

Examine the following argument:

Baseball fans have long argued that the city should build a downtown baseball stadium. If the city doesn't build a new stadium the team may leave, and a major city deserves a major league team. Furthermore, downtown's weather is superior to the wind of the present site, and public transportation to downtown would make the park more accessible.

In this example, four separate premises are offered for the conclusion.

Premise 1   If the city doesn't build a new stadium, the team may leave.

Premise 2   A major city deserves a major league team.

Premise 3   Downtown's weather is superior to the wind of the present site.

Premise 4   Public transportation to downtown would make the park more accessible.

∴ The city should build a downtown baseball stadium.

EXERCISE 3 A

Reducing Simple Arguments to Standard Form

Put each of the following arguments into standard form by first circling the joining words and transitional phrases, then identifying the conclusion, and finally identifying the premises. List the premises, numbering each separate statement, and write the conclusion using the symbol ∴. Leave out the joining words and phrases, because standard form identifies premises and conclusions, but write each premise and the conclusion as a complete sentence.

> *Example:* All politicians make promises they can't keep, and Jerry is nothing if not a politician. He will, therefore, make promises he can't keep.

1. All politicians make promises they can't keep.
2. Jerry is a politician.
   ∴ He will make promises he can't keep.

1. Because technical jobs are increasing more rapidly than other jobs, American high schools need to collaborate with industry in apprenticeship programs for those students who do not plan to attend college.

2. Because school vouchers would undermine public schools, permit discrimination, and transfer taxpayer money to those who need it least, private school parents, voters should not pass such legislation.

3. The student union building is ugly and uncomfortable. The preponderance of cement makes the building appear cold and gray both inside and out. Many of the rooms lack windows, so that one is left staring at the cement wall. The chairs are generally cheap and uncomfortable, while the poor lighting makes studying difficult, and the terrible acoustics make conversations almost impossible.

4. Abortion raises important moral questions, for abortion involves both a woman's right to privacy and the question of when life begins, and anything that involves personal rights and the onset of life raises serious moral questions.

5. Many biologists and gynecologists argue that life does not begin at conception. And the Supreme Court ruled in 1973 that to restrict a woman's right to have an abortion violates her right to privacy. These two facts lead us to believe that abortion should remain a woman's choice.

6. Capital punishment is not justified since with capital punishment, an innocent person might be executed, and no practice that might kill innocent people is justified.

7. Because some killers are beyond rehabilitation, society should have the right to execute those convicted of first-degree murder. More uniform implementation of the death penalty may serve as a deterrent, and victims' families are entitled to retribution. Furthermore, the costs of maintaining a prisoner for life are too great, and no state guarantees that life imprisonment means no parole.

8. In his celebrated work *On Liberty,* a defense of freedom of speech, John Stuart Mill argues that "power can be rightfully exercised over any member of a civilized community" only to "prevent harm to others." Because he maintains that no opinion, no matter how disagreeable, can inflict harm, it follows that we don't have the right to suppress opinion.

9. It makes sense for properly trained airline pilots to carry handguns as a last-ditch defense against terrorist takeovers. A recent undercover test by the Transportation Department showed airport screeners missing a significant number of knives and other potential weapons, and there aren't enough sky marshals to protect the thousands of daily flights. Stronger cockpit doors are a possibility, but retrofitting all airliners will take time. Pilots must have the means to save lives.

10. The Pope should allow priests to marry. Currently in the United States there is one priest for every 1,400 Catholics, and the average age of this one priest is 60. The Church needs more priests, and surely more young men would join the priesthood if celibacy were not required. And a majority of American Catholics are in favor of allowing priests to marry. In fact, before the eleventh century, priests and popes did marry.

AMBIGUOUS ARGUMENT STRUCTURE

Sometimes the precise direction of an argument seems ambiguous; what is offered as conclusion and what is meant as supporting premise can be unclear. In such cases, it is important to look for what is most reasonable to believe, to give *the benefit of the doubt.* Try each assertion as the conclusion and see if the premises provide logical support for it, beginning with what seems most likely to be the intended conclusion.

Closely allied with the benefit of the doubt is the ancient methodologic principle known as **Occam's razor.** Named for William of Occam, a 14th-century European philosopher, this principle advocates economy in argument. As William of Occam put it, "What can be done with fewer assumptions is done in vain with more." In other words, the simplest line of reasoning is usually the best. Newspaper columnist Jon Carroll invoked Occam's razor when commenting on the O. J. Simpson trial: "I am not a juror; I am not required to maintain the presumption of innocence. I used **Occam's razor,** a tool that has served me well before. The simplest explanation is usually the true one; if a wife is killed, look to the husband."

Medicine too follows this principle as Dr. Lisa Sanders tells us in *Diagnosis,* a *New York Times Magazine* column:

> . . . [Y]ou should strive to come up with the simplest possible explanation for the phenomena you observe. In medicine, that means we try to find a single diagnosis to explain all that we see in a patient. **Occam's razor,** it's called—the art of shaving the diagnosis to the simplest most elegant solution.

EXERCISE 3B

Reducing an Editorial to Standard Form

Put the argument presented in the following editorial into standard form.

Solves Surplus Problem

To the Editor:

At last, someone else—Elizabeth Joseph (Op-Ed, May 23)—has put into words what I have been silently thinking for some time: Polygamy makes good sense.

Ms. Joseph writes from the perspective of a wife. I write from the perspective of a divorced working mother. How much more advantageous it

Nurit Karlin

would be for me to be part of a household such as Ms. Joseph describes, rather than to be juggling my many roles alone.

If polygamy were legal, the problem—and I see it as a problem—of the surplus of extra women would disappear rapidly. No matter how many polemics there may be in favor of the free and single life-style, a divorced woman can feel extra in today's society, more so if she has children, which can isolate her from a full social life. How much easier to share the burdens—and the jobs.

When more women can rediscover the joys of sisterhood and co-wifehood (which are as old as the Bible), and overcome residual jealousy as a response to this type of situation, I think our society will have advanced considerably.

Frieda Brodsky
Brooklyn, New York

WRITING ASSIGNMENT 5

Creating a Political Handout

The following handout urges Californians to vote "no" on Proposition 174. This proposition (like other school voucher initiatives) would require the state to give parents vouchers to apply to their children's tuition if they choose private schools over public. This issue is currently being debated at the national level as well. As you will recognize, the content of this handout is essentially an argument in standard form: premises in support of a conclusion. Each premise is then developed and supported by a sentence or two.

After evaluating the effectiveness of this handout, create one of your own in support of or in opposition to a current political issue or campus issue. If the topic you choose is a ballot issue, refer to the Voter's Guide in your area for help in identifying the major premises. Pay special attention as well to the format and visual appeal of your document. Your computer program may allow you to add graphics to your design.

Five *Good* Reasons to Oppose the Vouchers Initiative

It provides no accountability.

- Though they would receive taxpayer dollars, the private and religious schools would be wholly unaccountable to the taxpayers— or to anyone other than their owners. Anyone who could recruit just 25 youngsters could open a "school." It would not need to be accredited, to hire credentialed teachers, or to meet the curriculum, health, and safety standards governing the public schools.

It undermines "neighborhood" schools, making large tax hikes likely.

- The initiative would strip our public schools of 10 percent of their funding—even if not one student transferred to a private or religious school—to give vouchers to students currently in non-public schools. Either the public schools would be devastated—or hefty tax increases would be needed . . . not to improve education in the public schools, but to pay for subsidizing private, religious, and cult schools.

It permits discrimination.

- Private and religious schools could refuse admission to youngsters because of their religion, gender, I.Q., family income or ability to pay, disability, or any of dozens of other factors. In fact, they wouldn't even have to state a reason for rejecting a child.

It transfers taxpayer money to the rich.

- Rich parents already paying $7,000 to $10,000 or more in private school tuition would now gain $2,600 from the vouchers—a form of "Robin Hood in reverse."

It abandons public school students.

- The children left behind, in the public schools, would sit in classrooms that were even more crowded—and that had even less money, per student, for textbooks, science equipment, and other materials and supplies.

Vote No on Prop. 174
California Teachers Association/NEA • 1705 Murchison Drive • Burlingame, CA 94010

STANDARD FORM, ESSAY ORGANIZATION, AND REVISION

When we put arguments into standard form, we ask critical questions: Is this assertion the conclusion, the focus of the argument? Or is it a premise supporting the conclusion? Or does it support another premise? Asking and answering questions such as these sharpens our analytical skills and enables us to read more critically. But analyzing argument structure also has specific application to writing.

Standard form can provide an outline of the argument, an excellent aid in essay organization and one you can use either to plan your essay or to revise it.

Such an outline states the thesis of the essay—the conclusion of the argument—and each premise signals a new point to be developed.

If you have thought out your argument carefully before you start writing, you will find that putting it in standard form can lead to a good working outline from which to proceed. Or you may find that you can impose standard form on your argument only when you have done some writing. (Remember writing's power to actually generate ideas.) This kind of outlining is particularly helpful in revising your paper.

After writing a rough first draft of your argument, if time permits, put it away for a few hours. When you return to it, approach it as if you were not the writer but a reader. Set aside concerns of style, coherence, and mechanics; focus exclusively on the bones of the argument—the conclusion and the premises that support it. Write this skeleton of your draft in standard form. Now you are in an ideal position to evaluate the foundation of your argument—before proceeding to matters of development (well-supported premises), coherence, style, and mechanics.

WRITING ASSIGNMENT 6

Responding to an Editorial

From a newspaper or an online magazine, choose an editorial with which you disagree. Then reduce it to standard form. Next, write a response expressing your objections to the piece and your view of the issue. Conclude by putting your argument into standard form.

ARGUMENT AND EXPLANATION—DISTINCTIONS

As you elaborate support for premises in written argument, you often rely on explanation—of terminology, of background, of your reasoning—but you must not lose sight of your purpose, which is to persuade your reader of the wisdom of your position.

In **argument,** you present reasons for your conclusion in order to convince someone of your point of view.

In **explanation,** on the other hand, you are clarifying why something has happened. Look at these examples:

Don't go to that market because it's closed for renovation.
Don't go to that market because the prices are higher than anywhere else and the checkout lines are slow.

In the first example, we are given an explanation of why the market is closed. In the second, we are given two reasons, two premises, for not shopping at that market—it's too expensive and the checkers are slow. This is an argument.

This distinction between explanation and argument may play a crucial role in your understanding of specific writing assignments and save you wasted effort on a false start. Is the instructor asking for an explanation, information on a particular subject, or is he asking you to write an argument, to take and support a position? The following exercise should help to clarify further this important distinction.

EXERCISE 3C

Distinguishing Arguments from Explanations

The following two pieces both appeared in newspapers, the first written by a journalist, Elizabeth Bumiller, the second by a professor and former veterinarian, Lisa Fullam. One presents an argument while the other offers an explanation. Read them both carefully and decide which is which. Keep in mind that the writer of an argument **takes a position** and attempts to persuade the reader of the rightness of that position. Explain your answer with references to specific passages in both pieces.

Bush Remarks Roil Debate over Teaching of Evolution

ELIZABETH BUMILLER

1 A sharp debate between scientists and religious conservatives escalated Tuesday over comments by President Bush that the theory of intelligent design should be taught with evolution in the nation's public shcools.

2 In an interview at the White House on Monday with a group of Texas newspaper reporters, Mr. Bush appeared to endorse the push by many of his conservative Christian supporters to give intelligent design equal treatment with the theory of evolution. Recalling his days as Texas governor, Mr. Bush said in the interview, according to a transcript, "I felt like both sides ought to be properly taught." Asked again by a reporter whether he believed that both sides in the dabate between evolution and intelligent design should be taught in the schools, Mr. Bush replied that he did, "so people can understand what the debate is about." . . .

3 On Tuesday, the president's conservative Christian supporters and the leading institute advancing intelligent design embraced Mr. Bush's comments

while scientists and advocates of the separation of church and state disparaged them. At the White House, where intelligent design has been discussed in a weekly bible study group, Mr. Bush's science adviser, John H. Marburger 3rd, sought to play down the president's remarks as common sense and old news. . . .

Intelligent design, advanced by a group of academics and intellectuals   4
and some biblical creationists, disputes the idea that natural selection—the force Charles Darwin suggested drove evolution—fully explains the complexity of life. Instead, intelligent design proponents say that life is so intricate that only a powerful guiding force, or intelligent designer, could have created it.

Intelligent design does not identify the designer, but critics say the the-   5
ory is a thinly disguised argument for God and the divine creation of the universe. Invigorated by a recent push by conservatives, the theory has been gaining support in school districts in 20 states with Kansas in the lead." . . .

Of God and the Case for Unintelligent Design
LISA FULLAM

As the theory of intelligent design again hits the news with President Bush's   1
encouragement this week that the theory be taught in schools alongside evolution, I have one question: What about unintelligent design?

Take rabbit digestion, for example. As herbivores, rabbits need help   2
from bacteria to break down the cell walls of the plants they eat, so, cleverly enough, they have a large section of intestine where such bacterial fermentation takes place. The catch is, it's at the far end of the small intestine, beyond where efficient absorption of nutrients can happen. A sensible system—as we see in ruminant animals like cattle and deer—ferments before the small intestine, maximizing nutrient absorption. Rabbits, having to make do with an unintelligent system, instead eat some of their own feces after one trip through, sending half-digested food back through the small intestine for re-digestion.

Horses are similarly badly put together: They ferment their food in a   3
large, blind-ended cecum after the small intestine. Unlike rabbits, they don't recycle their feces—they're just inefficient. Moreover, those big sections of hind gut are a frequent location for gut blockages and twists that, absent prompt veterinary intervention, lead to slow and excruciating death for the poor horse. The psalmist writes: "God takes no delight in horses' power." Clearly, if God works in creation according to the simplistic schemes of the intelligent design folks, God not only doesn't delight in horses, but seems positively to have it in for them.

Furthermore, why wouldn't an intelligent designer make it possible for   4
animals to digest their natural food without playing host to huge populations
of bacteria in the first place: Couldn't mammals have been equipped with
their own enzymes to do the job?

But that's not all: Consider mammalian testicles. In order to function   5
optimally, they need to be slightly cooler than the rest of the body and so
are carried outside the body wall in the scrotum. Why would one carry
one's whole genetic potential in such a vulnerable position? Clearly it's
not a gonad problem in general—ovaries work just fine at body temperature and are snuggled safely within the pelvic girdle for protection. But for
testicles, nope—the scrotum is jerry-rigged to allow for a warm-blooded
animal to keep his testicles cool. Surely an intelligent designer could have
figured out a way for testicles to work at body temperature, as ovaries do.

Here's another: Do you know anyone beyond the age of 20 or so who   6
has not had a backache? Let's face it: The human body is that of a quadruped
tipped up on end to walk on only two legs. The delicate and beautiful cen-
tilever curve of the human spine compensates (but not enough) for the odd
stresses that result from our unusual posture. Perhaps the God of intelligent design has a special place in his plan for chiropractors? And what
about the knee? Between the secure ball-and-socket of the hip and the
omnidirectional versatility of the ankle is a simple hinge joint, held together only by ligaments (including the anterior cruciate ligament) whose
names are known to athletes and sports fans because they're so easily and
frequently injured. Again, unintelligent design.

The real problem with intelligent design is that it fails to account for the   7
obvious anatomical and physiological making-do that is evident of so much
of the natural world. Evolutionarily minded folks see this as the result of genetic limitations and adaptations accumulated in specialization for certain
environments, while the intelligent design folks are left with a designer who
clearly cannot have been paying close attention.

While there are extremely precise and fine-tuned mechanisms in nature,   8
there is also lots of evidence of organisms just cobbled together. For instance, take marsupials, who give birth to what in other animals are analo-
gous to fetuses, then have to carry them around in what amounts to an ex-
terior uterus until the offspring are ready to face the world.

As a theist who sees natural evolution not as a theory but as well-   9
established observation, I take comfort in the catch-as-catch-can of the
natural world. I have every confidence that an all-loving creator walks in
and with the natural world as it struggles to fruition, cheering on our evolutionary triumphs (let's hear it for the opposable thumb!) and standing in
solidarity with the evolutionary misfits and misfires, like rabbit guts and
horses generally.

Isn't this how God walks in and with us in our individual lives as well,   10
cheering us on, emboldening us and consoling us in our often misguided

attempts to live well and do right, and standing in compassion and solidarity with us when we fail, and loving us into trying again? And isn't this a more compelling vision of God, and truer to the biblical God who comes again and again to offer salvation to erring humankind, than that of a designer who can't quite seem to get things right?

LOGICAL RELATIONSHIPS BETWEEN IDEAS—JOINING WORDS AND COHERENCE

Joining words and transitional phrases are especially important in written argument because the strength of an argument is in part dependent on the clarity of the relationships between the premises and the conclusion. Joining words are essential for conveying a logical sequence of thought. If logical connections are missing, the reader cannot follow the line of reasoning and either stops reading or supplies his own connections, which may not be the ones intended.

As an example of the kind of **"choppy"** or **disjointed writing** that results from the omission of logical connections, look at the following excerpt from former President Bill Clinton's Inaugural Address.

> (1) When our Founders boldly declared America's independence to the world and our purpose to the Almighty, they knew that America to endure would have to change. (2) Not change for change's sake but change to preserve America's ideals—life, liberty, the pursuit of happiness. (3) Though we march to the music of our time, our mission is timeless. (4) Each generation of Americans must define what it means to be an American.

Although sentence 1 relates to sentence 2, sentences 3 and 4 fail to relate to these first two sentences or to each other. The result: a correct but incoherent paragraph. Joining words may not "fix" this paragraph—incoherence is sometimes the result of problems in organization that can't be remedied by the mere addition of joining words. But their use promotes **coherence,** showing your reader the logical connections between your ideas.

Joining words fall into three categories: coordinating conjunctions, subordinating conjunctions, and transition words.

Note that, while the list of coordinating conjunctions is complete, the other two lists are partial, featuring only the most commonly used words from both categories.

JOINING CHART

Logical Relationship	Coordinating Conjunctions	Subordinating Conjunctions	Major Transitions
Addition	and		also, moreover
Contrast and Concession	but yet	while whereas although though even though	however on the other hand
Cause	for	because since as	
Result Effect	so and so	so that in that in order that	therefore thus hence consequently
Condition		if unless provided that	

Many of these words mean almost the same thing; they express the same logical connections between the ideas they join. For example, "but," "although," and "however" all express contrast, so we can join the following two ideas with any one of the three and arrive at a similar, if not identical, meaning.

I love reality television, *but* I doubt that it reflects real life.

I love reality televison *although* I doubt that it reflects real life.

I love reality television; *however,* I doubt that it reflects real life.

Choice of Joining Words

So what determines our choice? Notice that the two sentences above joined by "but" and "although" are less formal in tone than the sentences joined by "however." We often find transition words such as "however," "moreover," "hence," and "consequently" in formal documents—legal briefs and contracts. In less formal writing, these words can be distracting, so the best writers use them sparingly. Try an "And" or a "But" instead of "Moreover" or "However" to open a sentence and save the transition words for **major transitions.**

On those occasions when we use transition words, it can often be effective for fluency to embed them within the clause rather than begin with them. For example:

> Kate loves foreign films and rarely sees American-made movies; *however,* her roommate prefers American gangster films. ["However" begins the clause.]
> Kate loves foreign films and rarely sees American-made movies; her roommate, *however,* prefers American gangster films. ["However" is embedded within the clause.]

A REVIEW: PUNCTUATION OF JOINING WORDS

Coordinating conjunctions—put a comma before the conjunction when it joins two independent clauses unless the clauses are short.

> The homeless are creating and living in unsanitary conditions all over America, *so* cities must provide housing for them.

Subordinating conjunctions—introductory subordinate clauses [clauses that begin with a subordinating conjunction] are usually followed by a comma.

> *Although* the homeless are creating and living in unsanitary conditions all over America, cities are not providing needed housing.

When a subordinate clause follows the main clause, the comma is usually omitted.

> Cities are not providing needed housing *even though* the homeless are creating and living in unsanitary conditions all over America.

Transition words—transitional words and phrases, because they do not join sentences but only connect ideas, should be preceded by a semicolon or a period when they come between two clauses.

> The homeless are creating and living in unsanitary conditions all over America; *therefore,* cities must provide adequate housing for them.

If, in the preceding example, a comma rather than a semicolon preceded "therefore," many readers would consider it a run-together sentence or comma splice.

When a transition word is embedded within a clause, it is usually set off with commas.

> The homeless are creating and living in unsanitary conditions all over America; cities, *therefore,* must provide adequate housing for them.

EXERCISE 3D

Joining Sentences for Logic and Fluency

Make this disjointed argument cohesive and logical by joining sentences with appropriate joining words. You don't need to change the sequence of sentences.

> Obstetricians perform too many Cesareans. They can schedule deliveries for their own convenience. They can avoid sleepless nights and canceled parties. They resort to Cesareans in any difficult delivery to protect themselves against malpractice suits. Cesareans involve larger fees and hospital bills than normal deliveries. Cesarean patients spend about twice as many days in the hospital as other mothers. The National Institutes of Health confirmed that doctors were performing many unnecessary Cesarean sections. They suggested ways to reduce their use. The recommendation was widely publicized. The obstetricians apparently failed to take note. In the 1980s, the operation was performed in 16.5 percent of United States' births. In the 1990s, 24.7 percent of the births were Cesareans. Today, the percentage is even higher.

Revising for Coherence

Joining words are one important tool available to writers to promote coherence—a logical flow—in their writing. Sentence focus, a consistent sentence subject that reflects the rhetorical subject (see Chapter 8), is another. But since coherence comes from content as well as from style, no textbook could specify every conceivable option available to writers. So a writer, when revising a draft, must keep his audience in mind, never forgetting to take his reader with him as he moves from sentence to sentence and paragraph to paragraph. The writer must be conscious of the gulf that exists between himself and his reader. The reader's only access to the mind of the writer is through the words on the page; the reader has no other access to the writer's thoughts.

HIDDEN ASSUMPTIONS IN ARGUMENT

Even when arguments appear to be well supported with premises, and, where necessary, logical relationships are signaled with joining words, many real-life arguments come to us incomplete, depending on **hidden assumptions,** unstated premises and conclusions. Sometimes a missing premise or conclusion is so obvious that we don't even recognize that it is unstated.

The president is a republican, so he is opposed to gun control. [Missing premise: Republicans are opposed to gun control.]

Ken is lazy and lazy people don't last long around here. [Missing conclusion: Ken won't last long around here.]

Since I've sworn to put up with my tired Honda until I can afford a BMW, I must resign myself to the old wreck for a while longer. [Missing premise: I can't afford a BMW now.]

Filling in the omitted assumptions here would seem unnecessarily pedantic or even insulting to our intelligence.

Literature, by its nature elliptical, depends on the reader to make plausible assumptions:

Yon Cassius has a lean and hungry look; such men are dangerous.
—SHAKESPEARE, *JULIUS CAESAR*

Shakespeare assumes his audience will automatically make the connection—Cassius is a dangerous man. But not all missing assumptions are as obvious or as acceptable. At the heart of critical thinking lies the ability to discern what a writer or speaker leaves **implicit**—unsaid—between the lines of what he has made **explicit**—what he has clearly stated.

Dear Abby's readers took her to task for a response she made to a man who complained that because he shared an apartment with a man, people thought he was gay. She called this rumor an "ugly accusation." The implicit assumption here is that homosexuality is ugly, an assumption many of her readers—both gay and straight—objected to. One reader asked, "If someone thought this man was Jewish, Catholic or African American—would you call that an 'ugly accusation'?" Dear Abbey apologized.

A new kind of therapy called philosophical counseling is based on the belief that many personal problems stem from faulty logic, from irrational assumptions. One practitioner of this therapy, Elliot D. Cohen, gives as an example of such faulty reasoning the assumption that one should demand perfection from oneself and others. He teaches his clients critical thinking skills so that they can identify and correct such damaging assumptions.

Law professor Patricia J. Williams, in *The Alchemy of Race and Rights,* examines the implicit assumptions that led to the death of a young black man in New York. In this incident, three young black men left their stalled car in Queens and walked to Howard Beach looking for help, where they were surrounded by eight white teenagers who taunted them with racial epithets and chased them for approximately three miles, beating them severely along the way. One of the black men died, struck by a car as he tried to flee across a highway; another suffered permanent blindness in one eye.

During the course of the resultant trial, the community of Howard Beach supported the white teenagers, asking "What were they [the three black teenagers] doing here in the first place?" Examining this question, Williams finds six underlying assumptions:

Everyone who lives here is white.

No black could live here.

No one here has a black friend.

No white would employ a black here.

No black is permitted to shop here.

No black is ever up to any good.

These assumptions reveal the racism that led the white teenagers to behave as they did and the community to defend their brutality.

Dangers of Hidden Assumptions

Examine this seemingly straightforward argument:

John is Lisa's father, so clearly he is obligated to support her.

What's missing here? The premise that all fathers are obligated to support their daughters (or their children) is omitted. But would everyone find this premise acceptable under all conditions? Probably not. What about the age factor? What about special circumstances: Lisa's mother has ample means while John is penniless and terminally ill? Or Lisa was legally adopted by another family, John being her birth father?

The danger with such incomplete arguments lies in more than one direction. A writer may leave his readers to supply their own assumptions, which may or may not coincide with those of the writer. If the issue is controversial, the risks of distorting an argument increase. Or, writers may deliberately conceal assumptions to hide an unsound, often misleading argument. Watch for these in advertising and politics. If you are on the alert for such deceptions, you are better able to evaluate what you read and hear and thus protect your own interests.

Look at the unstated assumption in the following example:

Echoing the arguments of the National Physicians for Social Responsibility, a prominent archdiocese refused to participate in a federal civil defense program that taught ways of preparing for nuclear war. They objected to instructions for teachers and students which recommended that "if there should be a nuclear flash, especially if you feel the warmth from it, take cover instantly in the best place you can find. If no cover is available, simply lie down on the ground and curl up." Their objections were leveled not at the specific suggestions but at the underlying unstated assumption: that nuclear war is survivable. In the words of the Board: "To teach children that nuclear war is a survivable disaster is to teach them that nuclear war is an acceptable political or moral option."

Did the federal civil defense program deliberately conceal an assumption, or did it fail to think critically about the instructions issued to schools?

Currently, some politicians are in favor of privatizing Social Security, the governemnt administered retirement plan. They argue that individuals should have the right to invest their own retirement savings. But this argument is based on the following unstated assumptions—that everyone has the necessary knowledge to invest successfully in the stock market and that the stock market will perform well for each individual when he or she reaches retirement age. How realistic are these assumptions?

Hidden Assumptions and Standard Form

To help sort out the stated and unstated assertions in an argument, it can be illuminating to write out the argument in standard form. This means including the important hidden assumptions so the complete argument is before you and putting brackets around these assumptions to distinguish them from stated premises and conclusions.

Examples:

1. Harold is a politician so he's looking out for himself.

    a. [All politicians look out for themselves.]

    b. Harold is a politician.

    ∴ Harold is looking out for himself.

2. Products made from natural ingredients promote good health, so you should buy Brand X breads.

    a. Products made from natural ingredients promote good health.

    b. [Brand X breads are made from natural ingredients.]

    ∴ You should buy Brand X breads.

3. Products made from natural ingredients promote good health, and Brand X breads are made from natural ingredients.

    a. Products made from natural ingredients promote good health.

    b. Brand X breads are made from natural ingredients.

    ∴ [You should buy Brand X breads.]

EXERCISE 3E

Identifying Hidden Assumptions

A. The following arguments are missing either a premise or a conclusion. Put them into standard form, adding the implicit premise or conclusion; then place brackets around the missing assumptions you have inserted. A word to the wise: As with all argument analysis, find the conclusion first and then look for what is offered in its support.

1. Maggie is a musician, so she won't understand the business end of the partnership.
2. Those who exercise regularly increase their chances of living into old age, so we can expect to see Anna around for a very long time.
3. I never see Sophie without a book; she must be highly intelligent.
4. That is not a star because it gives steady light.
5. Those who buy stock on margin lose their money eventually. Yet that is what Sam is doing.
6. College enrollments are declining. But if that is so, then fewer new faculty will be hired. It follows that before long college faculties will become more conservative.
7. The Western industrialized nations will resolve the energy crisis if they mobilize all the technological resources at their disposal. If financial incentives are sufficiently high, then the mobilization of resources will occur. The skyrocketing cost of energy—as a result of increased oil prices—has produced just such sufficiently high financial incentives. The conclusion is clear.
8. "Most professional athletes don't have a college degree and so have no idea how to handle the big salaries suddenly dumped in their laps." (Harry Edwards, college professor and financial consultant for professional athletes)
9. Having become so central a part of our culture, television cannot be without its redeeming features.
10. **CONVICTED:** U.S. Petty Officer 3/c **Mitchell T. Garraway, Jr.,** of premeditated murder in the stabbing of a superior officer. The military court must now decide his sentence; its options include the death penalty. The last execution carried out by the Navy took place in 1849. (*Newsweek*)
11. From a letter to the *Sacramento Bee* after an article reporting that a nursing mother had been evicted from a downtown department store cafeteria (thanks to Perry Weddle of Sacramento State University for this one):

    It was inhumane to deny this woman the right to nurse her baby in the cafeteria because she was simply performing a natural bodily function.

    (Where will this argument take you once you supply the suppressed assumption?)

B. The following article appeared in the news section of several major newspapers. Read it carefully and supply the hidden assumption it seems to be leading us to. Why would the writer choose to make this assumption implicit?

Robert Redford's Daughter Rescued

SALT LAKE CITY—Shauna Redford, daughter of actor Robert Redford, was rescued when her car plunged into a river, authorities said yesterday.

They said Redford was wearing a seatbelt and suffered only minor injuries in the accident Friday. Redford, 23, of Boulder, was rescued from her partially submerged auto by three other motorists, who saw her vehicle crash through a guardrail into the Jordan River, eight miles south of Salt Lake City.

The Utah Highway Patrol said the three rescuers released Redford's seatbelt, pulled her from the car and carried her to the riverbank.

She was held at a hospital overnight for observation and released.

Last summer, Sidney Wells, 22, a Colorado University student who had dated Shauna Redford, was shot and killed in Boulder. Police said the killing may have been drug related.

C. Look closely at the following cartoons from the *New Yorker Magazine* archives. What do they suggest about relationships between men and women in the workplace in the 1950s? What hidden assumptions are they based on?

1. RICHARD TAYLOR, 1958

"Three more months and he reaches mandatory retirement age, thank God."

"Notice, class, how Angela circles, always keeping the desk between them..."

Now look at this recent cartoon. What unstated assumptions about relationships between men and women are suggested here?

A SUCCESSFUL WEDDING PARTY
RETURNS FROM THE HUNT

D. Find one advertisement or political cartoon in print journalism that clearly depends for its message on one or more unstated assumptions. Clip or photocopy the ad, write out the principal argument in standard form, including the missing assertions, and bring it to class to discuss with classmates.

Hidden Assumptions and Audience Awareness

As stated above, politicians and advertisers may deliberately suppress assumptions in order to manipulate the public. We will assume that we, as careful writers, do not share this goal and would not deliberately leave important assumptions unstated. At the same time, we don't want to bore our readers by spelling out unnecessary details. How do we determine what material to include, what to leave out?

George Lakoff and Mark Johnson, in their book *Metaphors We Live By*, point out that meaning is often dependent on context. They offer the following sentence as an example.

We need new sources of energy.

This assertion means one thing to a group of oil executives and quite another to an environmental group. The executives may assume the writer is referring to more offshore drilling, whereas the environmentalists may think the writer is referring to greater development of solar or other alternate sources of energy.

As writers, we must consider our audience carefully and understand the purpose for which we are writing. We make choices about which assumptions must be made explicit according to our knowledge of the reader. Are we writing for an audience predisposed to agree with us or for one that is opposed to our point of view? Are we writing for readers who are knowledgeable about the subject or ignorant? The answers to these questions help us to determine what material to include and what to omit.

You may find it helpful to have a friend, one who is unfamiliar with your topic, read a draft of your paper. Such a reader may help you spot assumptions that need clarification.

EXERCISE 3F

Identifying Your Reader

A common feature of many publications today is a section called "Personals." *The Nation* and the *New York Review of Books* (both probably in your library) and many local periodicals, including some campus papers, carry "Personals." What follows are four such ads, two from women who advertised in a public television magazine, and two from men who advertised in the *Daily Californian*, the University of California at Berkeley student newspaper. Form four groups and choose one of the following ads to analyze and respond to together.

From the *Daily Californian:*

> **MALE UCB student,** 25, 6'1", interested in music, religion, literature, nature, etc. seeks Lithuanian woman with beautiful soul—witty, pretty, intellectual, virtuous—for fun, friendship, maybe more.
> **ENGLISH/MUSIC major,** 25, would like to meet witty, intellectual, attractive female (pref. math/physics/other science major) for concerts, foreign films & after dinner activities.

From a public television magazine:

> **Sensual Blue-eyed Blonde,** successful entrepreneur, 30, 5'4", who is attractive, well traveled, well read, and has a great sense of humor, seeks a spiritual, self-aware single white male, 30–45, 5'10" or taller, who is worldly but grounded, successful but sensitive, healthy but not fanatical and open to pursuing a long-term commitment. Note and photo appreciated.
> **Pretty Woman, International** travel, Ivy education, health career, would like to meet professional man, 35–50, for tennis, dancing, bear hugs and possible first-time family. Photo appreciated.

Your aim is to understand the writer of the ad, who will then become the audience for your response. Read the ad of your choice carefully. What kind of person is the writer? What can you infer about his or her character, personality, and values? What does the publication he or she chose to advertise in reveal about the writer? Read between the lines: What hidden assumptions are buried there?

After completing your analysis, as a group write a brief response informed by your knowledge of the writer of the ad. If time permits, reading these responses to the class might be entertaining.

SUMMARY

In logic, the word *argument* has a special meaning, referring to rational discourse composed of **premises** and a **conclusion** rather than to a fight. It is useful to be able to recognize premises and conclusions in order to fully understand what an argument is proposing. Expressing arguments in **standard form** is a helpful strategy for understanding arguments.

Understanding the structure of arguments can be useful to writers when considering the organization of their own written arguments.

The logical connections between assertions in argument can be signaled by **conjunctions** and **transitional phrases** to promote a logical flow of prose and ideas.

Arguments are frequently presented with some of the premises or the conclusion implied rather than stated. Sometimes such **hidden assumptions** are obvious, but in other instances they can be misleading and need to be made explicit. Recognizing hidden assumptions in argument is an important part of critical thinking.

KEY TERMS

Argument   a rational piece of discourse, written or spoken, which attempts to persuade the reader or listener to believe something; composed of at least one premise in support of a conclusion.

Conclusion   the key assertion in an argument, the statement that the other assertions support; the point one hopes to make when presenting an argument.

Explanation   an attempt to clarify why something has happened or why you hold a given opinion.

Explicit   clearly stated, distinctly expressed.

Hidden assumptions   missing, unstated premises and conclusions in arguments; assertions that are necessary to recognize in order to fully understand an argument.

Implicit   suggested so as to be understood but not plainly expressed.

Joining words   words or phrases that indicate, or signal, the logical relationship between assertions in an argument. "Therefore" and its synonyms signal a conclusion; "because" and its synonyms signal a premise.

Occam's razor   a principle of argument that advocates economy, maintaining that the simplest line of reasoning is usually the best.

Opinion   a provisional judgment or belief, requiring proof or support; a first step in developing an argument.

Premise   a reason that supports the conclusion in an argument.

Standard form   an argument reduced to its essence, its principal premises and conclusion listed in simple outline form, with premises numbered and conclusion stated at the end.

CHAPTER 4

Written Argument

I told him he ought not simply to state what he thinks true, but to give arguments for it, but he said arguments would feel as if he was dirtying a flower with muddy hands. . . . I told him I hadn't the heart to say anything against that, and that he had better acquire a servant to state the arguments.

—Bertrand Russell

In Chapter 3, we focused on the structure of argument, distinguishing between premises and conclusions and reducing arguments to these two basic components. But how do we begin to **write** an argument?

FOCUSING YOUR TOPIC

A first critical step is to **focus** and refine the topic. At one time or another, we have all been part of heated political discussions between friends or family members. Grandfather states that taxes are too high. Cousin Susan points out that corporations do not pay their fair share, while Dad shouts that the government funds too many social programs and allows too large a number of immigrants to enter the country. These discussions are often discursive and unsatisfying because they are not focused on one clear and precise **question at issue.**

For an argument to be successful, one person does not necessarily have to defeat another; one point of view does not have to be proven superior to another. An argument can also be considered successful if it opens a line of communication between people and allows them to consider—with respect—points of view other than their own. But if an argument is to establish such a worthwhile exchange, it must focus first on a single issue and then on a particular question at issue.

The Issue

An **issue** is any topic of concern and controversy. Not all topics are issues since many topics are not controversial. Pet care, for instance, is a topic but not an issue; it has no **argumentative edge.** Laboratory testing of animals, on the other hand, is an issue. In the hypothetical family discussion above, three issues are raised: taxes, immigration, and government-funded social programs. No wonder such a discussion is fragmented and deteriorates into people shouting unsupported claims at one another.

Where and how do you find appropriate topics for an argument? In your work or personal life you might need to write an argument that has a real-world purpose. Why product X is superior to all other brands and how using it will turn a customer's business around. Why you are the most qualified applicant for the job. For your classes, you are often assigned topics. But sometimes in a writing class you are asked to select a topic of interest to you. Newspapers, in your community and on your campus, can suggest issues, as can news broadcasts. The Internet has opened up a vast new world of information from which you might select a topic once you have identified a broad category that interests you. Although it can be useful to choose a subject that you know something about, particularly if you want to take a strong stand right away, don't be afraid of exploring new areas. In a freshman history class some years ago, one of us was handed the unknown name *Leon Trotsky*. That required paper led to a whole new world of knowledge: Russia, the Soviet Union, the Russian Revolution, and communism. Your writing assignments can be a way of opening new worlds.

The Question at Issue

Whether you choose your own issue or are assigned one, the next step is to select one **question at issue**—a particular aspect of the issue under consideration. **Cloning,** for instance, is an issue that contains many distinct questions at issue:

Should all efforts to clone humans be banned by the federal government?

Should decisions about cloning be left to the states?

Should cloning of animals be encouraged for scientific research?

Should cloning of personal pets be permitted?

Should human cloning be permitted to help a sibling survive?

Could cloning lead to a rebirth of the eugenics movement?

A writer who does not focus on one and only one question at issue risks producing a disorganized essay, one that is difficult to follow because the readers will not be sure they understand the point the writer is arguing. Writing on the issue of whether or not cloning of animals should be encouraged for scientific research, one student kept drifting away from that question at issue to something else of keen interest to her, should cloning of pets be permitted? Since both her **questions at issue** were part of the **same issue,** cloning, and hence related, she was unaware that her paper was going in two different directions. The result was a disorganized, disjointed essay reflecting muddled thinking.

The following diagram illustrates that a single issue may contain any number of separate and distinct questions at issue. Your task as a writer is to isolate a particular question at issue and stay focused on it.

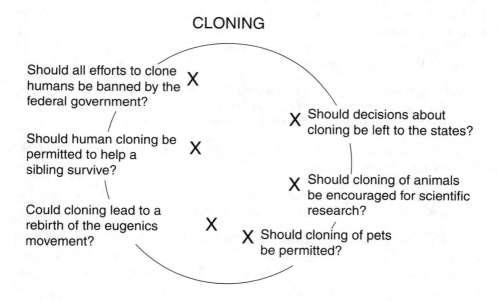

The Thesis

The final step in establishing the focus of an essay is determining the **thesis.** Although the issue and question at issue state, respectively, the subject and focus of the paper, they are neutral statements; they do not reveal the writer's opinion, nor should they. To encourage objective analysis, the question at issue should be expressed in neutral rather than biased or emotionally charged language. The **thesis,** however, states the writer's position, her response to the question at issue, the *conclusion* of her argument, the primary claim she is making. Your thesis takes central stage in both the final paper you write and the thinking you do as you conduct your research and prepare drafts. It controls the evidence you gather and clarifies the stand you want to take.

Suppose you want to write a paper about cloning and narrow the issue to a more focused question at issue:

Should cloning of animals be encouraged for scientific research?

You might start with a sentence that states the topic:

The cloning of animals began in 1997 when Scottish embryologist Ian Wilmut announced to an astonished world that he and his colleagues had successfully cloned Dolly, the sheep.

Yes, your reader would say. You're right on target with the topic, but what about the argumentative edge? Where is your opinion? What have you to prove in such a statement? Not much so far. Not many people would argue with the fact that Dr. Wilmut cloned Dolly. Once you have estabished a little background on your topic, you need to make a statement about what you want to prove in your paper.

Perhaps you want to convince your reader that scientists should be allowed to proceed with animal cloning:

Although many people are concerned that any form of cloning could eventually lead to the cloning of humans, such fears should not inhibit those seeking further scientific knowledge through the cloning of animals.

Or you may want to join others who have argued that cloning animals can set the stage for cloning humans:

Because the cloning of animals could lead some scientists to try to clone humans, even animal cloning is too dangerous to be permitted.

Both of these statements assert a position on a question at issue, both have an argumentative edge. In either case, you need to provide detailed examples of the benefits or problems created by animal cloning and explain why such evidence supports your case. With either thesis statement, you will have pinned down your ideas so that you have a road map to guide you as you search for and sift through the evidence necessary for supporting your position.

Sometimes when you begin exploring a topic for a paper, you may not know your position. You may need to learn more about the question at issue through research before arriving at a conclusion. If, however, your question at issue is clear and precise, you can proceed without a definite thesis or with only a tentative one since the writing process itself will help you to arrive at one (refer to Chapter 1).

You don't necessarily have to arrive at a completely yes-or-no response to the question at issue. For example, if the question at issue is whether or not school administrators should have the right to censor student newspapers, your response may not be an unequivocal yes or no but a qualified response:

School administrators should not have the right to censor student newspapers unless an article is libelous.

In essays by professional writers, the thesis is sometimes indirectly stated; it may be implicit rather than explicit. For instance, writer Sheila Koran argues in an essay that gay and lesbian couples should have the same legal spousal rights as married couples. She never directly states this thesis as she describes the life she lives with her mate, a life like any other family's, but the point is clearly made; the reader is never confused about the purpose of the essay. In general, the more experienced the writer, the more she is able to write a focused essay without an explicit thesis. But for the most part, writer and reader are best served by a clearly defined thesis.

IN SUMMARY: You should take the following steps as you prepare your topic:

Select an **issue** that is debatable.

Narrow that issue to a focused **question at issue.**

Write a "working" **thesis** that makes an assertion about this question at issue; your thesis states your opinion on the question at issue.

Two Kinds of Thesis Statements

Note the two examples of thesis statements that follow. How do they differ? How might the difference affect the paper that follows?

(a) Children's access to the Internet should be controlled in the home and at schools and libraries.

or

(b) Access to the Internet should be controlled, because children need protection from pornography and sexual predators.

An **open thesis** (a) states the writer's opinion but not the reasons for her opinion. A **complete thesis** (b) includes both the writer's opinion and at least some of the reasons or premises that support this conclusion.

Which thesis statement is preferable? It is a matter of choice, the writer's choice. Some writers fear that the complete thesis will not capture the reader's interest, believing that if all the reasons for the conclusion are given in the thesis, the reader's curiosity will not be aroused. On the other hand, a writer may prefer the greater clarity of the "complete" thesis. In any case, even if a writer chooses the open thesis approach, at some point in the process she should be just as clear about the reasons for her position as the writer who chooses the complete thesis.

As a general guideline to assist you in deciding the most suitable thesis approach to take, consider the complexity of the topic, the length of the paper, the needs of your audience, and the purpose of your project. In a long paper on a complex topic, the reader may welcome the clarity of the complete thesis or at least a modified one, but in a short essay on a simple topic, the complete thesis is probably not necessary and may be too mechanical.

A thesis is not necessarily restricted to one sentence. In fact, it's not unusual for a complete thesis to require a paragraph. As your work progresses and new ideas change your thinking, you may need to revise your thesis. You may also find yourself refining the language of your thesis during the final editing process. But a well thought out and clearly expressed thesis guides both writer and reader.

EXERCISE 4A

Identifying the Issue, Question at Issue, and Thesis

Complete the following sets by supplying the missing element.

1. ***Issue:*** _____.

   Question at Issue: Should a woman who donates her eggs to an infertile woman receive significant financial compensation?

   Thesis: If a woman chooses to use her body to help another, she has every right to demand a high fee.

2. ***Issue:*** Fuel economy standards.

   Question at Issue: Should the government have the right to set fuel economy standards for American auto makers?

   Thesis: _____.

3. ***Issue:*** Genetic engineering of crops.

   Question at Issue: _____.

   Thesis: The genetic engineering of crops should continue to have the support of our government and farmers.

4. For the following pair, supply two examples of a thesis: (1) an open thesis and (2) a complete thesis (with premises).

   Issue: Gambling on the Internet.

   Question at Issue: Should gambling on the Internet be available and unrestricted?

   Open Thesis: _____.

   Complete Thesis: _____.

SHAPING A WRITTEN ARGUMENT— RHETORICAL STRATEGIES

What do we mean by *rhetorical*? The term **rhetoric** has various shades of meaning, but the following definition adapted from the Greek philosopher Aristotle provides the most useful approach for our purposes: "The art of using language to good effect, to prove, to convince, to persuade."

And thus to argue. The structure of written argument as we know it today dates back to the orations of the Greeks and Romans. The following features of classical argument, modified by contemporary rhetoric, can serve us well as long as we recognize that they are options, not requisite components. We write to communicate, not to fit a formula or fulfill a set of narrow expectations.

The Introduction

How you begin your argument depends on the issue, the audience, and your own style. The key question is: How much can you expect your readers to know about your question at issue? If your subject has received a great deal of recent media attention, you probably do not need to supply much background. If, on the other hand, your subject is obscure or technical, then you will have to give your readers the necessary background information—the history of the case or the specific circumstances that give rise to the present problem—so that they can understand the argument to follow.

If not much background is required, you may begin your essay with a relevant **narrative,** either actual or fictional, which illustrates your question at issue. For example, if your subject is euthanasia, you may describe a day in the life of a terminally ill patient. Such a scene captures the reader's interest—not a necessity but sometimes a valuable **rhetorical strategy.** A relevant **quotation** can also provide an interesting way into your argument. Or you may choose to open with an **opposing view** and build your argument on a **refutation** of what is often the prevailing wisdom on an issue.

No matter what approach you choose, you have considerable flexibility. Your introduction may be a single paragraph or run to two or three paragraphs depending on the strategies you choose and the amount of background required. Usually, you will state your **thesis** somewhere in the introductory paragraphs so that your reader is clear about the purpose of the essay.

For a variety of introductory strategies, examine the following three essays in this chapter. Art Hoppe, in "Pro-Choice and Pro-Life (p. 96) begins by stating his position on the complex issue of abortion. The author of "Rap

Takes a Bum Rap" (p. 105) includes an analogy and a statement of what Rap is not before stating his thesis. The introduction to "College Athletes—Special Admissions?" (p. 101) provides relevant background on flexibility in college admissions, leading up to the writer's position on special admission standards for college athletes.

The Development of Your Argument

Once again, the possibilities, although not infinite, are numerous. You need to present as many strong **premises** in support of your position as necessary. These in turn have to be elaborated, explained, and defended with as much specific detail, example, and illustration as you can provide. You may draw on personal experience and research to support your position. Called in classical rhetoric the *confirmation* of your position, this support should be connected explicitly to your thesis unless the logical ties are self-evident. As the Greek philosopher and rhetorician Plato said in the *Phaedrus*, "What is stated outright will be clearer than what is not."

Sometimes one premise requires a whole paragraph or more. Others may need only a few sentences and can be effectively grouped with additional premises. Audience and purpose as well as your topic play a role in your choices. Here are two examples of paragraphs lifted from the middle of student essays, one that develops a single premise in some detail, another that groups a series of premises together in one paragraph.

A single premise paragraph:

Since the NCAA (National Collegiate Athletic Association) policy of random drug testing was begun some years ago, public debate on this issue has increased, and the idea of drug testing for college athletes has been challenged for a variety of reasons. The strongest argument against drug testing of college athletes is that it is unconstitutional. An athlete should be entitled to the same constitutional rights as other citizens, and drug testing violates both the Fourth Amendment's provisions against unreasonable search and seizure and the Fifth Amendment's provision of the right to refuse to furnish potentially incriminating evidence about one's self. *Time* magazine reported that ". . . a number of judges have already ruled that mass testing violates workers' constitutional rights to privacy and protection from self-incrimination." In the case of Simone LeVant, the Stanford diver who has, so far, been the only athlete to challenge the NCAA drug tests in court, the *New York Times* reported that Judge Peter G. Stone of the Santa Clara County Superior Court agreed with the athlete and her attorney that mandatory urine tests were an obtrusive, unreasonable, and unconstitutional invasion of privacy.

A multipremise paragraph:

Although it is a controversial proposition, legalizing drugs has many advantages. First of all, it will free the now overburdened legal system to do its job dispensing justice. Cases will be processed with greater speed because the system won't be overwhelmed with drug cases. With the legalization of drugs, violent drug-related crimes will decrease. As a result, prisons will be less crowded, which in turn will allow serious offenders to serve longer terms. Legalizing drugs will free law enforcement officials to combat other serious crimes more effectively. With the money saved from law enforcement and legal procedures, a more effective campaign of educating the public on the maladies of drugs can be mounted, and more money will be available for the rehabilitation of drug addicts. Finally, by legalizing drugs, we can slow down the spread of AIDS among IV drug users, who will be able to get clean needles and not have to share with other drug addicts, many of whom are infected with the AIDS virus. The positive results of legalizing drugs definitely outweigh the negative consequences.

How Many Premises Should an Argument Have?

It would seem that the greater the number of premises, the stronger the argument, but this quest for quantity should not be at the expense of quality; in other words, weak or questionable premises should not be included just to increase the number of premises. It's possible to have a strong argument with only two or three premises if those premises are convincing and are developed in detail.

The Conclusion

We have no simple rule of thumb here other than to suggest you conclude your essay rather than simply stop. If your paper is long and complex, you need to help your reader by briefly summarizing where you have been and what you propose. If you present only a tentative or partial thesis in the introduction, then you need to be sure that your final position is clear in the conclusion. If, as a result of your argument, you have definite recommendations for action, your conclusion can carry such suggestions.

You and your readers should feel satisfied at the close of your paper. This does not mean that every paper needs a long and redundant formulaic conclusion. Once again, we refer you to the sample essays in Exercise 4F for models.

And so your argument assumes its shape. Commenting on effective rhetoric, Plato summed it up in his *Phaedrus:*

Every discourse, like a living creature, should be so put together that it has its own body and lacks neither head nor feet, middle nor extremities, all composed in such a way that they suit both each other and the whole.

A DIALECTICAL APPROACH TO ARGUMENT

Effective argument is more than the straightforward presentation of a thesis, premises, and their support. Persuasive argument depends on **dialectical thinking.** What do we mean by dialectical? Dialectic is the art of arriving at the truth by disclosing the contradictions, the views contrary to your own, in an opponent's argument, and overcoming them.

As philosopher Georg Hegel saw it, the dialectic is a **process** of change whereby an idea, a **thesis,** is transformed into its opposite, **antithesis.** The combination of the two is then resolved in a form of truth, **synthesis.**

The English philosopher John Stuart Mill was trained by his father to argue both sides of every question and was taught that you had no right to a belief unless you understood the arguments for its opposite.

Eleanor Roosevelt advised women in politics to "argue the other side with a friend until you have found the answer to every point which might be brought up against you." We would second her advice.

And cognitive psychologist Piaget maintained that one mark of a maturing mind is the ability to take another's point of view and thus be capable of considering two conflicting views on the same issue.

Addressing Counterarguments

To take this dialectical approach to argument, you as a writer must pay careful attention to **counterarguments,** to opposing views, thus acknowledging the beliefs of those readers who might hold them. But, one might ask, why aid and abet the opposition by calling attention to their arguments? For a number of good reasons, such strategies can actually strengthen your own position.

1. By **anticipating** your opponent's reasoning, you can often disarm the opposition. The "I recognize that . . ." approach can be very effective, showing the writer's knowledge of the opposition's viewpoint.

2. You can make your own position stronger when you state and then **refute** opposing premises by demonstrating their weakness or falseness. Writer Louis Menand recognized this point when he wrote, "Every idea or piece of knowledge worth having is, in part, a response to ideas or knowledge less worth having. Refuting a bad argument makes a good argument stronger." You must handle refutation tactfully, however,

if you hope to convince those opposed to your position. If you treat them with contempt, as though they are shortsighted and thickheaded for holding the position they do, you only alienate them and defeat your own purpose, which is to have your views heard.

3. By addressing counterarguments to your position, you also appear more reasonable, more fair. You become a credible source and are seen not as narrow-minded, dogmatic, or unheedful of others' views, but as broad-minded and aware of complexity and so ultimately as more intelligent, and reliable.

4. And when you **acknowledge** the possibility of merit in some of your opponents' reasoning, you have taken the ultimate step in establishing yourself as a "generous" thinker. Arguments are rarely truly one-sided, no matter how strong your convictions. When you can **concede** a point, you move closer to a middle ground, opening a line of communication and thus increasing your chances of winning your final point.

5. You may even discover weaknesses and contradictions in your own thinking as you sort through the reasoning of your opponents. It is not easy to abandon cherished beliefs, but clear thinkers sometimes must.

How Much Counterargument?

How much counterargument should writers include in their papers? There is no precise answer. If the writer has strong refutations for every one of the opposition's premises, then she may want to address all these counterarguments. If, on the other hand, a writer thinks the premises she has to support her conclusion are stronger than her refutation of the opposition, she may want to include only a minimum of counterargument. In any case, a writer cannot ignore the most compelling opposing premises even if they provide the greatest challenge to the writer's own view.

For a paper in favor of the medical use of marijuana, the writer would have to deal with the fact that currently marijuana is a federally controlled drug which, like cocaine and heroin, is subject to legal controls. Precisely how the writer would present such a counterargument would depend on the evidence she presents and the precise position on the issue she decides to take. Once again, this is where the wording of the thesis is important.

Refutation and Concession

As you can see from this discussion, there is more than one way to address counterarguments. But address them you must, since to present a contradictory position and then leave it alone would confuse your reader. Here are two possible responses.

1. **Refutation:** Present a counterargument and then explain why this position is false, misleading, irrelevant, or weak; discredit it in some well-reasoned way.

From a student essay in support of a law sanctioning active euthanasia:

Counterargument

Refutation

Some say death and suffering are in keeping with God's universal plan for humanity. The dying process, no matter how long or how agonizing, has both spiritual and moral purpose, functioning to prepare people for the painless eternity of heaven. **To believe this argument though, one must believe there is life after death and many do not. So why can't people live and die in accordance with their own value system? Let both the religious and secular have some control of their own destiny; give those who choose to die that alternative, while honoring the belief of those who do not.**

2. **Concession:** Recognize the merit of a counterargument and so concede that point or (as in our example below) a feature of it. If, for example, you are arguing in favor of euthanasia and want to refute the counterargument that euthanasia is a form of murder, you might begin this way:

Concession

Counterargument

Although I also believe that life is sacred and murder is wrong, I don't think that ending the life of a brain-dead patient is equivalent to murder since in the true sense of the word "life," this patient is not living.

Visually, the relationship between counterargument and refutation and concession looks something like this:

Counterargument

Refutation   Concession

Rogerian Strategy

For a deeper appreciation of concession, we turn to the psychology of communication, particularly the work of Carl R. Rogers (1902–1987), a psychotherapist and communication theorist. Carl Rogers recognized that people tend to establish barriers and to grow more rigid in their beliefs when threatened and are thus less open to alternatives. If we view argument, whether spoken or written, not as a hostile contest between adversaries but as a dialogue, we may find a more responsive audience and thus have greater success with changing people's opinions. We need to develop *empathy*—the ability, in Rogers' words, "to see the expressed idea and attitude from the other person's point of view." It is through empathy that we can most successfully understand another's position and so concede appropriate points, often gaining rather than losing ground in the process. The reader will feel less threatened as the writer reduces the gap between them and replaces hostile judgment with "mutual communication."

A British politician turned to Rogerian strategy when Iran and Britain were in a political crisis over the publication of Salmon Rushdie's *The Satanic Verses*, a novel that offended Muslims to such a degree that the Ayatollah Khomeini, then the ruler of Iran, called on Muslims around the world to kill Rushdie, sending the author into hiding for 10 years. The British government, while providing the author with continuous police protection, tried to temper Iran's fury. Britain's foreign secretary, Sir Geoffrey Howe, in a BBC radio broadcast meant to be heard by Iran, delivered the following message:

> We do understand that the book itself has been found deeply offensive by people of the Muslim faith. We can understand why it has been criticized. It is a book that is offensive in many other ways as well. We are not upholding the right of freedom to speak because we agree with the book. The book is extremely rude about us. It compares Britain with Hitler's Germany. We don't like that any more than people of the Muslim faith like the attacks on their faith.

He concluded with his belief that no matter how offensive its content, "nothing in the book could justify a threat to the life of the author." His comments were meant to forge a bond of empathy between the British and the Iranians—both groups, both governments were criticized by Rushdie—so of course, the British understood the anger of the Iranians. Through this mutual understanding, the foreign secretary hoped to persuade Iran to withdraw its demand that Rushdie be assassinated. We wish we could claim success for Rogerian strategy in this instance, but in fact, it was not until the Ayatollah Khomeini died that the death sentence was lifted from Rushdie's head.

To write a convincing argument, you must present yourself as a reasonable, sympathetic person who respects your reader. Note how the two professional writers in the essays that follow use counterargument and concession to create reasoned arguments.

EXERCISE 4B

Analyzing Counterargument, Concession, and Refutation

1. Read each essay critically. Then, for **each selection,** identify, in writing, the writer's position and one example each of counterargument, refutation, and concession.

2. For class discussion, be prepared to discuss how effectively each author used all these rhetorical strategies.

Could It Be That Video Games Are Good for Kids?

STEVEN JOHNSON

Dear Sen. Clinton: I'm writing to commend you for calling for a $90-million study on the effects of video games on children, and in particular the courageous stand you have taken in recent weeks against the notorious "Grand Theft Auto" series. — 1

I'd like to draw your attention to another game whose nonstop violence and hostility has captured the attention of millions of kids—a game that instills aggressive thoughts in the minds of its players, some of whom have gone on to commit real-world acts of violence and sexual assault after playing. — 2

I'm talking, of course, about high school football. — 3

I know a congressional investigation into football won't play so well with those crucial swing voters, but it makes about as much sense as an investigation into the pressing issue of Xbox and PlayStation2. — 4

Your current concern is over explicit sex in "Grand Theft Auto: San Andreas." Yet there's not much to investigate, is there? It should get rated appropriately, and that's that. But there's more to your proposed study: You want to examine how video games shape children's values and cognitive development. — 5

Kids have always played games. A hundred years ago they were playing stickball and kick the can; now they're playing "World of Warcraft," "Halo 2" and "Madden 2005." And parents have to drag their kids away from the games to get them to do their algebra homework, but parents have been dragging kids away from whatever the kids were into since the dawn of civilization. — 6

So any sensible investigation into video games must ask the "compared to what" question. If the alternative to playing "Halo 2" is reading "The Portrait of a Lady," then of course "The Portrait of a Lady" is better for you. But it's not as though kids have been reading Henry James for 100 years and then suddenly dropped him for Pokemon. — 7

Another key question: Of all the games that kids play, which ones re-   8
quire the most mental exertion? Parents can play this at home: Try a few
rounds of Monopoly or Go Fish with your kids, and see who wins. I suspect
most families will find that it's a relatively even match. Then sit down and
try to play "Halo 2" with the kids. You'll be lucky if you survive 10 minutes.

The great secret of today's video games that has been lost in the moral   9
panic over "Grand Theft Auto" is how difficult the games have become.
That difficulty is not merely a question of hand-to-eye coordination; most of
today's games force kids to learn complex rule systems, master challenging
new interfaces, follow dozens of shifting variables in real time and prioritize
between multiple objectives.

In short, precisely the sorts of skills that they're going to need in the   10
digital workplace of tomorrow.

Consider this one fascinating trend among teenagers: They're spending   11
less time watching professional sports and more time simulating those
sports on Xbox or PlayStation. Now, which activity challenges the mind
more—sitting around rooting for the Green Bay Packers, or managing an
entire football franchise through a season of "Madden 2005": calling plays,
setting lineups, trading players and negotiating contracts? Which challenges the mind more—zoning out to the lives of fictional characters on a
televised soap opera, or actively managing the lives of dozens of virtual
characters in a game such as "The Sims"?

On to the issue of aggression, and what causes it in kids, especially   12
teenage boys. Congress should be interested in the facts: The last 10 years
have seen the release of many popular violent games, including "Quake" and
"Grand Theft Auto"; that period also has seen the most dramatic drop in violent crime in recent memory. According to Duke University's Child Well-Being
Index, today's kids are less violent than kids have been at any time since the
study began in 1975. Perhaps, Sen. Clinton, your investigation should explore
the theory that violent games function as a safety valve, letting children explore their natural aggression without acting it out in the real world.

Many juvenile crimes—such as the carjacking that is so central to   13
"Grand Theft Auto"—are conventionally described as "thrill-seeking"
crimes. Isn't it possible that kids no longer need real-world environments to
get those thrills, now that the games simulate them so vividly? The national
carjacking rate has dropped substantially since "Grand Theft Auto" came
out. Isn't it conceivable that the would-be carjackers are now getting their
thrills on the screen instead of the street?

Crime statistics are not the only sign that today's gaming genera-   14
tion is doing much better than the generation raised during that last
cultural panic—over rock 'n' roll. Math SAT scores have never been
higher; verbal scores have been climbing steadily for the last five years;
nearly every indicator in the Department of Education study known as the
Nation's Report Card is higher now than when the study was imple-
mented in 1971.

By almost every measure, the kids are all right.   15

Of course, I admit that one charge against video games is a slam dunk.   16
Kids don't get physical exercise when they play a video game, and indeed
the rise in obesity among younger people is a serious issue. But, of course,
you don't get exercise from doing homework, either.

Pro-Choice and Pro-Life

ART HOPPE

Like millions of Americans in this strangely divided country, I am both pro-   1
choice and pro-life. I'm both opposed to abortion, and I'm In favor of keeping them legal.

A *New York Times* CBS News poll the other day reported that a majority   2
of the respondents agreed that abortion was morally abhorrent. Yet a third
of these same people thought the act should be justified under the law.

This sounds like a cop-out. It's what I believe, too.   3

An abortion, by definition, is the killing of an unborn human being. No   4
one likes abortion, not even the most ardent advocate of a woman's right to
do what she wishes with her own body. An abortion is an act of desperation. Everyone from Pope John Paul II to Faye Wattleton would agree that
the better course is to avoid unwanted pregnancies.

Oddly enough, it is people on the liberal side of the political spec-   5
trum—people like me—who should be even more vigorously opposed to
abortion than the organized pro-lifers. It is we who prattle incessantly about
the sanctity of human life. It is we who oppose the death penalty—not for
the sake of the condemned criminal, but for the sake of us who execute
him. The future of the human race will never be secure, we preach, until we
renounce killing our own species for any reason.

How wondrous it is, then, that conservatives generally oppose abortion   6
and favor capital punishment, while liberals hold precisely the opposite
paradoxical viewpoint.

So how do I justify legalizing abortion? First of all, I think of a fertilized   7
egg—two microscopic cells, the spermatozoon and the ovum, joined together. It seems almost laughable to confer constitutional rights on something the size of an amoeba. And I find it equally hard to identify with the
reptilian-like embryo in the first stages of pregnancy.

The pro-lifers will argue that the sperm and the ovum, when joined,   8
are a potential human being, perhaps another Shakespeare or Beethoven.
To kill even this microscopic dot, they say, is outright murder. But
surely the same human potential lies in the sperm and the egg when still
separate.

Yet it has become morally acceptable to prevent them from joining, ei-   9
ther by contraception or, as the Catholics would have it, by the rhythm
method. Heaven only knows how many billions of sperm or hundreds of
ova perish unfulfilled in each of our lifetimes.

At the same time, I'm opposed to population control. I hate the argu- 10
ment of the pro-choice people that abortion is for the sake of the unwanted
child—that the mother is nobly saving her unborn from a life of poverty,
lovelessness or other deprivation. I say everything that's born, struggles to
be born; everything that's alive desperately wants to be alive—or, in the
case of humans, has the rarely exercised option of ending it all. Abortions
are committed for the sake of the parents.

So abortion, it seems to me, is a selfish act, a morally deplorable act. Yet 11
I irrationally support its legality. In the final analysis, it's because I am not
sure of my own arguments. I like to think that if I were a pregnant woman, I
would refuse an abortion. But that's merely what I like to think.

And if I'm not sure of the path through this tangled moral thicket, who 12
am I to force my way on others? At the very least, it's a controversial moral
choice. And, being controversial, I think only the mother can make it.

To force a woman to have a baby against her will requires the ultimate 13
in self-righteousness. God save us from the self-righteous.

When There Is No Other Side

What makes an issue worth arguing? While there are no fast rules, issues inappropriate for argument fall into three general categories. Some are so personal
or so self-evident that they don't lend themselves to intelligent debate. Take
for example the following claims:

Chocolate ice cream is far superior to strawberry.

or

Free, quality education should be provided for all children in America.

Neither proposition lends itself to the kind of exploration we have been
discussing in this chapter, in the first instance because it concerns a personal
and insignificant preference, and in the second because no one could in all se-
riousness argue against such a proposition.

A third, and more compelling, category is that in which the issue is simply
too offensive to the majority of writers or readers. Arguments advocating racial
bigotry or denial of the Holocaust, for example, fall into this category. Sometimes there is no other side worth defending.

Columnist Ellen Goodman illustrates how issues with no defensible other
side have affected newspaper reporting.

At the end of the 19th century, when African Americans were strung like
"strange fruit" from Southern trees, the *New York Times* required every story
about lynching to include a quote from a segregationist justifying the hanging.
At some point, the absurdity of that journalistic "evenhandedness" struck home
to the editors. Murder is not a story with "another side."

I mention that footnote to my profession's history because I've always found something odd in the notion that "balance" is a seesaw, outfitted with exactly two seats for opponents whose views are carefully and equally weighted. A given story may have 15 sides . . . or one.

When terrorists struck on September 11, there was only one side. No editor demanded a quote from someone saying why it was fine to fly airplanes into buildings. . . .

FOR AN EFFECTIVE ARGUMENT

Choose an issue worth arguing.

Express your thesis clearly.

Support your own position as thoroughly as possible.

Present relevant opposing views (counterarguments).

Provide appropriate concessions and refutations.

Develop empathy with your audience.

LOGICAL JOINING OF CONTRASTING AND CONCESSIVE IDEAS

To express contrast and concession, so necessary for effective written argument, you need to manipulate your sentences to create a coherent flow of ideas and to convey logical relationships. We introduced principles of logical joining with the discussion of conjunctions in Chapter 3 and continue that discussion here.

EXERCISE 4C

Expressing Contrast and Concession

Below are three different attitudes on smoking in public places. Read the passages carefully, examine the logical relationship between ideas, then state the position of each writer and explain how you reached your decision.

1. The battle continues. Whereas some contend that smoking, as a direct threat to health, should be banned in all public places, others maintain that this is too extreme a measure. Medical evidence demonstrates that cigarette smoke is harmful to nonsmoking bystanders as well as to smokers, but smokers argue that their emotional health is at stake. While nonsmokers claim that medical costs from health problems justify such restrictions of personal choice, smokers point out that such discrimination threatens their constitutional civil rights.

2. Although most people recognize that smoking is a direct threat to health, prohibiting smoking in public constitutes a new form of discrimination.

3. While banning smoking in public can create serious problems for smokers, current medical evidence strongly supports those who insist on a completely smoke-free environment.

As you have no doubt noticed, it is through the different choices of joining words that these writers established their slant on the issue here. Let's review these distinctions:

Coordinating Conjunctions	Subordinating Conjunctions	Major Transitions
Contrast:	**Contrast and Concession:**	**Contrast and Concession:**
but yet	while whereas although though	however on the other hand

The Concessive Sentence

The degree to which subordinating conjunctions express concession can vary according to the content of the sentence. In sentence 3 above, the writer recognizes the merit of a counterargument. But in some cases you may simply acknowledge your opponent's position without really conceding it, as in the following example:

Although smokers defend their constitutional rights, the health of a non-smoker should come first.

EXERCISE 4D

Making Rhetorical Choices

Take a stance on the issue of general education requirements by combining the first two sentences in number 1, using the appropriate joining word to reflect your position (your argument's "conclusion"). Then combine the following pairs of sentences so that the paragraph will be logically "shaped" to support your position and reveal appropriate concessions.

1. Many educators argue for a broad and rigorous series of required general education courses.

   Others claim that students should not have to spend so much time on general courses outside their chosen majors.

2. A general education program often means that students can't graduate in the customary four years and so must delay their careers.

Graduates with a broad liberal arts background tend to be promoted more consistently than their more narrowly trained competitors.

3. Most students can't afford to prolong their graduation.

   The nation can't afford a workforce of specialists uninformed about the world and unprepared in literacy and thinking skills.

4. Students are not inclined to learn in mandatory classes where they are not interested in the material.

   Undergraduates are often unaware of what's available on a college campus or what their interests might be, until they are exposed to a variety of subjects.

MORE ON COHERENCE

While you can manipulate ideas with joining words to signal relationships at the sentence level, you also need to develop rhetorical patterns of coherence throughout your paper. The form of your paper can take many shapes, but you want the whole to be held together by an almost invisible glue. Your thesis should guide you as you build paragraphs and create a thread that weaves its way from opening sentence to conclusion. The result will be a unified whole. Every sentence should follow from the sentence before it; each paragraph must follow logically from the one preceding it. As a writer, you take your reader's hand, never letting that reader stray from the flow of your argument. If you were to cut your paper into individual paragraphs, shake them up, and throw them in the air, a stranger should have no difficulty putting them together in the original order. The same is true of sentences within a paragraph.

To accomplish this **logical flow** from sentence to sentence, you will arrange points in a logical sequence, select joining conjunctions and major transitions carefully, and repeat or echo **key words** to keep your reader focused on your train of thought. Pronouns, those words that refer back to nouns (his, him, hers, her, they, this, that, these), can help relate one sentence to another, as can synonyms for nouns when repetition begins to sound monotonous. For more on keeping ideas connected within a paragraph, see Sentence Focus—Techniques for Sharpening the Flow of Ideas and Parallel Structure in Chapter 8.

A caution: Coherence devices should not be heavy-handed or too obvious. Remember to go lightly on the major transitions (however, therefore, on the other hand). It is the logical progression of your ideas that is important, not the deployment of conjunctions alone.

EXERCISE 4E

Identifying Coherence Strategies

To be sure that your papers are coherent, return to the essay you wrote for Writing Assignment 3, "Reconstructing the Lost Tribe." Make a copy and then cut the paper into separate paragraphs. Shuffle the paragraphs and bring the pieces to class. Exchange your paper with a classmate and see if you can reconstruct each other's work in the order the writer intended. If you encounter difficulties, consult with your partner to see what coherence strategies she needs to provide for a better flow of ideas from paragraph to paragraph.

Your instructor may suggest that you postpone this exercise until you can use a copy of Writing Assignment 8, "Taking a Stand," which follows later in this chapter.

SAMPLE ESSAYS

To help you see some of the rhetorical features of effective written argument in action, we have selected three examples representing a variety of topics for you to examine closely. The first two are by students, the third by a professional journalist. (The first essay, "College Athletes—Special Admissions?" illustrates how to document electronic sources. See also Chapter 9.)

EXERCISE 4F

Identifying Rhetorical Features of Argument

In the first essay, we identify the elements of written argument presented in this chapter. In the second and third essays, we ask you to do the same.

thesis

premises

counterarguments

refutations

concessions (You'll find that some concessions reflect Rogerian strategy.)

College Athletes—Special Admissions?

There are many different types of students, among them, those who do well 1
academically without really trying; those who do well but have to exert a lot
of time and energy to do so; those who don't do well but could if given the
right opportunity and set of circumstances; and those who don't do well but
do excel in other areas. High school students who have excellent academic
records will have little trouble meeting rigorous admissions requirements and

getting accepted to an academically competitive school. But there are many students who don't necessarily have that choice. Many students with less outstanding academic records must rely on other strengths to allow them an equal chance at a good education. One of the most common strengths a student can have besides academic proficiency is athletic skill. Because each individual, regardless of academic record, has something important to offer a college or univeristy, and because the world isn't clearly divided into "those who are smart" and "those who are not smart," I feel it is crucial for schools to be flexible in their admissions policies. Therefore, although some might argue that it is not fair for academically competitive colleges and universities to continue admitting accademically ill-equipped student athletes, I think it is crucial, both for the sake of the student athlete and the school.

Thesis–2 premises

2

Many people argue that admitting inferior students simply because they are good athletes is unfair to those students under consideration for their academic records alone, that this practice discriminates against or constitutes unfair treatment of qualified applicants who aren't athletically inclined. But, in fact, as a matter of policy, colleges and universities accept a certain number of academically ineligible students, called "special admits," under several separate programs. Special admits are usually students with outstanding specialized talents (in music, dance, theatre, art, for example), or from overseas, or with unique life experiences, not to mention legacies with family connections, as well as students from disadvantaged backgrounds. So, why not consider those with superior athletic ability?

Counterargument

Refutation

3

Others complain about the number of student athletes who don't graduate, claiming that schools waste their time and money on these students who never complete a degree. I agree that the statistics are frightening. Overall graduation rates for scholarship athletes are low. But if viewed in context, in comparison to all dropout rates, the picture takes on a different light, as suggested in an article a few years ago in The Wall Street Journal.

Counterargument

Concession

> Many people claim that only a small proportion of students who attend college on an athletic scholarship ever obtain a degree; but this is true of all entering freshmen in our colleges, since fewer than half emerge with degrees (McCormick).

Refutation

And in a more recent article in U.S. News & World Report, Ben Wildavsky claims that

> . . . scholarship athletes at Division 1 schools actually graduate at a rate slightly higher than the overall student population: 58 percent versus 56 percent, according to the NCAA's latest annual report. The athletes' rate is up a bit compared with 1985 but has generally held steady since the NCAA passed controversial new academic requirements known as Proposition 48 in 1986 (2).

Wildavsky cites Duke University's athletic program as an outstanding example of success, with a graduation rate of 90 percent for scholarship athletes versus a 93 percent average for all Duke students (2).

Counterargument

Some would argue that unprepared students admitted on athletic abil- 4
ity alone are at a severe disadvantage with even less time for academic pur-
suits than those more proficient. But most academically competitive schools
now have special academic counselors trained to deal with the needs and
problems of the student athlete. Specialized programs like San Francisco
State's PLUK (Please Let Us Know) Program are there to see that athletes be-

Refutation

come better equipped intellectually, strengthening academic skills which
may have been neglected in the past due to athletic participation. Bolster-
ing the high academic achievement of its student athletes, Duke recognizes
the pressures they face and provides exceptional "access to tutoring and
coaching in study skills—particularly time management" (Wildavskv 2).
While expensive academic support may not be the norm everywhere, the
days of trying to shuffle athletes through the academic system, using them
for their athletic skills with no regard for their own well-being, are waning.

Concession

I agree that the academic performance of many student athletes re- 5
mains a challenge. But in the meantime, it would be wrong not to allow
these student athletes a chance to mature and gain social and intellectual
skills that will help them wherever they go after college. In its "Big Ten Resolution on Intercollegiate Athletics" (representing 10 mid-western universities), the Committee on Institutional Cooperation stated:

> . . . Participation in committed athletic training and competition
> can be deeply rewarding for students as a field of personal excel-
> lence, and can foster character through discipline, team member-
> ship, and the mutual respect expressed in fair play. Skilled coaches
> can offer outstanding leadership to college athletes, and exemplify
> standards of dedication, expertise, and sportsmanship that comple-
> ment and enrich the academic missions of their campuses (1).

Refutation

Skip Prosser, the men's basketball coach at Wake Forest University, added
to this position: "I've seen so many kids [college basketball players], given
the opportunity, become great ambassadors for Wake Forest or wherever"
(Suggs 4). And reviewing a recent book on the subject, Reclaiming the
Game: College Sports and Educational Values, John Thelin comments "one
can attribute important educational values to varsity sports participation
that are not strictly academic. . . . We cannot assume a sport subculture is
necessarily antithetical to the proper values of the college experience"
(108–109).

Premise

Allowing schools the option to admit such student athletes might be 6
the only way these students could attend college. Their high school records
might be so poor that they wouldn't be accepted anywhere on academics
alone. In addition, many such students may not be able to afford tuition
and would be excluded from scholarships unless money was available for
athletes as well as scholars. In on-going efforts to raise graduation rates for
college athletes, the National Collegiate Athletic Association (NCAA) has
been recommending more demanding academic requirements. However,

coaches charge that they will knock more black players out of college. "They're legislating against African-American individuals," fulminates Jim Harrick, the men's basketball coach at the University of Georgia. . . . Most of the top basketball players are black, and coaches like Mr. Harrick fear any move could jeopardize their efforts to recruit the best players (Suggs 2).

Premise

Besides, college sports programs provide one of the very few avenues 7 available for promising young athletes to fully develop the necessary athletic prowess necessary for attempting to break into professional sports. Since it is often the more academically competitive schools that have the resources to build and support reputable, widely recognized sports programs, these are the schools that young athletes need to attend in order to increase their chances of fulfilling their primary career goal—professional sports. This idea is similar to that of a superior academic student who wants to attend Harvard Business School to increase his or her chances of fulfilling a career goal in business. Those students with superior athletic ability shouldn't be discriminated against and kept out of the good colleges and universities.

Premise

While it's the student athletes themselves I'm most concerned with— 8 their right to higher education, including preprofessional training—the schools who accept these athletes benefit as well. Recruiting promising high school athletes can add significantly to a college's established sports program and a good sports program can, in turn, be a big factor in attracting desirable applicants, both academic and athletic. Winning teams add to the overall reputation of a school, both inside and outside its immediate geographical area. Schools with winning teams can attract many good applicants as well as casting the deciding vote for a student torn between two otherwise equal schools.

Premise

Successful sports programs can also greatly affect alumni giving and 9 community support for a school. Sports booster clubs, alumni, and parents of students, past and present, are some of the largest givers of financial support to colleges and universities. Giving to favorite teams can also spill over into donations to other areas of a university with overall giving increasing, especially if it has winning teams.

And so, for the good of the school, and more importantly, for the bene- 10 fit of students who might not otherwise have a chance to realize their dreams or goals, I feel it is of the utmost importance for schools to continue admitting student athletes, even those not academically qualified.

Works Cited

Big Ten Resolution on Intercollegiate Athletics. 2 Nov. 2001. 29 Apr. 2005 <http://www.math.umd.edu/~jmc/COIA/BigTen.html>.

McCormick, Robert E. "Colleges Get Their Athletes for a Song." The Wall Street Journal 20 Aug. 1995.

Suggs, Welch. "Who's Going to Play?" Chronicle of Higher Education 48 (26 July 2002). EBSCOhost. San Francisco State U., J. Paul Leonard Lib. 28 Apr. 2005 <http://0-weblinks1.epnet.com>.

Thelin, John R. "Reclaiming the Game: College Sports and Educational Values." <u>Journal of Higher Education</u> 76 (Jan/Feb 2005). EBSCO*host*. San Francisco State U, J. Paul Leonard Lib. 28 Apr. 2005 <http://0-weblinks3. epnet.com>.

Wildavsky, Ben. "Graduation Blues." <u>USNews.com</u> 18 Apr. 2002. 29 Apr. 2005 <http://www.usnews.com/usnews/edu/college/sports/articles/18graduation. htm>.

Rap Takes a Bum Rap

JOHN HERSCHEND

Since its birth, Rap music has taken the blame for many of the problems plaguing America's inner cities—violence, drugs, AIDS, you name it. But Rap music cannot take the blame for these problems any more than, say, soap operas can shoulder the blame for infidelity in America. Rap is an art form, a medium which expresses, enrages and educates like most other art forms. As Guru says in the introduction to his album *Jazzmataz*, Rap is "musical, cultural expression based on reality." It does not cause problems but, instead, expresses them just as some movies, television shows and other forms of music do. However, unlike most of the mindless violence depicted in popular movies, Rap is a constructive outlet which brings attention to our country's problems in a creative, innovative and sometimes positive fashion. 1

In fact, the roots of rap are based in creativity and innovation. With its humble beginnings in the black ghettoes as filler between songs at parties, Rap has become a multi-million dollar business and one of the most established forms of new music in the past decade. The original idea was simple: two turntables and a microphone. The DJ, in command of the turntables, manipulates the records in order to form a beat or provide snippets of musical accompaniment. The "MC" then "busts out" in a fit of rhyme based stories, usually about the DJ's ability to "spin" or the MC's ability to "rap." However, as rap became more and more popular, the rappers began focusing their attention on the larger issues of life in the ghetto—violence, drugs, and oppression—forming two separate branches of Rap. 2

The first is known as "gangsta" rap, a rough mix of extreme violence and heavy rhythms, sounding something like broken glass on an inner city basketball court. The second is hip-hop, a jazz based, dance mix which is much more complex and layered than gangster. The music of hip-hop evokes the feel of a smoky, Soho jazz club in the 1950s while the words relate stories of ghetto life in the 1990s. The message of hip-hop is upbeat, oftentimes offering solutions or alternatives to the problems rather than focusing solely on them. Although gangsta and hip-hop differ in their style and message, both forms are important for their ability to educate and to offer a creative outlet. 3

Rap's ability to educate its listeners is an often overlooked but crucial ele-   4
ment of the music. Several groups envision the music as their way to speak
directly to kids. Groups such as the Bay Area's Disposable Heroes of Hipho-
prisy believe that they, as Rap artists, are the only role models the children
may have and therefore work to fill their music with thoughts on politics,
environmentalism and other social issues in hopes of raising the conscious-
ness of their listeners. Many of their songs are like quick morality plays. For
instance, on the Disposable Heroes' album, *Hypocrisy Is the Greatest Luxury,*
they have a song entitled "The Language of Violence" about a boy who
goes to jail for killing another boy. In the song, the killer is caught and sent
to jail where he is raped by the inmates. The song follows a more philosophical vein and asks: "is this a tale of rough justice in a land where there's
no justice at all. Who is really the victim? Or are we all the cause, and victim of it all." Lyricist Michael Franti's aim is to get the kids who might commit acts of violence to think not only of the immediate physical consequences of their actions, but of the larger picture of violence and
victimization. He says that "death is the silence in this circle of violence."
The same is true of other rap artists such as the Digable Planets, The Phar-
cyde and Guru. These groups fill their albums with a smoky coolness of life
on the streets and the choices available to the kids. They tell stories of
street life with a more positive and hopeful edge, working to expand the
vision of the listener, to help them see beyond the ghetto. Their music
doesn't seek to exploit or cause violence but rather paint a picture of reality
and offer alternatives.

But not all Rap music offers such positive alternatives. A good portion   5
of Rap, particularly gangsta, offers little or no alternatives. It simply paints
a picture of a bleak world where the gun is king. And it is here where Rap
foes focus their efforts and here where I would agree with them. They say
that Rap glamorizes the violence on the streets. They say that kids look to
these groups as heroes and follow their lyrics as a zealot Christian might
follow the Bible. In fact, a recent *Newsweek* article entitled *A Gangster
Wake-Up Call* questions whether kids will "change their attitudes about
money, sex, and violence now that gangster rap appears to be doing a
drive-by on itself?" In essence, the article is assuming that Rap is the only
place that kids get these ideas. The article is about the death (due to
AIDS) of Eazy-E, one of the first major Rap stars, and the jailing of three
other Rap superstars because of their violent ways. It seems that the Rap
foes are making an important point: Rap stars live the life they sing about.
But all this is presupposing the fact that the listeners of Rap are motivated
by the lyrics to take action in the streets. In fact, it completely bypasses
the notion that violence has existed in our streets before Rap and that the
musicians, particularly the ones indicated in the *Newsweek* article, are victims of these streets.

Rather than say that Rap lyrics are a cause of street violence, I would   6
like to offer the idea that violence is the cause of Rap lyrics, and that our

society seems to have a double standard when it comes to judging the violence of Rap music versus the violence of popular cinema and television. If we are to isolate Rap for its violence what, then, do we make of movies today? Or while we're on the subject, how about many popular TV shows? It seems that violence is an obsession with Americans and still we don't indict these shows as being the cause of it. They are accepted and even called "artistic," and works of genius. For instance, in "Vox Populi," an article which appeared in *The Atlantic* magazine, Francis Davis credits Quentin Tarantino for his subtle handling of an extremely violent scene in *Reservoir Dogs*. In the scene, a captive cop is bound to a chair while Mr. Blonde, played by Michael Madsen, dances around with a razor in his hand, eventually cutting off the cop's ear and dousing him in gasoline. Davis is impressed with the scene because it takes our emotions for a ride. He writes about the scene, saying that Madsen "does a series of graceful little dance steps to Stealers Wheel's 'Stuck in the Middle with You,' and closes in on his defenseless, screaming captive. 'Was that as good for you as it was for me?' Madsen asks the cop afterward. . . . Madsen might also be asking those of us who sat through the scene without averting our eyes."

Davis feels that this form of violence is more acceptable because it is complex and plays with the audience's emotions. Conversely, Rap artist Ice-T was forced, due to heavy protest from police organizations, to remove the song *Cop Killer* from an album with the same name. The police groups, who felt that the album encouraged kids to kill police officers, won their argument and Ice-T had to pull the song and change the name of the album. Interestingly enough, Tarantino did not meet the same criticism and was praised by many for his "genius" in handling the violence of the police scene. A double standard? To say that one form of violence is better or more acceptable than another is ridiculous. The hard edges of gangsta Rap are no different than Tarantino's violence. By stating that the violence of movies and TV shows does not cause acts of aggression while at the same time indicting Rap music as a reason for aggression, we set an absurd double standard.

Rap music is violent because it reflects the real life struggles of life on the inner city streets. And although this is not an appealing vision for many, it is still a telling story, one that deserves attention. Of course many songs are often blown out of proportion, but the kernel of struggle is still discernible. When groups sing about drive-bys, drugs and beer drinking, it's because the singers grew up with these realities. These are not imaginary issues that are drummed up to sell records; they are the incidents of real life for many kids in America. Rap music is a window to real life, an expression of frustration and a way for Americans to understand what is going on in our streets. This is not to validate the violence, but to say that the expression is a positive release for both listener and singer, something that should not be so readily ignored and dismissed.

We look to expression—music, literature, cinema—as a way of release.   9
Indeed, it is powerful; it can change hearts and minds. But expression is ultimately a product of experience. It is an interpretation of life and all the
emotions that go along with it—fear, love, anger, happiness—feelings as
old as our ability to express them. Rap, as a member of this community,
cannot and should not be singled out as the cause of violence. It is an expression of life in our inner cities, a vision that is sometimes hopeful and
sometimes violent but always based in reality. And if we listen without
prejudice, we might begin to hear the words behind the violence. We
might even be able to begin focusing on the real factors of ghetto life
rather than constantly blaming the messenger for the delivery of bad
news.

Works Cited

Davis, Francis. "Vox Populi." <u>Constellations: A Contextual Reader for
Writers</u>. 2nd ed. Ed. John Schilb, et al. New York: HarperCollins, 1995:
603–610.

Marriott, Michel. "A Gangster Wake-Up Call." <u>Newsweek</u> 10 Apr. 1995:
74–76.

A Case for Affirmative Action

CYNTHIA TUCKER

Why are many Americans—white Americans, mostly—so upset about col-   1
lege admissions programs that take race into account for a handful of students whose test scores are slightly below standards? Why are programs
that boost the chances of black and brown students so controversial, while
similar programs that benefit white students go without notice?

For example, the country's premier colleges and universities have   2
long reserved places for the lesser-achieving children of their well-heeled
graduates and donors. At the University of Georgia, family connections
are one of the dozen or so factors—along with race—used to assess about
20 percent of its applicants who don't quite meet academic standards. In
other words, a kid whose test scores and grades are not quite good
enough may get into Georgia anyway if his mom or dad is a graduate.

That practice allows weaker students—most of them white—to be ad-   3
mitted at the expense of better students. Yet no one bemoans it as an assault on the vaunted "meritocracy."

College admissions also grant athletic "preferences," a device that hap-   4
pens to benefit many kids—black, white, and brown—who otherwise could
not get near their chosen college. For some reason, a black kid with low
SATs who can score touchdowns and generate a lot of money for the university is not nearly as offensive as a black kid with low scores who just
wants an education.

To be fair, some criticism of college admissions efforts is legitimate.   5
Awarding scholarships based on race makes no sense, since they would often

end up giving financial aid to the black upper-middle-class but not to the white poor. Besides that, poorly run affirmative-action programs, such as the contracting set-aside program run by the city of Atlanta, tend to generate resentments that splash over onto better-run and more necessary programs.

But much criticism of affirmative action in college admissions is based on myth, misunderstanding and—how shall I say this?—simple bigotry. Affirmative-action programs exist only in 25 percent to 40 percent of the nation's institutions of higher learning; the other 60 percent to 75 percent accept all applicants. So the controversy centers around the nation's most prestigious institutions. 6

Admission to those elite colleges is highly competitive, because a diploma from Harvard or Emory nearly guarantees a financially rewarding career. Rejected white applicants, looking for an explanation for their failure, often believe they were unfairly supplanted by an unqualified minority student. 7

Consider, however, an analogy used by Thomas Kane of the Brookings Institution, likening affirmative action in colleges to the handicapped parking space: 8

> Eliminating the reserved space would have only a minuscule effect on parking options for non-disabled drivers. But the sight of the open space will frustrate many passing motorists who are looking for a space. Many are likely to believe that they would now be parked if the space were not reserved.

Scaling back affirmative action would cripple the prospects for black participation in this nation's economic, political and social elite. William Bowen, former president of Princeton University, and Derek Bok, former president of Harvard University, recently conducted a landmark study of affirmative action at 28 elite institutions, including Atlanta's Emory University. They found that black graduates of those colleges go on to earn advanced degrees—medicine, law, MBAs—at slightly higher rates than their white counterparts, and also become more active in civic affairs. 9

Because America proffers advancement through education, programs to enhance educational opportunities for students of color remain critical—perhaps more important than any other form of affirmative action. Since my grandfathers would not have been admitted to white universities, it does not seem unreasonable to create a form of "legacy" for their descendants. 10

FOUR APPROACHES TO WRITING ARGUMENTS

The next four writing assignments all focus on argument. Writing Assignment 7 serves as preparation for Writing Assignment 8. Writing Assignment 9 presents a more complex and thus more challenging approach to an issue. Writing

Assignment 10 focuses on working collaboratively with classmates on complex issues chosen by the class.

WRITING ASSIGNMENT 7

Arguing Both Sides of an Issue

The Topic

Below is a list of proposals advocating a position on a social issue. Choose **one** and write two arguments, one **defending** and one **refuting** the proposal. For each argument, convey clearly the position you are taking by writing a short thesis (the conclusion of your argument) at the top of the page. For each position, provide relevant reasons (premises) that are, to the best of your knowledge, accurate although not fully developed yet. You will have two separate papers with a paragraph for each premise. Although each paragraph should be written coherently with fluent sentences, you don't, at this stage, need to provide logical transitions between paragraphs for a coherent whole. And you need not provide an introduction or conclusion. All this will come later in Writing Assignment 8, 9, or 10.

Make your selection with care, for you will be spending considerable time on this one issue.

1. The use of car phones while a driver is in motion should be prohibited.

2. The military draft should be reinstated.

3. Internet users should be permitted to download music without cost.

4. Online gambling should be prohibited by federal law.

5. Even if economics is not a factor, the mother of a young child or children is still justified in choosing to work outside the home.

6. Government should provide support for stem cell research.

7. The Golden Gate Bridge and other unprotected spans should have suicide barriers.

8. Athletes are being unfairly singled out for using performance-enhancing drugs.

9. The SAT should be considered a necessary component of college admission criteria.

10. Fast food restaurants should take responsibility for the nation's growing obesity rate.

11. Nationwide standardized tests throughout elementary and secondary school have a negative effect on education.

12. Parents should be allowed to choose the sex of their child.

13. Medical research on animals should be forbidden by law.

14. Girls 17 and under should be required to obtain parental permission before having an abortion.

15. Video games foster violent behavior among young people.

16. Women are underrepresented in the sciences because they are discriminated against.

OR

Women are underrepresented in the sciences because of innate differences between the sexes.

If another issue interests you more, you may write on it. Be sure the issue is one worth arguing from both sides and can be expressed as a proposal similar to those above. You may, of course, change any of the given topics to suit your own purpose. Be sure to consult with your instructor before selecting an alternative topic.

Audience

A wide range of your peers: those who would agree with you, those who would disagree, and those who have not, as yet, formed any opinion.

Purpose

To present both sides of a controversial issue so you and your readers are forced to consider alternatives to one position.

WRITING ASSIGNMENT 8

Taking a Stand

The Topic

In this essay, take a stand on the issue you debated in Writing Assignment 7, constructing as persuasive an argument as possible. Your **thesis** should express your position either for or against the proposition you addressed in the previous assignment.

To support your position fully, draw on the **premises** you presented in Writing Assignment 7, discarding reasoning that seems weak or irrelevant, adding reasons where you find gaps in your earlier paper. Strengthen your argument with as much data as you think necessary to make your case. As you expand your argument, you will need to consult outside sources—newspapers, magazines, books, and carefully evaluated Web sites—for supporting information. Be sure to cite all references. For guidelines on documentation, consult Chapter 9, your English handbook, or Internet guides.

To address **opposing views,** select the most important premises from your list of arguments on the other side of your position and briefly address them, acknowledging, conceding, and refuting in the manner best suited to your stand on the issue. Do not elaborate the opposing views in the same way you will develop your own premises.

For help in organizing your paper, refer to the sample essays in Exercise 4F.

Important: To complete the assignment, include the following attachments written out on a separate sheet as an introductory page:

1. Your issue, question at issue, and thesis
2. Your principal argument set out in standard form (see Chapter 3)

Audience

The same as for Writing Assignment 7.

Purpose

To present a convincing, balanced, fair argument for your position on a controversial issue in order to persuade your readers to adopt your point of view.

A CHECKLIST OF ESSENTIAL COMPONENTS FOR WRITING ASSIGNMENT 8

A clear thesis to guide you as a writer and prepare your reader.

Support for this thesis—plenty of well-reasoned premises supported with examples and your own analysis.

Counterarguments with appropriate concessions and refutations.

Sentences logically joined for contrast and concession and overall coherence.

WRITING ASSIGNMENT 9

Exploring an Argument in Depth—An Alternative

Not all issues lend themselves to a pro or con, yes or no argument. In Writing Assignment 7, you argued two opposing positions on the same question at issue, and then in Writing Assignment 8 took a position on that issue. For this paper, address an issue in more of its complexity, considering arguments from as many sides as possible and coming to a conclusion that seems reasonable in light of your in-depth exploration. Such topics often present paradoxes in which two contradictory claims may both merit approval. In such a conclusion, you may incline to one position or another or may settle for explaining and clarifying the issues without going so far as to make a definitive decision.

The Topic

Choose a current controversial issue of interest to you, one that suggests more than a simple pro and con approach. Because you will present a number of viewpoints, you must make sure your readers know which point of view you are expressing at any given point in the paper. Clear and logical transitions between points will help you accomplish this, as will smooth attributions of quotations and references to the ideas of others (see Chapter 9).

Be prepared to face a degree of chaos as you sort out the different perspectives. Don't be afraid of the inevitable confusion that a more complex issue often produces. It is through such a thinking and writing process that critical thinking takes place.

Audience

The same as for Assignments 7 and 8.

Purpose

To clarify your audience's understanding of a complex, controversial issue.

A CHECKLIST FOR WRITING ASSIGNMENT 9

An introduction that presents the question at issue with appropriate background, acknowledges its complexity, and suggests your thesis even though you may not be taking a clear stand either pro or con.

A detailed discussion of arguments for as many positions as possible.

Refutations and concessions as appropriate for a thoughtful examination of alternatives.

Your personal recommendation on the issue, based on an evaluation in which you weigh the strengths and weaknesses of the positions you have presented, or a call for further investigation, or a summary of possible alternatives.

WRITING ASSIGNMENT 10

Collaborating on a Complex Issue—A Group Approach

Here we offer an alternative approach to writing the kind of argument presented in Writing Assignment 9. Rather than preparing your paper on your own, you will be working with a group of classmates. Once out in the world, writing for business, politics, for many jobs, you will find that much of the writing you do is collaborative.

The Topic

Each member of the class will submit two or three controversial issues. From this list, the class will select four or five topics around which research groups will form on the basis of preference. You should end up with groups of five or six students.

Here are the guidelines for working with classmates to construct a written argument:

1. The research group for each topic will meet in class to narrow the issue to a specific question at issue.

2. Students will conduct research to find at least one relevant article each that addresses the question at issue. They will make copies for members of the group. Because these articles are to represent the various positions on the question at issue, members of the group must confer to ensure that the articles together reflect the diverse points of view.

3. Students will reduce the central argument of their own articles to standard form (see Chapter 3).

4. Each group will meet as often as necessary, in class and out as time permits, to share and discuss these materials. Members of each group will also have an opportunity to discuss the organization and development of their papers and to suggest additional research if necessary.

5. The class will choose whether students complete these papers on their own or work together as a group to compose one final product as a fully collaborative effort.

6. Each group may want to select the best paper to read to the class, or, in the case of collaborative papers, there should be time to hear them all.

Audience

The same as for Writing Assignments 7, 8, and 9.

Purpose

To present different perspectives on an issue and to engage or persuade an audience through collaborative effort.

SUMMARY

Convincing arguments usually contain an introduction to the topic, a **thesis** stated or clearly implied, well-supported **premises,** acknowledgment of **opposing views,** and a conclusion. Successful written argument depends on a **dialectical approach** in which writers address both their own position and the views of others.

A well-written argument requires joining sentences for logic and fluency and developing coherent links to express relationships.

Collaboration on the production of a written argument can be helpful and reflects the process often used in the working world.

KEY TERMS

Concession   a statement that grants the opposing view.

Counterargument   an opposing view in an argument.

Dialectic   a method of argument that systematically weighs contradictory ideas.

Empathy   the ability to see and understand an idea or issue from the other person's point of view.

Issue   any topic of concern and controversy.

Question at issue   a particular aspect of the issue under consideration.

Refutation   an explanation of why a position is false or weak.

Rhetoric   the art of using language to good effect, to prove, to convince, to persuade.

Rogerian strategy   an explicit effort to see ideas from an opponent's point of view; the cultivation of empathy with the opposition; a concept derived from the research of psychologist Carl Rogers.

Thesis   a statement of a writer's position; in argument, a response to the question at issue, the conclusion of the central argument in an essay.

CHAPTER 5

The Language of Argument— Definition

"When I use a word," Humpty Dumpty said in rather a scornful tone, *"it means just what I choose it to mean—neither more nor less."*
— LEWIS CARROLL, *ALICE THROUGH THE LOOKING GLASS*

"If you would argue with me, first define your terms."
—VOLTAIRE

In Chapter 4, we discuss how to construct written arguments that explore an issue in depth and address opposing views. Now we'd like to concentrate on the precise use of language, on paying close attention to how we choose our words, and thus on how we make our meaning precise and clear to others. It is important that we know the meaning and the power of the words we use, and that when we write, our readers, to the degree possible, share our understanding of these words. When we cannot assume that our readers share an understanding of our terms, we need to define them.

DEFINITION AND PERCEPTION

Controlling the Discourse

Ellen Willis, writing in *Rolling Stone,* admonishes us, "Find out who controls the definitions, and you have a pretty good clue who controls everything else." Toni Morrison, in her novel *Beloved,* illustrates the brutal oppression of slavery with the story of the slave Sixo. When the school teacher accused him of stealing the shoat (a piece of pork), Sixo claimed he wasn't *stealing* but *improving his property.* The teacher beat Sixo "to show him that definitions belonged to the definers—not the defined."

Alice responded to Humpty Dumpty's claim in the opening quotation of this chapter with, "The question is, whether you *can* make words mean so many different things." Humpty Dumpty continued, "The question is, which is to be master—that's all."

Nowhere is the precision of language more important than in politics. Yet nowhere is meaning more likely to be manipulated. Writing in the *New York Times Magazine,* political writer Matt Bai explained how the Republican party controlled the language of debate during the 2004 election and how subsequently the Democrats tried to regain control by "framing" the issues themselves. While widely debated, the term "framing" was generally understood to mean choosing the language to **define** controversial issues and thus establish positive contexts for political arguments. Bai discussed the Republican's successful invention of terms like "tax relief" and "partial-birth abortions" to cast a favorable aura around their policies of low taxes and opposition to abortion. But he also pointed out that Republican senators made a mistake when they used the phrase "nuclear option" to describe their decision to abolish the filibuster. This misstep in language choice alienated many and allowed the Democrats to reframe the discussion in their terms and accuse the Republicans of "changing the rules in the middle of the game," threatening time-honored "checks and balances," and being guilty of an "abuse of power." Such phrases "framed" the Democrats' arguments in the favorable light of constitutional tradition and preserved the Senate's right to filibuster.

Defining Ourselves

Our definitions can reveal how we see people—as individuals and collectively. In his book *Days of Obligation,* writer Richard Rodriguez points out that American feminists have appropriated the word *macho* "to name their American antithesis," a man who is "boorish" and "counterdomestic." But Rodriguez tells us that in Mexican Spanish "*machismo* is more akin to the Latin *gravitas.* The male is serious. The male provides. The Mexican male never abandons those who depend upon him." As this example illustrates, when different cultures share languages, shifts in meaning often occur, reflecting cultural bias.

Feminist Gloria Steinem pointed out our culture's sexual bias in its traditional definitions of the following terms, definitions that have played crucial roles in determining how women and men view themselves and others:

> *work:* something men do, go to; as distinguished from housework and childcare, which is what women do
>
> *art*: what white men produce
>
> *crafts:* what women and ethnic minorities do

Fortunately, these definitions are changing. Indeed, we have historical precedent for scientific definitions shifting to conform to new ways of thinking. In the nineteenth century, alcoholism was defined as criminal behavior.

When the term was redefined as an illness after World War I, considerable progress in treatment became possible.

Conversely, when the American Psychological Association recently stopped classifying homosexuality as an illness, the homosexual community was understandably gratified by the revision of a definition it found unjust and damaging.

Definition and the Social Sciences

In a study on child abuse and health, which we cite in Chapter 7, the researchers first had to define child abuse before they could determine its effect on women's health. They separated child abuse into three categories—emotional, physical, and sexual. Then they defined each category.

> *emotional abuse:* repeated rejection or serious physical threats from parents, tension in the home more than 25 percent of the time, and frequent violent fighting among parents.

> *physical abuse:* strong blows from an adult or forced eating of caustic substances; firm slaps were excluded.

> *sexual abuse:* any nonvoluntary sexual activity with a person at least five years older.

Researchers interviewed 700 women from a private gynecological practice and tabulated their responses according to these categories. Without clear-cut definitions to guide them, social scientists would be left with subjective impressions rather than quantifiable results.

In law, definitions often need to be revised to avoid unfair applications as society changes. Such was the case when SUVs slipped though a giant loophole in the tax code inadvertently left gaping. To help small businesses and farmers, the government provided tax credits and accelerated depreciation for small trucks, vehicles defined not by function but by their weight—more than 6,000 pounds. Into this provision slipped the SUV, once rare for personal use but for many years now a popular family vehicle. A variety of professional people could receive a tax break for driving very large, very expensive SUVs to work and around town. To achieve fairness, we need new definitions: "work vehicles" and "passenger vehicles."

LANGUAGE: AN ABSTRACT SYSTEM OF SYMBOLS

Abstract words can present particular difficulties when it comes to stipulating precise meaning. But language itself, whether it refers to an **abstraction** (politics) or a **concrete** object (a given politician), is an abstract system of symbols. The word is not the thing itself, but a *symbol* or *signifier* used to represent the thing we refer to, which is the *signified*. For example, the word "cat" is a symbol or signifier for the animal itself, the signified.

"Cat"

THE SYMBOL or SIGNIFIER
(the word)

THE SIGNIFIED
(the thing being referred to)

But meaning is made only when the signified is processed through the mind of someone using or receiving the words. This process serves as an endlessly destabilizing force. Whenever a speaker, writer, listener, or reader encounters a word, a lifetime of associations renders the word, and thus the image it conjures up, distinct for each individual.

As literary theorist Stanley Fish points out, meaning is dependent not only on the individual but also on the context, situation, and interpretive community. To illustrate this point, let's look at the word "host." It means one thing if we are at a party, something different if we're discussing parasites with a biologist, and something else entirely if we are at church. Hence, the context or situation determines our understanding of "host."

If, however, you are not a member of a religion that practices the ritual of communion or are not conversant with parasitology, then you may understand the meaning of "host" *only* as the giver of a party. You are not part of the interpretive community, in this case a religious community or a scientific discipline, that understands "host" as a consecrated wafer, a religious symbol, or as an organism on which another lives.

Even when the signified is concrete, individual experience and perception will always deny the word complete stability; the range of possible images will still be vast. Take the word "table." Nothing of the essence of table is part of the word "table." Although most words in English (or any modern language) have roots and a history in older languages, the assignation of a particular meaning to a given term remains essentially arbitrary. While all English speakers share a *general* understanding of the word "table," each user or receiver of this word, without having considerably more detail, will create a different picture.

If the symbolic representation of a **concrete,** visible object such as a table is as unstable as our discussion suggests, think how much more problematic **abstract** terms must be. Were we to substitute the abstraction "freedom" for the concrete "table," the range of interpretations would be considerably more diverse and much more challenging to convey to others. Visual pictures, which arise when concrete objects are signaled, don't come to mind as readily when we refer to abstractions, a distinction that led Shakespeare to explain why poets must give "to airy nothing a local habitation and a name."

In the following poem, Thomas Lux explores the "endlessly destabilizing force" of language as readers, even when reading the same text, make it uniquely their own.

THE VOICE YOU HEAR WHEN YOU READ SILENTLY

is not silent, it is a speaking
out-loud voice in your head: it is spoken,
a voice is saying it
as you read. It's the writer's words,
of course, in a literary sense
his or her "voice" but the sound
of that voice is the sound of your voice.
Not the sound your friends know
or the sound of a tape played back
but your voice
caught in the dark cathedral
of your skull, your voice heard
by an internal ear informed by internal abstracts
and what you know by feeling,
having felt. It is your voice
saying, for example, the word "barn"
that the writer wrote
but the "barn" you say
is a barn you know or knew. The voice
in your head, speaking as you read,
never says anything neutrally—some people
hated the barn they knew,
some people love the barn they know
so you hear the word loaded
and a sensory constellation
is lit: horse-gnawed stalls,
hayloft, black heat tape wrapping
a water pipe, a slippery
spilled chirrr of oats from a split sack,
the bony, filthy haunches of cows . . .
And "barn" is only a noun—no verb
or subject has entered into the sentence yet!
The voice you hear when you read to yourself
is the clearest voice: you speak it
speaking to you.

EXERCISE 5A

Reading Language

1. In this poem, what is the difference between the voice of the writer and the voice of the reader?

2. What is the significance of the exclamation mark at the end of the following lines?

   And "barn" is only a noun—no verb
   or subject has entered into the sentence yet!

3. What is Lux saying about language and the act of reading?

The Importance of Specificity

Semanticist S. I. Hayakawa discussed the idea of an abstraction ladder in which language starts on the ground, so to speak, with an object available to our sense of perception, and moves up to concepts abstracted from, derived from, the concrete source—for example, from a specific cow to livestock to farm assets to assets. He stressed that our powers of abstraction are indispensable. "The ability to climb to higher and higher levels of abstraction is a distinctively human trait without which none of our philosophical or scientific insights would be possible." But he cautioned against staying at too high a level of abstraction.

> The kind of "thinking" we must be extremely wary of is that which *never* leaves the higher verbal levels of abstraction, the kind that never points *down* the abstraction ladder to lower levels of abstraction and from there to the extensional world:
>
> "What do you mean by *democracy*?"
> "Democracy means the preservation of human *rights*."
> "What do you mean by *rights*?"
> "By rights I mean those privileges God grants to all of us—I mean man's inherent privileges."
> "Such as?"
> "Liberty, for example."
> "What do you mean by *liberty*?"
> "Religious and political freedom."
> "And what does that mean?"
> "Religious and political freedom is what we enjoy under a democracy."

The writer never moves down to the essential lower levels on the abstraction ladder, and a discourse consisting only of abstractions, devoid of concrete details and examples, is necessarily vague, often difficult for the reader to understand, and, in this definition of democracy, circular.

To avoid the confusion that unclarified abstractions can generate, Hayakawa suggested pointing down "to extensional levels wherever necessary; in writing and speaking, this means giving **specific examples** of what we are talking about," grounding our arguments in experience.

Compare the empty, circular definition of democracy Hayakawa quotes above with the concrete illustrations that illuminate E. B. White's celebrated World War II definition of the same term.

> We received a letter from the Writers' War Board the other day asking for a statement on "The Meaning of Democracy." It presumably is our duty to comply with such a request, and it is certainly our pleasure. Surely the Board knows what democracy is. It is the line that forms on the right. It is the don't in don't shove. It is the hole in the stuffed shirt through which the sawdust slowly trickles; it is the dent in the high hat. Democracy is the recurrent suspicion that more than half of the people are right more than half of the time. It is the feeling of privacy in the voting booths, the feeling of communion in the libraries, the feeling of vitality everywhere. Democracy is a letter to the Editor. Democracy is the score at the beginning of the ninth. It is an idea that hasn't been disproved yet, a song the words of which have not gone bad. It's the mustard on the hot dog and the cream in the rationed coffee. Democracy is a request from a War Board, in the middle of a morning in the middle of a war, wanting to know what democracy is.

Such specificity is what writer Annie Dillard values when she says, "This is what life is all about: salamanders, fiddle tunes, you and me and things . . . the fizz into **particulars**." And what novelist Vladimir Nabokov prizes when he asks us to "Caress the details, the divine **details**."

EXERCISE 5B

Levels of Specificity

Good writing requires that general concepts or categories be illustrated by specific examples. To practice providing the kind of concrete, specific detail Dillard and Nabokov talk about above, rank the words and phrases in the following lists, giving a "1" to the most general, with higher numbers moving through each level of specificity. You may find more than one item on a given level.

	2	1	4	3	2
Example:	actors;	performers;	Bill Murray;	movie actors;	singers;

4	4	3
Mariah Carey;	Jennifer Aniston;	pop singers

1. painting
   work of art
   Whistler's Mother
   American painting
   painting by Whistler
2. shuffle
   move
   amble
   walk slowly
   travel on foot
   drive
   walk
3. sport
   doubles
   five-card draw
   boxing
   card games
   activity
   poker
   tennis
   bridge
   singles
   welterweight fight
4. negative characteristic
   characteristic
   cheating
   unethical characteristic
   plagiarism
5. novel
   modern American novel
   reading
   The Grapes of Wrath
   fiction
   literature

> novel by Steinbeck
> modern novel

6. vertebrates
   Alaskan huskies
   biped
   Chris Rock
   woman
   dogs
   animals
   quadruped
   Jessica Simpson
   man
   cat
   Siamese cats
   basset hounds

Abstractions and Evasion

Sometimes abstractions and evasive language are used, consciously or unconsciously, to confuse, distort, conceal, or evade, in short, to manipulate others—a practice Hemingway laments in his war novel, *A Farewell to Arms:*

> I was always embarrassed by the words sacred, glorious, and sacrifice and the expression in vain. We had heard them, sometimes standing in the rain almost out of earshot, so that only the shouted words came through, and had read them, on proclamations that were slapped up by billposters or other proclamations, now for a long time, and I had seen nothing sacred, and the things that were glorious had no glory and the sacrifices were like the stockyards at Chicago if nothing was done with the meat except to bury it. There were many words that you could not stand to hear and finally only the names of places had dignity. Certain numbers were the same way and certain dates and these with the names of the places were all you could say and have them mean anything. Abstract words such as glory, honor, courage, or hallow were obscene beside the concrete names of villages, the numbers of roads, the names of rivers, the numbers of regiments and the dates.

Hemingway eloquently indicates the power of concrete nouns to honor the dead.

During debates on the complex environmental issue of preserving wetlands, the first President Bush declared that "all existing wetlands, no matter how small, should be preserved." But when pressured by real estate, oil, and mining interests to open protected wetlands to development and exploration, Bush expediently redefined the word, a definition that left at least 10 million acres of wetlands unprotected. Such examples lend fresh meaning to our earlier claims of power for those who control the definitions.

British writer George Orwell addressed the political significance of language in his celebrated essay, "Politics and the English Language," claiming that

> political speech and writing are largely the defense of the indefensible. . . . Defenseless villages are bombarded from the air, the inhabitants driven out into the countryside, the cattle machine-gunned, the huts set on fire with incendiary bullets: this is called *pacification*."

"Pacification" is an example of a **euphemism** which deliberately obscures the reality of war.

Euphemism and Connotation

Euphemisms—indirect, less expressive words or phrases for sensitive ideas— are sometimes justified as a means of sparing feelings: Someone passed away rather than died, or a fat person is referred to as big-boned. But we must be

" 'Born in conservation,' if you don't mind. 'Captivity' has negative connotations."

particularly wary of language that deliberately camouflages precise meaning. A few years ago, when opposition to building the controversial MX missile grew heated, the proponents began to call the missiles "peacemakers," hoping to deflect public reaction away from the notion of an arms buildup.

As suggested by the elephants' conversation, euphemisms can give a positive connotation to a negative experience. Many words carry both a denotative and a connotative meaning. **Denotation** refers to the basic dictionary meaning of a word, separate from its emotional associations. **Connotation** means the suggestive or associative implications beyond the literal, explicit sense of a word. For example, think of the words *bachelor* and *spinster*. Both refer to (denote) an unmarried adult. But now consider the connotation. In our culture, one word carries a positive connotation, the other a negative one. The two words, *slender* and *skinny*, both mean thin. But one would be a compliment, the other not.

EXERCISE 5C

Beware the Euphemism

1. Below is a list of paired terms or phrases. For each, briefly explain how the language of the second phrase dulls or deflects the meaning, and thus the reality, of the initial term, and discuss why you think such euphemistic language crept in. For some of these terms, you may need to do a little research in order to fully understand the meaning.

TERM		EUPHEMISM
1) drilling for oil	/	exploring for energy
2) foreign	/	offshore
3) taxes	/	revenue enhancement
4) tax cuts	/	tax relief
5) collateral damage	/	civilian losses
6) cloning	/	"somatic cell nuclear transfer"
7) shot by a fellow soldier	/	friendly fire
8) face wrinkles	/	laugh lines

2. From newspapers, magazines, television, or the Internet find a current example of usage that you think represents a manipulative euphemism. Advertising is often a good source of deceptive language. Explain the difference between the denotative and the connotative meaning and why the euphemism seemed necessary.

DEFINITION IN WRITTEN ARGUMENT

Appositives—A Strategy for Defining Terms Within the Sentence

As we have illustrated in this chapter, abstract terms need illustration with specific, concrete examples, and words that might be obscure to a general audience need defining so that our readers understand what we mean. How does a writer define terms without derailing the organization and flow of the paper or paragraph? Often, the answer is to use **appositives—noun phrases (or pronouns) placed beside other nouns (or pronouns) to elaborate on their meaning.** We illustrate this relationship with an arrow pointing from the appositive to the noun it modifies.

Appositives usually follow the nouns they modify:

> The <u>Sacramento River</u>, *the main* <u>*source*</u> *of surface water in a state where distrust of centralized governmental authority has historically passed for an ethic*, has its headwaters in the far northern ranges of Siskiyou County.

By placing important detail in an appositive, shown here in italics, writer Joan Didion says a lot about both a California river and the state where it flows, all in one fluent sentence. But writers may also introduce a sentence with an appositive:

> *An expression of frustrated* <u>*rage*</u>, <u>rap</u> tries to be outrageous in order to provoke strong reactions.

The phrase "an expression of frustrated rage" modifies "rap." Such additions allow a writer to include essential information or background details that may not warrant separate sentences. You can expand meaning even as you remain reasonably economical in sentence length.

> The first scene of the opera *Die* <u>*Walkure*</u>, *the* <u>*second*</u> *of the four operas making up Richard Wagner's Ring Cycle*, takes place in the house of <u>Hunding</u>, *a fierce* <u>*warlord*</u>.

EXERCISE 5D

Recognizing Appositives

In the three passages that follow, identify the appositives and the nouns they modify by underlining the appositives and drawing an arrow pointing to the nouns or pronouns they modify.

1. A descriptive passage with examples

The Evertons are introduced to a second national peculiarity, one they will soon recognize on the streets of Ibarra and in towns and cities beyond. It is something they will see everywhere—a disregard for danger, a companionship with death. By the end of a year they will know it well: the antic bravado, the fatal games, the coffin shop beside the cantina, the sugar skulls on the frosted cake.

—HARRIET DOERR, *STONES FOR IBARRA*

2. Identification

Cotton Mather was an exception, one who so fully accepted and magnified the outlook of his locality that he has entered folklore as the archetypal Puritan, not only a villainous figure in the pages of Hawthorne, William Carlos Williams and Robert Lowell, but an object of parody even to his fellow townsmen in 18th-century Boston.

—LARZER ZIFF, *THE NEW YORK TIMES BOOK REVIEW*

3. Definition

As Baranczak points out, Milosz [Nobel Prize–winning poet] rejects symbols in favor of metonymy and synecdoche, those figures of speech which represent a whole by a thing allied to it or by a part of it.

—HELEN VENDLER IN *THE NEW YORKER*

Appositives and Argument

Appositives in arguments are useful, allowing you to define terms, expand and emphasize ideas, and show opposing points of view in the same sentence, as illustrated in the following example:

A unilateral attack on a foreign enemy, *a policy that was considered difficult and dangerous by many, but one that was vigorously promoted by a number of hardline strategists*, means the U.S. would strike without the support of other nations.

Two views on American foreign policy are juxtaposed in one strong sentence. And you will find appositives helpful when identifying sources within the text of your paper:

S. I. Hayakawa, *a noted semanticist*, points out that advertising and poetry are alike (162).

Punctuation of Appositives

Punctuation choices are simple and logical. In most cases, the appositive phrase is set off from the noun it modifies with commas, as we illustrate above. If you want greater emphasis, you can do as Harriet Doerr did and use a dash: "It is something they will see everywhere—*a disregard for danger, a companionship with death.*"

Occasionally, when an appositive ends a sentence, a colon is appropriate for even sharper emphasis. This is a good choice when you're concluding a sentence with a list.

> The President gave his reasons for going to war: *Hussein was amassing weapons of mass destruction; he was securing uranium from Africa; he was a ruthless killer of Kurds and Shiites; he was threatening authorized U.S. air surveillance.*

EXERCISE 5E

Creating Appositives

Most of you already use appositives to some extent in your writing whether you recognize them or not. But a little conscious practice may expand your use of this handy device.

A. Combine the following sets of sentences by reducing one or more sentences to appositives. You may find more than one way to combine them.

> **Example:**
>
> A unilateral attack on a foreign enemy was considered difficult and dangerous by many. It means the U.S. would strike without the support of other nations.
>
> becomes
>
> A unilateral attack on a foreign enemy means the U.S. would strike without the support of other nations, *a policy that was considered difficult and dangerous by many.*
>
> or
>
> A unilateral attack on a foreign enemy, *a policy that means the U.S. would strike without the support of other nations,* was considered difficult and dangerous by many.

1. New York has long been the destination of America's adventurous young. It is a city of danger and opportunity.

2. Punk was a return to the roots of rock 'n' roll. It was a revolt against the predictability of disco.

3. People have very different ideas about the meaning of poverty. It is a condition that to some suggests insufficient income, to others laziness, and to still others a state of unwarranted discomfort.

4. Writing ability can have far-reaching effects on a college graduate's future accomplishments. Writing ability is the capacity to generate and organize relevant ideas, compose coherent sentences, choose precise diction, control mechanics.

5. According to the lieutenant's testimony during his court-martial, he was simply following orders as any military man is trained to do. These orders came from his commanding officers.

6. When the Soviets sent troops into Vilnius, Vytautas Landsbergis isolated himself and members of his government in a fortified parliament building. Vilnius is the capital of Lithuania and Landsbergis was the Lithuanian president.

7. Over time, psychiatrists have expanded the definition of the term "addiction." It is a word whose meaning has undergone revision to cover a broader range of compulsive behaviors. These compulsions now include sex, television viewing, designer clothes, shopping, computers. These extend to a whole spectrum of dependencies.

8. Concrete has spread over wider and wider areas of the American landscape. It has covered not just the weed patches, deserted lots, and infertile acres but whole pastures, hillsides, and portions of the sea and sky.

B. Write a sentence about your major, your job, or another interest, being sure to include a related technical term. Then add an appositive that defines or illustrates the term.

C. In your next essay or in a revision of a previous assignment, write and identify at least five appositives.

Extended Definition

Because abstract terms and concepts can be misunderstood and manipulated, you must take care to establish precise meaning when writing a persuasive argument. Before you take a position on abortion for instance, you need to define when you think life begins. Before mounting an argument on gun control, you need to define what you think the wording of the Second Amendment means and stipulate the particular firearms you're considering. You must also consider your audience, what terminology might be unfamiliar to them.

Note how student Nathan Yan (see Chapter 9) defines the AP test early in his essay. If he were writing this piece for an AP class, he would not need to define *advanced placement,* but writing for a newspaper, he knows many readers will be unfamiliar with such tests and thus, without clarification, will not continue reading his argument. Note how smoothly he has integrated his definition into the flow of his paper:

> The AP tests are nationwide standardized tests administered by the private College Board Association. Successfully passing an AP test will count toward college credit and, depending on the college or university, may grant exemptions from certain general education courses. For many high schools it represents the highest class level for students taking a particular course.

Texas politicians and educators understand the role of definition. In 2004 the Texas Board of Education approved new definitions of marriage for the state's high school and middle school textbooks. Where formerly the texts used terms like "married partners," the Board agreed to rewrite the definition of marriage as a "life-long union between a husband and a wife," thus conforming to Texas law banning gay marriage.

Sometimes an entire argument depends on the meaning of a particular word to make its case. Note how Andrew Sullivan, an editor at *The New Republic*, and William Bennett, former Secretary of Education, clarify their opposing positions on gay marriage. Both provide their own carefully defined understanding of the term "marriage" to mount their very different arguments.

Let Gays Marry
ANDREW SULLIVAN

"A state cannot deem a class of persons a stranger to its laws," declared   1
the Supreme Court last week. It was a monumental statement. Gay men and lesbians, the conservative court said, are no longer strangers in America. They are citizens, entitled, like everyone else, to equal protection—no special rights, but simple equality.

For the first time in Supreme Court history, gay men and women were   2
seen not as some powerful lobby trying to subvert America, but as the people we truly are—the sons and daughters of countless mothers and fathers, with all the weaknesses and strengths and hopes of everybody else. And what we seek is not some special place in America but merely to be a full and equal part of America, to give back to our society without being forced to lie or hide or live as second-class citizens.

That is why marriage is so central to our hopes. People ask us why we   3
want the right to marry, but the answer is obvious. It's the same reason anyone wants the right to marry. At some point in our lives, some of us are lucky enough to meet the person we truly love. And we want to commit to that person in front of our family and country for the rest of our lives. It's the most simple, the most natural, the most human instinct in the world. How could anyone seek to oppose that?

Yes, at first blush, it seems like a radical proposal, but, when you think   4
about it some more, it's actually the opposite. Throughout American history,
to be sure, marriage has been between a man and a woman, and in many
ways our society is built upon that institution. But none of that need change
in the slightest. After all, no one is seeking to take away anybody's right to
marry, and no one is seeking to force any church to change any doctrine in
any way. Particular religious arguments against same-sex marriage are rightly
debated within the churches and faiths themselves. That is not the issue
here: there is a separation between church and state in this country. We are
only asking that when the government gives out civil marriage licenses,
those of us who are gay should be treated like anybody else.

Of course, some argue that marriage is by definition between a man   5
and a woman. But for centuries, marriage was by definition a contract in
which the wife was her husband's legal property. And we changed that. For
centuries marriage was by definition between two people of the same race.
And we changed that. We changed these things because we recognized
that human dignity is the same whether you are a man or a woman, black
or white. And no one has any more of a choice to be gay than to be black or
white or male or female.

Some say that marriage is only about raising children, but we let child-   6
less heterosexual couples be married (Bob and Elizabeth Dole, Pat and Shel-
ley Buchanan, for instance). Why should gay couples be treated differently?
Others fear that there is no logical difference between allowing same-sex
marriage and sanctioning polygamy and other horrors. But the issue of
whether to sanction multiple spouses (gay or straight) is completely separate from whether, in the existing institution between two unrelated adults,
the government should discriminate between its citizens.

This is, in fact, if only Bill Bennett could see it, a deeply conservative   7
cause. It seeks to change no one else's rights or marriages in any way. It seeks
merely to promote monogamy, fidelity and the disciplines of family life
among people who have long been cast to the margins of society. And what
could be a more conservative project than that? Why indeed would any conservative seek to oppose those very family values for gay people that he or
she supports for everybody else? Except of course, to make gay men and lesbians strangers in their own country, to forbid them ever to come home.

Leave Marriage Alone
WILLIAM BENNETT

There are at least two key issues that divide proponents and opponents of   1
same-sex marriage. The first is whether legally recognizing same-sex unions
would strengthen or weaken the institution. The second has to do with the
basic understanding of marriage itself.

The advocates of same-sex marriage say that they seek to strengthen   2
and celebrate marriage. That may be what some intend. But I am certain that

it will not be the reality. Consider: the legal union of same-sex couples would shatter the conventional definition of marriage, change the rules which govern behavior, endorse practices which are completely antithetical to the tenets of all of the world's major religions, send conflicting signals about marriage and sexuality, particularly to the young, and obscure marriage's enormously consequential function—procreation and child rearing.

Broadening the definition of marriage to include same-sex unions   3
would stretch it almost beyond recognition—and new attempts to expand the definition still further would surely follow. On what principled ground can Andrew Sullivan exclude others who most desperately want what he wants, legal recognition and social acceptance? Why on earth would Sullivan exclude from marriage a bisexual who wants to marry two other people? After all, exclusion would be a denial of that person's sexuality. The same holds true of a father and daughter who want to marry. Or two sisters. Or men who want (consensual) polygamous arrangements. Sullivan may think some of these arrangements are unwise. But having employed sexual relativism in his own defense, he has effectively lost the capacity to draw any lines and make moral distinctions.

Forsaking all others is an essential component of marriage. Obviously it is   4
not always honored in practice. But it is the ideal to which we rightly aspire, and in most marriages the ideal is in fact the norm. Many advocates of same-sex marriage simply do not share this ideal; promiscuity among homosexual males is well known. Sullivan himself has written that gay male relationships are served by the "openness of the contract" and the homosexuals should resist allowing their "varied and complicated lives" to be flattened into a "single, moralistic model." But that "single, moralistic model" has served society exceedingly well. The burden of proof ought to be on those who propose untested arrangements for our most important institution.

A second key difference I have with Sullivan goes to the very heart of   5
marriage itself. I believe that marriage is not an arbitrary construct which can be redefined simply by those who lay claim to it. It is an honorable estate, instituted of God and built on moral, religious, sexual and human realities. Marriage is based on a natural teleology, on the different, complementary nature of men and women and how they refine, support, encourage and complete one another. It is the institution through which we propagate, nurture, educate and sustain our species.

That we have to engage in this debate at all is an indication of how   6
steep our moral slide has been. Worse, those who defend the traditional understanding of marriage are routinely referred to (though not to my knowledge by Sullivan) as "homophobes," "gay-bashers," "intolerant" and "bigoted." Can one defend an honorable, 4,000-year-old tradition and not be called these names?

This is a large, tolerant, diverse country. In America people are free to   7
do as they wish, within broad parameters. It is also a country in sore need of shoring up some of its most crucial institutions: marriage and the family,

schools, neighborhoods, communities. But marriage and family are the greatest of these. That is why they are elevated and revered. We should keep them so.

EXERCISE 5F

Defining Marriage

1. William Bennett believes that "broadening the definition of marriage to include same-sex unions would stretch it almost beyond recognition— and [that] new attempts to expand the definition still further would surely follow." Among these "new attempts" he suggests group marriages, polygamy, and incest. How does Sullivan address these charges?

2. What concession does Sullivan grant to forces opposed to same-sex marriage? (See Refutation and Concession in Chapter 4.)

3. How does Sullivan refute the traditional definition?

4. Why does Sullivan see same-sex marriage as "a deeply conservative cause"?

WRITING ASSIGNMENT 11

Determining Your State's Position on Gay Marriage

Write a paper in which you explore the position on gay marriage taken in your state and discuss your reaction to this position. If your state hasn't yet taken action on the subject, you may select another state.

Audience

The instructor, other members of the class, and possibly members of your state legislature.

Purpose

To explain your state's position on a controversial issue and present your opinion.

WRITING ASSIGNMENT 12

Composing an Argument Based on a Definition

Step 1

Choose a word from the list of abstract terms below, think about its implications for a few minutes, and then start writing a definition that captures its meaning and significance for you. Using a freewriting approach (see Chapter 1), keep going for about twenty minutes. If time and your instructor permit, do this in class; you will find the combination of spontaneity and structure imposed by writing during class to be an aid to composing. You can't get up to make a phone call or make a sandwich. Volunteers can enlighten (and entertain) the class by reading these drafts aloud.

addiction	heroism
alcoholism	law
art	leader
business	maturity
courage	political correctness
cult	pornography
defeat	progress
depression	sexual harassment
education	terrorism
gossip	violence

Step 2

With more time for reflection and revision, take the spontaneous draft you have written and, in two or three pages, expand and edit your definition. In the process of defining your term, arrive at a significant point and support your position.

You need to argue your point, to use the term you are defining as a springboard for a complete written argument. As the discussion in this chapter has emphasized, you must include specific detail to animate your abstraction.

If time permits, multiple definitions of the same term can be read to the class for comparison and discussion.

Here are some possible strategies for writing an extended definition; do not feel compelled to use them all.

- Stipulate your precise meaning, but don't begin with a dictionary definition unless you plan to use it or disagree with it.
- Provide examples of the term.
- Explain the function or purpose of the term.
- Explore etymology (origin and history of a word). The most fruitful source for such explorations is the *Oxford English Dictionary*, a multi-volume work available in most college libraries and a dictionary well worth your acquaintance. Use the history of a term to help make a point.
- Examine the connotations of the term.
- Discuss what it is not (use this sparingly).
- Draw analogies. Here you will want to be precise; be sure the analogy really fits. (See "False Analogy," p. 150.)

Audience

The instructor and other members of the class.

Purpose

To make the definition of a term the focal point of an argument.

Extended definitions: Here are three short examples from students, all a little shorter than what we expect from this assignment.

Imagination

In *The Seven Year Itch*, a movie made in the fifties, Marilyn Monroe makes it clear that she thinks imagination is an asset when she wistfully sighs, "I have a lot of things, but imagination is not one of them." Carl Jung would agree with Marilyn that imagination is an asset. In his book *Psychological Times*, written in 1923, he says, "Without this playing with fantasy no creative work has ever yet come to birth. The debt we owe to the play of the imagination is

1

incalculable." What is this thing that two very different people both think is important to have?

The *New Oxford Dictionary* defines imagination as "The creative faculty   2
of the mind in its highest aspect; the power of framing new and striking intellectual conceptions." Yes, that definitely sounds like a positive thing to have. But there is something left out of that definition for imagination. How do you know if you have it, and as Marilyn thinks, is it possible not to have it?

I'm sure Carl Jung would have felt that his work fit the *New Oxford Dic-*   3
tionary's definition, thus making him a man with imagination. This would be a great topic for a poll in *People Magazine*—Name a person you think has imagination. Agatha Christie and Picasso immediately come to my mind. We have proof of their imagination in novels and artwork. But even if you can't force yourself to write a letter, and drawing leaves you cold, it doesn't mean you don't have imagination. After all, we all have certain things in common with Agatha Christie and Picasso.

We can all think, and imagination is a function of our minds. It is the   4
forming of new ideas by using the knowledge we already have. If you've ever toyed with different solutions to a situation before making a decision about it, you've used your imagination. If you've ever had to get the cork out of a wine bottle without a corkscrew, or pondered over a perfect gift for someone special, you've used your imagination. Next time you open the cabinet and swear you have nothing for dinner, yet come up with something anyway, applaud yourself for using your imagination.

Everyone has imagination. The definition in the *New Oxford Dictionary*   5
may make it sound like only masterpieces qualify as works of imagination. But we all have it, we just use it in different ways. Think about your own definition of imagination, and just by that you've proved you have it.

Different Approaches to the Same Term

Radical [1]

The word "radical" has been defined in the *Oxford English Dictionary* as "going   1
to the root or origin, touching or acting upon what is essential and fundamental." Thus, a radical reform is said to be a fundamental, "thorough reform." In a political sense, an advocate of "radical reform" was described as "one who holds the most advanced views of political reform on democratic lines, and thus belongs to the extreme section of the Liberal party." While this may have been a commonly accepted usage of the term in England at the time, the word "radical" has drifted away from its original specific meaning to a rather vague term for anyone who appears to be trying to disrupt the status quo.

In the late 1800s and early 1900s, socialists, Communists, and anarchists   2
alike were popularly categorized by the general American public with the

term "radical." With the controversy surrounding the political goals of these different activists, "a radical" was at the very least a controversial figure. More often than not, the word "radical" brought to mind some sort of disruptive character, a nonspecific image of an extremist, most probably from the far left. On the political spectrum the "radical" is still viewed as an individual on the extreme left, opposite the "right" or "conservative" parties. "Conservatives" holding radically different views and goals are not normally termed "radicals"; they are merely part of the "ultraright."

3   The term "radical" today is used less as a description of political intent and more as a critique of overall manner and appearance. While many of the "radicals" in the 1960s did indeed advocate numerous political reforms, the general public was more impressed by their personal character and style of advocacy. It is not surprising that when asked to define "a radical," most individuals conjure up a vague image of some young person wearing ragged clothes and long hair. It is a pity that in this society, where progressive change is so essential, the term "radical" has been imbued with so much negativity, so many connotations that really have nothing to do with political reform.

Radical [2]

1   A radical is an algebraic symbol that tells a person to carry out a certain mathematical operation. The end result of this operation will tell a person the root or origin of a number or problem.

2   Recently, while in Los Angeles, I overheard someone describe a car as radical. I immediately thought to myself, something is wrong here. Radicals do not have engines. They may contain a number, like 32, underneath their top line, but never a stock Chevy 302 engine. It simply would not fit. When I asked this person why he called the car a radical, he replied, "Because the car is different and unusual." Once again, I thought to myself, he has made a mistake. Radicals are quite common. In fact, they are an essential part of most algebraic theories. I had to infer that this man knew nothing about algebra. If he did, he would have realized that radicals are not different or unusual at all, and would not have called the car one.

3   While I was in New York this past summer, I happened to see a group of people carrying signs of protest in front of the United Nations Building. As I watched them, a man came over to me, pointed at the group and muttered, "Radicals." I thought to myself, man are you ever wrong. Radicals do not carry signs saying, "Feed the Poor." They may carry a number, like 2, in their top right hand corner, but this number only means to find the root of a problem. It does not mean, "Feed the Poor."

4   These two events show that there is a great deal of misunderstanding throughout the country in regard to what a radical is. At their simplest level, radicals tell us to find the root of a problem. At their most complex level, they tell us the same thing.

STIPULATING PERSONAL MEANING

Through the centuries, people have been defining what they consider them-selves to be, using the term "man" in a number of inventive ways.

Plato

First, he put man in the class "biped" and differentiated him from others in the class by describing him as "a featherless biped." When his rival, Diogenes, pro-duced a plucked chicken, Plato had to add "having broad nails" as a further distinguishing characteristic.

Shakespeare

"What a piece of work is a man! How noble in reason! how infinite in faculty! in form, in moving, how express and admirable! in action how like an angel! in apprehension how like a god! the beauty of the world! the paragon of animals! And yet, to me what is this quintessence of dust? Man delights not me; no, nor woman neither." (*Hamlet*)

Ambrose Bierce

"An animal so lost in rapturous contemplation of what he thinks he is as to overlook what he indubitably ought to be. His chief occupation is extermina-tion of other animals and his own species, which, however, multiplies with such insistent rapidity as to infest the whole habitable earth and Canada." (*Devil's Dictionary*)

Inventing New Words to Fill a Need

Contemporary American writer Alice Walker sought to rectify some of the lin-guistic imbalance in gender representation when she coined the term *womanist* for her collection of nonfiction, *In Search of Our Mothers' Gardens: Womanist Prose.* Why, we might ask, did she need to invent such a word? We can assume that she experienced a condition for which there was no term, so she created one. A student came up with *strugglesome*, a term we're often tempted to use ourselves. Writer and performer Rich Hall created the word *sniglet* for "any word that doesn't appear in the dictionary, but should." Two ex-amples from his collection:

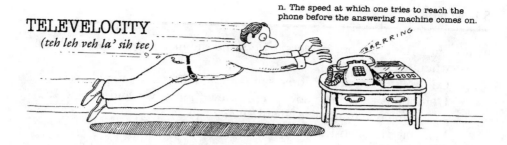

TELEVELOCITY
(teh leh veh la' sih tee)

n. The speed at which one tries to reach the phone before the answering machine comes on.

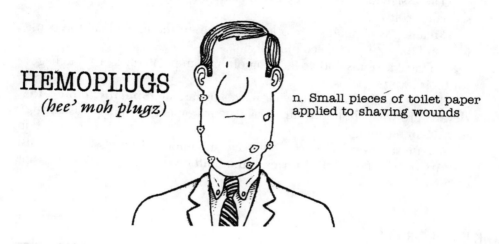

HEMOPLUGS
(hee' moh plugz)

n. Small pieces of toilet paper applied to shaving wounds

WRITING ASSIGNMENT 13

Creating a New Word

Now it's your turn to create a new word. Give the word an extended definition so that those in your class can see how to use it and why our culture needs such an addition to the language. Here, again, you have an opportunity to develop an argument, using your new word as a springboard.

Audience

The instructor and other members of the class.

Purpose

To identify a meaning in need of a name.

SUMMARY

It is important that our readers understand the meaning of the words we use when we write.

Controlling the **definitions** is important, particularly in politics.

Definitions can affect how people view themselves and others, "addiction" being one example of many such terms.

Language is an abstract system of symbols.

The assignation of a particular meaning to a given term remains essentially arbitrary.

Meaning is dependent to a large degree on the individual, the context, and the interpretive community.

Political systems and advertising often manipulate abstract language for their own purposes.

The power to abstract is what makes us human. **Specific, concrete details** are what flesh out our ideas so our readers can grasp, visualize, and retain meaning.

We must beware of evasive language and euphemisms.

Appositives help define terms at the sentence level.

KEY TERMS

Appositives   noun phrases placed beside nouns to elaborate on their meaning, useful for identifying, defining, explaining, and describing terms and concepts within the sentence.

Connotation   the suggestive or associative implications beyond the literal, explicit sense of a word.

Denotation   the basic dictionary meaning of a word, separate from its emotional associations.

Euphemism   an indirect, less expressive word or phrase, for a sensitive idea.

CHAPTER 6

Fallacious Arguments

Her reasoning is full of tricks
And butterfly suggestions,
I know no point to which she sticks;
She begs the simplest questions,
And, when her premises are strong
She always draws her inference wrong.

—*Upon Lebia Arguing* by Alfred Cochrane (1865–?)

WHAT IS A FALLACIOUS ARGUMENT?

To answer this question, we ask you to look carefully at two short arguments:

> Short people do not make good presidents.
> The democratic candidate is short.
> Therefore, the democratic candidate will not be a good president.

> Senator Smith was expelled from college for cheating on an exam.
> His wife divorced him because of his numerous affairs.
> Therefore, he is a man without honor, a politician who cannot be
>   trusted, and we should not support his National Health Bill.

Which of these two arguments is more persuasive? Technically, the line of reasoning in the first argument is logical because the two premises lead inescapably to the conclusion. There is nothing fallacious in the *form* of this argument. The difficulty lies in the first premise; it is an absurd claim and an unacceptable premise. This argument is not persuasive and would convince no one. (Look ahead to Chapter 7, "Deductive and Inductive Argument," for a detailed explanation of form and acceptability of premises.)

But what about the second argument? Would you be in favor of a National Health Bill created by such a man? Some might find it persuasive, believing that he could not propose worthwhile legislation. But because nothing in the premises indicates flaws in the bill—only flaws in the man— the conclusion is not logically supported. The bill may be worthwhile despite the nature of the man who proposes it. This then is a **fallacious argument,** an argument that is persuasive but does not logically support its conclusion.

Because fallacious arguments are both appealing and abundant, we as critical readers and writers must guard against them. The first step in this defense is to familiarize ourselves with the most common fallacies. Fallacious reasoning may be intentional, as is sometimes the case with unscrupulous merchandisers and politicians, or it may be an innocent mistake resulting from fuzzy thinking or unexamined bias. In any case, if we are familiar with fallacies we can avoid them in our own thinking and writing. We can also spot them in the arguments of others, a skill that makes us wiser consumers and citizens.

There are many fallacies, a number of which tend to overlap. Our intention here is not to overwhelm you with an exhaustive list of fallacies and a complex classification scheme. Instead, we offer a list of the more common fallacies, presented in alphabetical order for easy reference.

Appeal to Authority

The opinion of an authority can support an argument only when it reflects his special area of expertise; the authority must be an expert on the subject being argued, as is the case in the following examples:

> The Surgeon General warns that smoking is injurious to health.
> Vladimir Horowitz, the internationally acclaimed pianist, preferred the Steinway piano.
> Studies conducted by the *Washington Post,* the *Los Angeles Times,* and CNN suggest that increasing numbers of parents object to video game violence.

But if the appeal is to an authority that is not appropriate, the appeal is fallacious, as is the case in the following example:

> Abortion to save the life of a mother is an irrelevant issue because a former surgeon general, a well-known pediatric surgeon, claimed that in all his years of surgical practice he had never seen a case in which such a dilemma had arisen.

The problem here is that a pediatric surgeon is not an appropriate authority on an issue involving obstetrics, a different medical specialty.

Fallacious appeals to authority are bountiful in advertising, which employs well-known actors and athletes to sell us everything from banking services to automobiles to coffee. Since many of these celebrities have no specialized knowledge—no authority—on the particular service or product they are promoting, they are not credible sources. For example, George Foreman, a boxer, gave his name to an appliance, the George Foreman Grill, though he has never been a chef or worked in the food industry.

Appeals to authority also appear in the form of **snob appeal** or **appeal to the authority of the select few.** The following advertisement for a resort hotel illustrates this fallacy, which appeals to people's desire for prestige and exclusivity:

Palmilla's not for everyone. The best never is.

Keep in mind that fallacious appeals to authority should not cause us to doubt all authorities but rather should encourage us to distinguish between reliable and unreliable sources. In constructing your own arguments, be prepared to cite, explain, and, if necessary, defend your sources when relying on authority.

Appeal to Fear

An appeal to fear attempts to convince by implicitly threatening the audience. Its efforts to persuade are based on emotion rather than reason. An ad for a business college uses this approach:

Will there be a *job* waiting when *you* leave college?

The ad attempts to frighten students by implying that unless they attend this business college, they will be unable to get a job after attending a four-year traditional college.

Former Senator Jesse Helms of North Carolina raised millions in campaign funds by sending voters a letter that contained the following warning:

Your tax dollars are being used to pay for grade school classes that teach our children that CANNIBALISM, WIFE-SWAPPING and the MURDER of infants and the elderly are acceptable behavior.

Appeal to Pity

An appeal to pity attempts to win our sympathy in order to convince us of the conclusion. Like an appeal to fear, it appeals to our emotions rather than our intellect. Some students use this approach when arguing for a particular grade.

Professor Hall, I must get an A in your course. If you don't give me an A, I won't be able to go to law school.

As we know, a student's work in a course—papers, exams, participation—determines the final grade. The consequences of a grade, no matter how dire they may be, should have no effect in determining that grade.

Emotion may play a part in argument, but its role must be secondary, a backdrop to logical reasoning. In fact, effective arguments often begin with frightening statistics—"If nothing is done about global warming, the earth's temperature will increase 10 degrees by the year 2015 with disastrous consequences for our environment." Or they may begin with an emotional illustration. For example, an argument for mandatory fencing around all private swimming pools may open with a description of a mother caring for a child who is brain damaged as a result of almost drowning in a private pool. Either of these introductions will capture the emotions and interest of the audience, but they should be followed by facts, appropriate appeals to authority, and logical reasoning.

Begging the Question

When a person **begs the question,** he offers no actual support for his conclusion while appearing to do so. Instead, he may argue in a circle, just restating, as a premise, his conclusion in different words.

People like Dave Matthews' music because it is the most enjoyable music around.

The writer is simply stating that people find Dave Matthews' music enjoyable because it is enjoyable. He begs the question. "They like it" means the same as "They find it enjoyable."

Or, take a couple of classics:

Parallel lines will never meet because they are parallel.

... your noble son is mad.
Mad call I it, for to define true madness,
What is't but to be nothing else but mad?
—POLONIUS TO QUEEN GERTRUDE IN *HAMLET,* II.II

[We can discern something of Polonius' character from the manner of his argument.]

Money is better than poverty, if only for financial reasons.
—WOODY ALLEN

Even a president can be guilty of circular reasoning:

The reason I keep insisting that there was a relationship between Iraq and al Qaeda [is] because there was a relationship between Iraq and al Qaeda.

—PRESIDENT GEORGE W. BUSH

Some such fallacious arguments beg the question not by restating the conclusion but by supporting the conclusion with assumptions (stated or hidden) that are as much in need of proof as is the conclusion. For example, those opposed to rent control argue that rent controls should be removed because such decontrol could result in a significant rise in apartment construction and thus relieve the shortage of affordable rental units. A letter to the editor points out the weakness:

Editor: In your editorial concerning the housing crisis, you rely on one of the oldest rhetorical tricks of accepting as a given that which you could not possibly prove, that is, "There can be little question that removal of rent controls would result in a boom in apartment house construction. . . ." If rent control is such an important factor, construction should have been booming in the '80s before rent control laws existed in our state. It wasn't. . . .

Before we can accept the conclusion, the "truth" of the premise—that construction of new housing will increase if rent control laws are abolished—must be established.

"You know what I like about power? It's so damn empowering."

We can also encounter question begging (avoiding the issue) in the form of an actual question, a **loaded question.** An example:

Have you started paying your fair share of taxes yet?

First, the questioner would have to establish what he means by "fair share" and then establish that the person to whom he addressed the question had not been paying it.

In some arguments, just a single word—*reactionary*, *negligent*, *warmonger*, *deadbeat*—can beg the question. Be on the alert for such prejudicial language.

Double Standard

When an argument contains the fallacy of **double standard** (sometimes referred to as special pleading), it judges and labels the same act differently, depending on the person or group who performs the act.

Shannon Faulkner, the first woman ever admitted to the Citadel, a military college in South Carolina, dropped out in her first year. The other cadets cheered as she departed the campus, and the media covered her departure in great detail. What the jeering male cadets and the media ignored were the 34 other first-year students, all men, who also dropped out. Shannon Faulkner and her classmates made the same decision, but she was subjected to ridicule and close media scrutiny while her 34 male classmates were not; a double standard was applied.

Editorialist Cynthia Tucker accuses our government of having a double standard in its dealings with China and Cuba:

If diplomatic relations and free trade are a sound policy toward China, which restricts religious freedoms, limits free speech, builds nuclear weapons and poses a threat to its neighbors, doesn't the same apply to Cuba, which restricts religious freedoms, limits free speech, and has no nuclear weapons and poses no threat to its neighbors?

CARTOON © RHYMES WITH ORANGE—HILARY B. PRICE. KING FEATURES SYNDICATE.

Sometimes a double standard can be applied subtly though the manipulative use of language. A well-known defense lawyer, while discussing legal strategies on television, stated that he "prepares" his witnesses while the prosecution "coaches" theirs. "Prepares" suggests professional legal preparation for the courtroom, whereas "coaches" suggests that a witness is encouraged to say what the lawyer tells her to whether it is true or not. Both lawyers are working with their clients before trial, but the defense lawyer's subtle use of language casts a negative slant on opposing counsel.

Equivocation

Equivocation is the shifting of the meaning of a given term within a single argument. This fallacy stems from the often ambiguous nature of language. A term may be ambiguous because it has more than one meaning; for instance, the word "affair" may mean a party, a controversial incident, or an extramarital relationship. Look at this example:

> We are told by the government that to discriminate against a person in employment or housing is wrong and punishable by law. But we must discriminate when we hire an individual (Does he have the necessary experience?) or when we rent an apartment (Does he have sufficient income?). Discrimination is a necessary part of making such decisions.

The word "discriminate" is the culprit. In the first sentence, "discriminate" refers to prejudice, to denying an individual employment or housing because of his or her race, sex, or religion. In the second sentence, "discriminate" refers to making careful distinctions between applicants on the basis of relevant issues.

In writing our own arguments, we can avoid equivocation by defining all ambiguous terms and being consistent in our use of them. (See Chapter 5 for definition strategies.)

False Analogy

One creative way to mount an argument can be through analogy. An argument by analogy compares two or more things, alike in certain respects, and suggests that since they share certain characteristics, they probably share other characteristics as well. A doctor argues effectively for drug therapy over psychotherapy as the best treatment for schizophrenia or severe depression by comparing the brain to the heart. "The brain is an organ, like the heart, and like that organ, can malfunction as a result of biochemical imbalances."

But in a **false analogy,** one compares two things in which the key features are different. A mountain climber offers this analogy to minimize the danger of his sport:

> I don't want to die falling off a rock. . . . But you can kill yourself falling in the bathtub, too.
>
> —JOHN BACHAR

He is comparing two extremely dissimilar acts: climbing a mountain and taking a bath, one a sport, the other a daily routine. And while it is possible to kill oneself slipping in the bathtub, if we were to compare the number of deaths in proportion to the number of bathers and the number of mountain climbers, we would surely find a higher incidence of deaths resulting from mountain climbing than from bathing. To construct a more convincing analogy, the mountain climber should compare the risk in mountain climbing with that in another high-risk sport such as race car driving.

A "Dear Abby" reader writes in response to Abby's recommendation that young people use contraceptives for premarital sex: "We know that premarital sex is wrong, just as we know shoplifting is wrong." Dear Abby's reply points out the fallaciousness of this comparison.

> One of the most powerful urges inborn in the human animal is the sex drive. Nature intended it to ensure perpetuation of our species. It is not comparable with the temptation to swipe a candy bar or a T-shirt.

In debating whether or not it is appropriate for Miss America beauty contestants to have plastic surgery, those in favor of allowing such surgery compare it with other practices women use to improve their appearance, such as makeup and hair color. *Boston Globe* columnist Ellen Goodman points out that this analogy is false since cosmetics are superficial whereas cosmetic surgery, such as breast implants, is physically invasive. She then offers a more accurate analogy: Cosmetic surgery for beauty contestants is like steroids for athletes—each gives an unfair advantage to contestants involved in a competition.

The following letter to "Miss Manners" argues on the basis of analogy, an analogy that in her reply Miss Manners shows to be false:

Dear Miss Manners:

If I were to entertain someone at dinner whom I knew to be a vegetarian, I would make certain there would be plenty of things on the menu that a vegetarian could eat. Besides my lamb chop, there would be plenty of vegetables, breads, salads, etc. I would not feel compelled to become a vegetarian myself for the occasion.

Were I to dine at the home of vegetarians, I would expect of them a similar accommodation, so that in addition to their usual fare, they might serve me a small steak, perhaps, though of course they wouldn't need to partake of it themselves.

Miss Manners replies:

Gentle Reader:

You lose the argument. Here is the problem: Serving vegetables to guests does not violate your principles, nor does it make you a vegetarian. However, expecting your vegetarian friends to serve you something that they exclude from their households would require their violating their principles.

Reasoning by analogy is appealing because it is vivid and accessible and thus can be an effective argument strategy. But we must not accept analogies without careful examination. We must ask if the two things being compared are similar in ways that are significant to the point being made.

False Cause

The fallacy of **false cause** is also called **post hoc reasoning,** from the Latin *post hoc, ergo propter hoc,* which means "after this, therefore because of this." As this translation indicates, the fallacy of false cause assumes a cause–effect relationship between two events because one precedes another. It claims a causal relationship solely on the basis of a chronological relationship. Mark Twain uses this relationship for humorous effect:

I joined the Confederacy for two weeks. Then I deserted. The Confederacy fell.

We know, as Twain did, that his desertion did nothing to end the Civil War, but this fallacy is not always so obvious. Look at the following example:

Governor Robinson took office in 2000.
In 2002, the state suffered a severe recession.
Therefore, Governor Robinson should not be reelected.
(Hidden assumption: The governor caused the recession.)

Elected officials are often credited with the success or blamed for the failure of the economy. But, in fact, anything as complex as the economy is affected by numerous factors such as inflation, environmental changes, and fluctuations in the stock market. Elected officials may indeed affect the economy but are unlikely to be the sole cause of its success or failure.

In another example of post hoc reasoning, an author attributes his nephew's autism to a vaccination. A doctor criticizes the writer's conclusion in a letter to the *New York Times Book Review:*

> To the Editor:
>   There will always be people who are convinced that because the signs of mental retardation or a seizure disorder or autism first became evident after an immunization, then certainly the immunization caused their problems; millions of dollars have been awarded in damages because some such people served on juries.
>   For those people of reason who remember that **post hoc, ergo propter hoc** is a logical fallacy and not a standard of proof, let me state categorically that careful review of the literature confirms that a DPT shot might result in a fever or a sore leg or an irritable child. But it will not cause retardation, it will not precipitate epilepsy, and it never has and never will lead to autism.
>   DIANE LIND FENSTER, M.D.
>   GREEN BAY, WIS.

Some have argued that the atomic bombs we dropped on Hiroshima and Nagasaki caused Japan to surrender at the end of World War II. Others argue that this is a case of post hoc reasoning, that other factors such as Russia's threat to enter the war against Japan caused Japan to surrender, so that the killing of 110,000 Japanese, many of them women and children, was unnecessary.

Determining the cause of all but the simplest events is extremely difficult. Post hoc reasoning is appealing because it offers simple explanations for complex events.

False Dilemma

A **false dilemma** presents two and only two alternatives for consideration when other possibilities exist. For this reason, a false dilemma is often referred to as **either/or reasoning.**

In his essay, "Love One, Hate the Other," movie critic Mick LaSalle rails against what he calls "false polarities." He offers the following examples: Lennon *or* McCartney, Monroe *or* Bardot, Hemingway *or* Fitzgerald, Freud *or* Jung. He calls them false "because, in each case, two elements are arbitrarily set apart as opposites when they are not opposite at all, and the idea is that we must choose between the two when there's no legitimate need to do that."

Narrowing to two choices is a strategy designed to forestall clear thinking and force a quick decision. This kind of reasoning can be seductive because it reduces the often difficult decisions and judgments we must make by narrowing complex problems and issues to two simple options.

Columnist Anna Quindlen comments on how this either/or reasoning shaped the public's opinion and the trial of Erik and Lyle Menendez, two brothers accused of murdering their parents for financial gain.

. . . the question has become: venal rich kids or tormented victims? Which are the Menendez brothers? Few seem to consider a third possibility: maybe both. . . . Lyle and Erik [are] either tormented, abused child-men or cold-blooded climbers in Porsches. Not both. Never both.

Columnist Ellen Goodman offers an example of one young critical thinker who refused to accept the limits of either/or thinking.

Remember the story of Heinz, the man whose wife was dying for lack of medicine or the funds to buy it? Children are asked to decide whether it's OK for Heinz to steal the drugs. On the one hand it's wrong to break the law, on the other, it's wrong to let the woman die.

What I remember most about the Heinz dilemma is the response of an 11-year-old little girl named Amy, as described in Carol Gilligan's book, *In a Different Voice.* Amy didn't think that Heinz should steal the drugs because if he did he might end up in jail—and what would happen next time his wife needed the pills? Nor did Amy think she should die.

This 11-year-old refused to choose from column A or column B. She thought they should "talk it out," get a loan, or find another way out of the dilemma. Traditional moralists thought Amy was "illogical." But the truth was that she took the long, wide moral view—six steps down the road, up a side road and back to the main road. Amy stepped outside the multiple-choice questionnaire.

"Damn it, Eddie! If you don't believe in nuclear war and you don't believe in conventional war, what the hell kind of war do you believe in?"

What alternative has the speaker completely overlooked?

Hasty Generalization

A **hasty generalization** is a conclusion based on a sample that is too small or in some other way unrepresentative of the larger population.

> Students in Professor Hall's eight o'clock freshman composition class are often late. There's no doubt that people are right when they claim today's college students are irresponsible and unreliable.

In this case the sample is both unrepresentative and too small; unrepresentative because we would expect an eight o'clock class to have more late students than classes offered later in the day, and too small because one section can't represent an entire freshman class.

In Chapter 7, we ask students to collect hasty generalizations. Here are some of our favorites:

> Jocks can't type.
> Women in bridal departments are airheads.
> Anyone who listens to heavy metal is not intelligent.
> Older guests always arrive early.
> Everyone in the South is gun crazy.
> Everyone in Germany dances by themselves.
> Women who work full time have unsuccessful marriages.

It is impossible to avoid making generalizations, nor should we try. But we must examine the basis for our generalizations to determine their reliability (see Chapter 7).

One way to avoid this fallacy is to qualify your generalizations with words such as "many" or "some." Most of us would accept the claim that "some women are bad drivers" but would reject and be offended by the claim that "women are bad drivers."

Personal Attack

Often called by its Latin name, ***ad hominem*** ("against the man"), the fallacy of personal attack substitutes for a reasoned evaluation of an argument an attack against the person presenting the argument. The person is discredited, not the argument.

When Rachel Carson's *Silent Spring,* a seminal work on the health hazards of insecticides and pesticides, was published in 1962, a leading scientist (male) questioned her concern for future generations because she was a spinster who had no children. He attacked her personally, not her argument that certain commonly used chemicals caused cancer.

As a newspaper columnist, writer Jon Carroll often receives mail from readers who disagree with him. One such reader called him a "bunny hugger" for his protect-the-environment point of view. Carroll's response:

. . . here's a little rule: If you hurl ad hominems at people, you are forcing them to shut their ears. You could be Albert Bloody Einstein, and if you start your note with "Dear Idiot," your message will not come through.

Those given to Latin names like to label a particular kind of personal attack as *tu quoque*—"you also." In this instance, a person and thus his arguments are discredited because his own behavior does not strictly conform to the position he holds. We've all heard about the parent who drinks too much but admonishes his child about the dangers of drinking.

Anti-gun-control groups were delighted when Carl Rowan, a prominent Washington columnist and a staunch advocate of gun control, used an unregistered pistol to wound a young man who broke into his backyard. But Rowan's failure to follow his own beliefs does not necessarily make his argument for gun control a weak one.

Poisoning the Well

A person **poisons the well** when he makes an assertion that precludes or discourages an open discussion of the issue. This assertion will intimidate the listener, who fears that any resistance on his part will lead to a personal disagreement rather than a critical discussion.

Every patriotic American supports legislation condemning the desecration of the flag.

The listener must now prove his patriotism rather than express his doubts about the legislation, and the speaker avoids having to defend his conclusion with relevant premises.

Slippery Slope

We know the **slippery slope** fallacy by other names too: the domino theory, the ripple effect. One thing leads to another. People often claim that an action should be avoided because it will inevitably lead to a series of extremely undesirable consequences. Sometimes such a chain reaction is probable, but often it can be exaggerated for effect.

Writer Wendy Kaminer, reviewing *Under Fire: The NRA and the Battle for Gun Control,* presents one group's position on gun control:

What seems like reasonable restrictions on guns with no legitimate civilian purpose (assault rifles, for example) will lead inevitably to total prohibition of gun ownership that ends in virtual slavery at the hands of a totalitarian regime.

The argument here is that if we allow the government to take one step— the banning of assault weapons—the next step will be the banning of all guns—and the final step, loss of all freedom for all citizens. In this argument, the downward slope is more precipitous than the evidence warrants, leading to an erroneous conclusion.

Columnist William Safire points out that "Logicians are very cautious about *slippery slope* arguments because it is impossible to know beforehand, with absolute deductive certainty, that an 'if-then' statement is true." Careful reasoning helps us distinguish between probable and outrageous claims.

Straw Man

In a **straw man** argument, a person creates and then attacks a distorted version of the opposition's argument:

> The candidate wants the federal government to house everyone, feed everyone, care for everyone's children, and provide medical care for everyone. And he's going to take 50 percent of every dime you make to do it.

This argument overlooks the candidate's proposal to reduce defense spending to meet his goals. Hence, this is an unfair presentation of the opposing view, but one that could be extremely effective in discouraging votes for the candidate. This is the purpose of a straw man argument: to frighten supporters away from the opponent's camp and into one's own. Columnist Ellen Goodman comments on this strategy in an essay titled "The Straw Feminist":

> The straw man has been a useful creature throughout history. Whenever people argued, he could be pulled together quickly out of the nearest available haystack, and set up as an opponent. The beauty of the straw man was that he was easily defeated. The straw man was also useful as a scarecrow. The arguments attributed to him were not only flimsy, they were frightening.
>
> So I wasn't surprised when the straw feminist was sighted burning her bra at a "Miss America" pageant. The fact that there never was a bra-burning was irrelevant. Feminists became bra-burners. Not to mention man-haters.

The straw feminist wanted to drive all women out of their happy homes and into the workforce. The straw feminist had an abortion as casually as she had a tooth pulled. The straw feminist was hostile to family life and wanted children warehoused in government-run day and night care. At times, the straw feminist was painted slightly pinko by the anticommunists or rather lavender by the antilesbians. But it was generally agreed upon that she was a castrating—well, you fill in the blank.

This creature was most helpful for discrediting real feminists but also handy for scaring supporters away.

> **A caution:** German philosopher Arthur Schopenhauer [1788–1860] pointed out that "it would be a very good thing if every trick could receive some short and obviously appropriate name, so that when a man used this or that particular trick, he could at once be reproved for

it." Fallacies provide us with those short and appropriate names for tricks or errors in reasoning, but we must not assume that all such errors can be labeled. Whenever we find fault with a particular line of reasoning, we should not hesitate to articulate that fault, whether or not we have a label for it. On the other hand, we must be careful not to see fallacies everywhere, perhaps even where they don't exist.

EXERCISE 6A

Identifying Fallacies

Identify by name the fallacies in each of the following arguments and justify your responses. You may want to turn to the end of the chapter for a chart of the fallacies.

> **Competition and collaboration:** An interesting approach to this exercise combines competition and cooperation. The class is divided into two teams who compete in identifying the fallacies, with team members cooperating on responses as an option.

1.

"It could go badly, or it could go well, depending on whether it goes badly or well."

2. "A group of self-appointed 'life-style police' are pushing to control many aspects of our daily lives. If they succeed, we lose our basic right to free choice. Today they're targeting smoking. What's next? Red meat?

Leather? Coffee? If fifty million smokers can lose their rights anyone can." (From an ad for the National Smokers Alliance.)

3. America: Love it or leave it.

4. You can't expect insight and credibility from the recent book *The Feminist Challenge* because its author David Bouchier is, obviously, a man.

5. Politicians can't be trusted because they lack integrity.

6. "We would not tolerate a proposal that states that because teenage drug use is a given we should make drugs more easily available." (Archbishop John R. Quinn in response to a National Research Council's recommendation that contraceptives and abortion be made readily available to teenagers.)

7. How long must we allow our courts to go on coddling criminals?

8. "I'm firm. You are stubborn. He's pig-headed." (Philosopher Bertrand Russell)

9. Anyone who truly cares about preserving the American way of life will vote Republican this fall.

10. "Why is it okay for people to choose the best house, the best schools, the best surgeon, the best car, but not try to have the best baby possible?" (A father's defense of the Nobel prize winners' sperm bank)

11. Socrates, during his trial in 399 B.C.: "My friend, I am a man, and like other men, a creature of flesh and blood, and not of wood or stone, as Homer says; and I have a family, yes, and sons, O Athenians, three in number, one almost a man, and two others who are still young; and yet I will not bring any of them hither in order to petition you for an acquittal." (Plato, *The Apology*)

12. "All Latins are volatile people." (Former Senator Jesse Helms, on Mexican protests against Senate Foreign Affairs subcommittee hearings on corruption south of the border)

13. Mark R. Hughes, owner of Herbalife International, was questioned by a Senate subcommittee about the safety of the controversial diet products marketed by his company. Referring to a panel of three nutrition and weight-control authorities, Hughes asked: "If they're such experts, then why are they fat?"

14. The Black Panthers—Were they criminals or freedom fighters? (From a television ad promoting a documentary on the radical group.)

15. When the Supreme Court ruled that school officials need not obtain search warrants or find "probable cause" while conducting reasonable searches of students, they violated freedoms guaranteed under the Bill of Rights. If you allow a teacher to look for a knife or drugs, you'll soon have strip searches and next, torture.

16. Since I walked under that ladder yesterday, I've lost my wallet and received a speeding ticket.

17. Sometimes, the *best* is not for everyone. (An ad for a "Parisian boutique")

18. "I'm being denied the right to own a semiautomatic firearm simply because someone doesn't like the way it looks. If you look at all the different automobiles out there, the majority of them travel on regular roads. So how do you explain the dune buggies or off-road vehicles? They're different, but you don't hear anybody saying, 'Why does anyone need to have a dune buggy or an off-road vehicle? What's wrong with your regular run-of-the-mill traditional automobile?' It's all a matter of personal preference." (Marion Hammer, president of the National Rifle Association)

19. We are going to have to ease up on environmental protection legislation or see the costs overwhelm us.

20. Any rational person will accept that a fetus is a human being.

21. A tax loophole is something that benefits the other guy. If it benefits you, it is tax reform.

22. Heat Wave Blamed for Record Temperatures Across U.S. (A Grass Valley *Union* headline)

23. The erosion of traditional male leadership has led to an increase in divorce because men no longer possess leadership roles.

24. "Just as instructors could prune sentences for poor grammar, so the principal was entitled to find certain articles inappropriate for publication—in this situation because they might reveal the identity of pregnant students and because references to sexual activity were deemed improper for young students to see."

25.

26. Now, all young men, a warning take, And shun the poisoned bowl; [alcohol] 'Twill lead you down to hell's dark gate, And ruin your own soul. (Anonymous, from Carl Sandburg, ed., *The American Songbag*)

27. While our diplomats in France were gathering intelligence, their diplomats in Washington were practicing espionage.

28. I recently read about a homeless man with a burst appendix who was turned away from a hospital emergency room to die in the street. It's obvious that hospitals don't care about people, only money.

29. Do the vastly inflated salaries paid to professional athletes lead them into drug abuse?

30. The Nuclear Freeze movement was misguided and dangerous from the beginning, dependent as it was on "unilateral" disarmament. (This is a common argument of the movement's opponents. Those supporting the Nuclear Freeze movement actually proposed "bilateral" disarmament.)

31. *Haemon:* So, father, pause, and put aside your anger. I think, for what my young opinion's worth, That, good as it is to have infallible wisdom, Since this is rarely found, the next best thing Is to be willing to listen to wise advice. *Creon:* Indeed! Am I to take lessons at my time of life From a fellow of his age? (Sophocles, *Antigone*)

32. S & W vegetables are the best because they use only premium quality.

33. In the presidential election of 2000, Al Gore challenged George W. Bush's victory on grounds of voter fraud in Florida. The electoral college votes, deciding the winner, hung in the balance, even though Gore held the lead in the popular vote. Some asserted that Gore should concede, just as Nixon did when John F. Kennedy won in 1960. In that election, votes for Kennedy in Illinois were said to have been fraudulently earned, although without the Illinois electoral votes, Kennedy still held his lead as he also held the lead in the popular vote.

34. Reading test scores in public schools have declined dramatically. This decline was caused by the radical changes in teaching strategies introduced in the 1960s.

35. Howard Dean, as head of the Democratic National Committee, claimed that the Republican party consisted of white Christians.

36. "I give so much pleasure to so many people. Why can't I get some pleasure for myself?" (Comedian John Belushi to his doctor in justification of his drug use)

37. "Editor: Now that it has been definitely established that nonsmokers have the right to tell smokers not to pollute their air, it follows that people who don't own cars have the right to tell car owners not to drive. Right?" (Jim Hodge, *San Francisco Chronicle*)

38. We must either give up some of our constitutional liberties to ensure that the government can protect us against terrorism or we will again fall prey to terrorists.

39. "Students should not be allowed any grace whatsoever on late assignments. Before you know it, they will no longer complete their work at all. If they don't do their assignments, they will be ignorant. If the students who are being educated are ignorant, then all of America will become more ignorant." (Thanks to a former student)

40.

TOM MEYER/SAN FRANCISCO CHRONICLE.

EXERCISE 6B

Analyzing a Short Argument

The following letter is not a genuine letter to the editor but a critical thinking test devised by educators. Test yourself by writing a critique of this deliberately flawed argument. It contains at least seven errors in reasoning, some of them fallacies that you have studied in this chapter, some of them weaknesses that can be identified and described but not labeled.

230 Sycamore Street
Moorburg
April 10

Dear Editor:
    Overnight parking on all streets in Moorburg should be eliminated. To achieve this goal, parking should be prohibited from 2 a.m. to 6 a.m. There are a number of reasons why an intelligent citizen should agree.
    For one thing, to park overnight is to have a garage in the streets. Now it is illegal for anyone to have a garage in the city streets. Clearly then it should be against the law to park overnight in the streets.
    Three important streets, Lincoln Avenue, Marquand Avenue, and West Main Street, are very narrow. With cars parked on the streets, there really isn't room for the heavy traffic that passes over them in the afternoon rush hour. When driving home in the afternoon after work, it takes me thirty-five minutes to make a trip that takes ten minutes during the uncrowded time. If there were no cars parked on the side of these streets, they could handle considerably more traffic.
    Traffic on some streets is also bad in the morning when factory workers are on their way to the 6 a.m. shift. If there were no cars parked on these streets between 2 a.m. and 6 a.m., then there would be more room for this traffic.
    Furthermore there can be no doubt that, in general, overnight parking on the streets is undesirable. It is definitely bad and should be opposed.
    If parking is prohibited from 2 a.m. to 6 a.m., then accidents between parked and moving vehicles will be nearly eliminated during this period. All intelligent citizens would regard the near elimination of accidents in any period as highly desirable. So we should be in favor of prohibiting parking from 2 a.m. to 6 a.m.
    Last month the Chief of Police, Burgess Jones, ran an experiment which proves that parking should be prohibited from 2 a.m. to 6 a.m. On one of our busiest streets, Marquand Avenue, he placed experimental signs for one day. The signs prohibited parking from 2 a.m. to 6 a.m. During the four-hour period there was *not one accident* on Marquand. Everyone knows, of course, that there have been over four hundred accidents on Marquand during the past year.

The opponents of my suggestions have said that conditions are safe enough now. These people don't know what "safe" really means. *Conditions are not safe if there's even the slightest possible chance for an accident.* That's what "safe" means. So conditions are not safe the way they are now.

Finally let me point out that the director of the National Traffic Safety Council, Kenneth O. Taylor, has strongly recommended that overnight street parking be prevented on busy streets in cities the size of Moorburg. The National Association of Police Chiefs has made the same recommendation. Both suggest that prohibiting parking from 2 a.m. to 6 a.m. is the best way to prevent overnight parking.

I invite those who disagree as well as those who agree with me to react to my letter through the editor of this paper. Let's get this issue out in the open.

Sincerely,

Robert R. Raywift

WRITING ASSIGNMENT 14

Analyzing an Extended Argument

From the following collection of editorials, choose one (or find one in a newspaper or periodical) on which to write an essay evaluating the argument. We suggest the following process for approaching this paper:

Analyze each paragraph of your chosen editorial in order. Compose a list of the fallacies you find in each paragraph—give names of fallacies or identify weaknesses in reasoning (not all weaknesses can be precisely named) and illustrate with specific examples from the editorial. Avoid the trap of being too picky; you won't necessarily find significant fallacies in every paragraph.

During this paragraph-by-paragraph analysis, keep the argument's conclusion in mind and ask yourself if the author provides adequate support for it.

Next, review your paragraph-by-paragraph analysis to determine the two or three major problems in the argument. Then group and condense your list of faults or fallacies and, in a coherently written essay organized around these two or three principal categories, present your evaluation of the argument. For example, if you find more than one instance of personal attack, devote one of your paragraphs to this fallacy and cite all the examples you find to support your claim. Follow the same procedure for other weaknesses. Identify each specific example you cite either by paraphrase or direct quotation, imagining as you write that the reader is not familiar with the editorial you are critiquing. In your introduction, briefly discuss the issue of the editorial you've chosen, possibly supplying background information not covered in the editorial itself.

Audience

College-age readers who have not read the editorial and who are not familiar with all of the fallacies listed in the text.

Purpose

To illustrate to a less critical reader that published arguments written by established professionals are not necessarily free of fallacious reasoning.

On Date Rape

CAMILLE PAGLIA

Humanities professor and cultural critic, *San Francisco Examiner*

Dating is a very recent phenomenon in world history. Throughout history, women have been chaperoned. As late as 1964, when I arrived in college, we had strict rules. We had to be in the dorm under lock and key by 11 o'clock. My generation was the one that broke these rules. We said, "We want freedom—no more double standard!" When I went to stay at a male friend's apartment in New York, my aunts flew into a frenzy: "You can't do that, it's dangerous!" But I said, "No, we're not going to be like that anymore." Still, we understood in the '60s that we were taking a risk. 1

Today these young women want the freedoms that we won, but they don't want to acknowledge the risk. That's the problem. The minute you go out with a man, the minute you go to a bar to have a drink, there is a risk. You have to accept the fact that part of the sizzle of sex comes from the danger of sex. You can be overpowered. 2

So it is women's personal responsibility to be aware of the dangers of the world. But these young feminists today are deluded. They come from a protected, white, middle-class world, and they expect everything to be safe. Notice it's not black or Hispanic women who are making a fuss about this— they come from cultures that are fully sexual and they are fully realistic about sex. But these other women are sexually repressed girls, coming out of pampered homes, and when they arrive at these colleges and suddenly hit male lust, they go, "Oh, no!" 3

These girls say, "Well, I should be able to get drunk at a fraternity party and go upstairs to a guy's room without anything happening." And I say, "Oh, really? And when you drive your car to New York City, do you leave your keys on the hood?" My point is that if your car is stolen after you do something like that, yes, the police should pursue the thief and he should be punished. But at the same time, the police—and I—have the right to say to you, "You stupid idiot, what the hell were you thinking?" 4

I mean, wake up to reality. This is male sex. Guess what, it's hot. Male sex is hot. There's an attraction between the sexes that we're not totally in control of. The idea that we can regulate it by passing campus grievance 5 committee rules is madness. My kind of feminism stresses personal responsibility. I've never been raped, but I've been very vigilant—I'm constantly reading the signals. If I ever got into a dating situation where I was overpowered and raped, I would say, "Oh well, I misread the signals." But I don't think I would ever press charges.

Boxing, Doctors—Round Two

LOWELL COHN

Sportswriter, San Francisco Chronicle

Before I went on vacation a few weeks ago, I wrote a column criticizing the American Medical Association for its call to abolish boxing. As you might have expected, I have received letters from doctors telling me I'm misinformed and scientifically naive. One doctor even said I must have had terrible experiences with doctors to have written what I wrote.   1

That just shows how arrogant doctors are. It never would occur to them that I might have a defensible position. If I disagree with them, it's because I'm ignorant.   2

Doctors are used to being right. We come into their offices sick and generally not knowing what's wrong with us. We are in awe of their expertise and afraid for our well-being. We have a tendency to act like children in front of them. "If you can only make me well, Doc, I will love you for life." Doctors, who start out as regular human beings, come to expect us to worship them. They thrive on the power that comes from having knowledge about life and death.   3

Which brings us to their misguided stand against boxing. Doctors are offended by injuries in boxing, although they don't seem as mortified by the people who die skiing or bike riding or swimming every year. You rarely hear a peep out of them about the many injuries football players sustain—that includes kids in the peewee leagues and high school. Why the outrage over boxing?   4

Because many doctors are social snobs. They see people from ethnic minorities punching each other in a ring and they reach the conclusion that these poor, dumb blacks and Latinos must be protected from themselves because they don't know any better. The AMA is acting like a glorified SPCA, arrogantly trying to prevent cruelty to animals. They would never dare preach this way to football players, because most of them went to college. Nor would they come out against skiing, because many doctors love to ski.   5

Boxers know the risks of taking a right cross to the jaw better than doctors, and they take up the sport with a full understanding of its risks. A man should have the right to take a risk. Doctors may want to save us from adventure, but there still is honor in freely choosing to put yourself on the line. Risk is why race-car drivers speed around treacherous tracks.   6

Danger is why mountain climbers continue to explore the mystery of Mount Everest. Yet doctors do not come out against auto racing or mountain climbing.

One physician wrote a letter to the Sporting Green saying the AMA's   7 position against boxing is based on medical evidence. As I read the letter's twisted logic, I wondered if the AMA causes brain damage in doctors. "Skiing, bicycle riding and swimming kill more people each year (than boxing)," he writes. "Obviously, far more people engage in those activities than enter a boxing ring."

Does his position make sense to you? We should eliminate boxing,   8 the sport with fewer negative consequences, but allow the real killer sports to survive. Amazing. If this doctor were really concerned with medical evidence, as he claims, he would attack all dangerous sports, not just boxing.

But he doesn't. The truth is, boxing offends the delicate sensibilities of   9 doctors. They don't like the idea that two men *intentionally* try to hurt each other. They feel more comfortable when injuries are a byproduct of a sport—although ask any batter who has been beaned by a fastball if his broken skull was an innocent byproduct.

In other words, doctors are making a moral judgment, not a medical   10 judgment, about which sports are acceptable. Every joker is entitled to ethical opinions, but doctors have no more expertise than you or I when it comes to right and wrong. If preaching excites them, let them become priests.

What if the AMA is successful in getting boxing banned? Will the sport   11 disappear? No way. As long as man is man, he will want to see two guys of equal weight and ability solve their elemental little problem in a ring. If the sport becomes illegal, it will drift off to barges and back alleys, where men will fight in secret without proper supervision. And then you will see deaths and maiming like you never saw before.

Whom will the AMA blame then?   12

Say Goodbye to SUVs

RICH LOWREY

Editor of the *National Review*

Drive your Lincoln Navigator around the block a few extra times while you   1 have the chance. If California Democrats have anything to say about it, the sport utilities vehicle will eventually be chased from the nation's streets. A bill that just passed the California Legislature, and will probably soon be signed into law by Governor Gray Davis, mandates that automakers make "the maximum feasible reduction" in carbon dioxide emissions. The only way to do this is to squeeze out bigger, heavier vehicles.

The vote won't just affect fuzzy-headed Californians who think it's prac- 2
tically a hate crime to drink nonorganic coffee and want their cars to run on rubber bands and propellers, but every driver in the country. A quirk in the Clean Air Act allows states to follow either federal or California pollution standards, making the Golden State a leader in environmental regulation. Also, automakers can't afford to simply forgo the California market, and therefore will probably have to manufacture all cars to meet California standards. California Democrats want, in effect, to save the planet on the backs of America's soccer moms.

Environmentalists tried to raise fuel-economy standards nationwide 3
earlier this year in Congress, but failed, because SUVs and other light trucks are so popular. In 36 out of the 50 states, sales of light trucks outpace sales of passenger cars. So, enviros opted for the California backdoor. The Golden State doesn't have many of those pesky unionized autoworkers who object to attempts by enviro activists to "act locally" by killing off their jobs.

An environmental group, the Bluewater Network, drafted the legisla- 4
tion, and it passed the Legislature by one vote after lobbying by U.S. Sens. John Kerry, D-Mass., and John McCain, R-Ariz., who had supported the failed regulatory push in Congress. The bill leaves it to the California Air Resources Board to determine what constitutes the "maximum feasible reduction." Whatever it is, it won't be enough to put a dent in "global warming" (if such a thing even exists). California vehicles, by one estimate, account for roughly one-tenth of 1 percent of all carbon dioxide released globally. This is not just a drop in the bucket, but a fraction of a drop in the bucket.

The Legislature explicitly ruled out new taxes as a way to achieve emis- 5
sions reductions, but the measures likely to be adopted will be taxes by a different name. To get consumers to stop buying light trucks, automakers will be forced to raise their prices.

Meanwhile, the most obvious way to reduce the fuel consumption of 6
cars is simply to make them lighter and smaller, and thus less likely to protect passengers from crashes. In response to another starry-eyed California mandate—for automakers to make 10 percent of their sales "zero emissions" cars by 2004—Ford has been marketing glorified golf carts.

There is no reason to believe that consumers, in their love affair with 7
SUVs, minivans and trucks, are making anything but a rational choice. The price of gasoline, adjusted for inflation, is less than it was in 1970, and can be less than a gallon of bottled water. Why not consume more of it in exchange for greater room, safety, pickup, towing power, etc.? But environmentalists think they know better. California liberals want government out of your bedroom, so it can meddle in your driveway instead.

KEY TERMS

Term	Description	Example
Appeal to authority (2 forms)	1. Appeals to an authority who is not an expert on the issue under discussion.	Abortion to save the mother is irrelevant because a pediatric surgeon has never seen a case in which such a dilemma has risen.
Snob appeal	2. Appeals to people's desire for prestige and exclusivity.	Pamilla's not for everyone. The best never is.
Appeal to fear	Implicitly threatens the audience.	Will there be a *job* waiting when *you* leave college?
Appeal to pity	Attempts to win sympathy.	Professor Hall, I must get an A in your course. If you don't give me an A, I won't be able to go to law school.
Begging the question	1. Offers no actual support; may restate as a premise the conclusion in different words.	Students like rock music because it is the most enjoyable music around.
Loaded question	2. Asks a question that contains an assumption that must be proven.	Have you started to pay your fair share of taxes yet?
Question-begging epithet	3. Uses a single word to assert a claim that must be proven.	Reactionary, negligent, warmonger, deadbeat.
Double standard	Judges and labels the same act differently depending on the person or group who performs the act.	China and Cuba both restrict religious freedoms and limit free speech. China has favored-nation status whereas Cuba is not recognized by the United States.
Equivocation	Shifts the meaning of a term within a single argument.	We are told that to discriminate in employment or housing is punishable by law. But we must discriminate when we hire an individual or rent an apartment.

Term	Description	Example
Fallacious argument	Persuasive but does not logically support its conclusion.	Senator Smith was expelled from college for cheating on an exam. His wife divorced him because of his numerous affairs. Therefore, he is a man without honor, a politician who cannot be trusted, and we should not support his National Health Bill.
False analogy	Compares two or more things that are not in essence similar and suggests that since they share certain characteristics, they share others as well.	I don't want to die falling off a rock. But you can kill yourself falling in the bathtub too.
False cause [Latin name: *post hoc, ergo propter hoc*]	Claims a causal relationship between events solely on the basis of a chronological relationship.	I joined the Confederacy for two weeks. Then I deserted. The Confederacy fell.
False dilemma	Presents two and only two alternatives for consideration when other possibilities exist.	Either you are in favor of recalling the mayor, or you are a supporter of her political platform.
Hasty generalization	Generalizes from a sample that is too small or in some other way unrepresentative of the target population.	Students in Professor Hall's eight o'clock freshman composition class are often late. Today's college students are irresponsible and unreliable.
Personal attack [Latin name: *ad hominem*]	1. Attacks the person representing the argument rather than the argument itself.	Because she is extremely wealthy, our mayor cannot properly represent this city

Term	Description	Example
Tu quoque ("you also")	2. Discredits an argument because the behavior of the person proposing it does not conform to the position he's supporting.	A teenager to his father: Don't tell me not to drink. You drink all the time.
Poisoning the well	Makes an assertion that will intimidate the audience and therefore discourage an open discussion.	Every patriotic American supports legislation condemning the desecration of the flag.
Slippery slope	Claims that an action should be avoided because it will lead to a series of extremely undesirable consequences.	What seems like reasonable restrictions on guns with no legitimate civilian purpose will lead inevitably to total prohibition of gun ownership that ends in virtual slavery at the hands of a totalitarian regime.
Straw man	Creates and then attacks a distorted version of the opposition's argument.	The democratic candidate wants the federal government to house everyone, feed everyone, care for everyone's children, and provide medical care for everyone. And he's going to take 50 percent of every dime you make to do it.

CHAPTER 7

Deductive and Inductive Argument

There is a tradition of opposition between adherents of induction and deduction. In my view, it would be just as sensible for the two ends of a worm to quarrel.

—ALFRED NORTH WHITEHEAD

Sometimes arguments are classified as inductive or deductive. Induction and deduction are modes of reasoning, particular ways of arriving at an inference. Different logicians tend to make different distinctions between deductive and inductive reasoning, with some going so far as to declare, as Whitehead did, that such a distinction is spurious. But classifications, if carefully made, help us to understand abstract concepts, and scientists and humanists alike often refer to patterns of reasoning as deductive or inductive. This classification also helps us to distinguish between conclusions we must accept and those we should question, a valuable skill for both reading critically and writing logically.

KEY DISTINCTIONS

The key distinctions between deduction and induction are generally seen as falling into two categories.

(1) Necessity Versus Probability

In a **deductive argument,** the conclusion will follow by *necessity* from the premises if the method of reasoning is valid, as in this familiar bit of classical wisdom:

1. All men are mortal.
2. Socrates is a man.
∴ Socrates is mortal.

In an **inductive argument,** the conclusion can follow only with some degree of ***probability*** (from the unlikely to the highly probable). British philosopher Bertrand Russell made the point implicitly but emphatically in *The Problems of Philosophy:* "The man who has fed the chicken every day throughout its life at last wrings its neck instead." The chicken reasons thus:

1. He has fed me today.
2. He has fed me this next day.
3. He has fed me this day too.
4. He has fed me yet another day, etc.
∴ He will feed me tomorrow.

The poor chicken has made a prediction, and a reasonable one, based on its past experience.

A related distinction here becomes clear. The premises of a deductive argument contain all the information needed for the conclusion, whereas the conclusion of an inductive argument goes beyond the premises. For this reason, some prefer the certainty of deduction to the probability of induction.

Ambroise Paré, an Italian Renaissance physician, revealed his distrust of induction when he defined inductive diagnosis as "the rapid means to the wrong conclusion." One assumes that he would have argued for the value of a few well-learned principles behind one's observations. In contrast, nineteenth-century Harvard professor and scientist Louis Agassiz urged his students to practice induction, to observe before making generalizations, believing that: "[A] physical fact is as sacred as a moral principle."

(2) From General to Specific, Specific to General

In a ***deductive*** argument, the inference usually moves from a generalization to a particular, specific instance or example that fits that generalization. Two examples:

1. All students who complete this course successfully will fulfill the critical thinking requirement.
2. Jane has completed this course successfully.
∴ Jane has fulfilled the critical thinking requirement.

1. Children born on a Saturday will "work hard for a living."
2. Nick was born on a Saturday.
∴ Nick will work hard for his living.

You may not believe this folk wisdom, especially if you were born on a Saturday, but the line of reasoning is still deductive.

In an ***inductive*** argument, the inference usually moves from a series of specific instances to a generalization.

1. Droughts have been more frequent in some areas.
2. Skin cancers related to ultraviolet rays have been increasing.
3. The tree line is moving north about 40 meters a year.
4. Polar ice has been melting more rapidly than in the past.
5. Oceans have been rising at measurable annual rates around the globe.

∴ Clearly, global warming is upon us.

*"Gentlemen, it's time we gave some serious thought
to the effects of global warming."*

Sometimes in inductive reasoning, we begin with a **hypothesis, an unproved theory or proposition,** and gather the data to support it. For instance, when Jonas Salk thought his vaccine would cure polio, he first had to test it inductively by administering it to a broad sample before concluding that the vaccine prevented polio.

THE RELATIONSHIP BETWEEN INDUCTION AND DEDUCTION

In Exercise 7B we ask you to distinguish between inductive and deductive reasoning, but in reality the two are inextricable. Consider the source for the generalizations upon which deductions are based. In some cases they seem to be the laws of nature, but more often than not we arrive at these generalizations by means of repeated observations. Throughout history, people have observed their own mortality, so we can now take that generalization—all people are mortal—as a given from which we can deduce conclusions about individual people. Induction has, in this case, led to a trusted generalization that in turn allows us a "necessary," or deductive, inference.

Humorists have sometimes turned these concepts on their heads. Here's Woody Allen reflecting on deduction: "All men are Socrates." And Lewis Carroll, in "The Hunting of the Snark," on induction: "What I tell you three times is true."

In a more serious approach, Robert Pirsig, in his philosophical novel *Zen and the Art of Motorcycle Maintenance*, attempts to explain deduction, induction, and the relationships between them in language we can all understand. These terms were never intended to be the exclusive domain of academics but, rather, descriptive of the ways in which we all think every day.

Note how the following excerpt from Pirsig's novel explains both the differences between induction and deduction and their dependence on one another.

Mechanics' Logic

Two kinds of logic are used (in motorcycle maintenance), inductive and deductive. Inductive inferences start with observations of the machine and arrive at general conclusions. For example, if the cycle goes over a bump and the engine misfires, and then goes over another bump and the engine misfires, and then goes over another bump and the engine misfires, and then goes over a long smooth stretch of road and there is no misfiring, and then goes over a fourth bump and the engine misfires again, one can logically conclude that the misfiring is caused by the bumps. That is induction: reasoning from particular experiences to general truths.   1

Deductive inferences do the reverse. They start with general knowledge and predict a specific observation. For example, if, from reading the hierarchy of facts about the machine, the mechanic knows the horn of the cycle is powered exclusively by electricity from the battery, then he can logically infer that if the battery is dead the horn will not work. That is deduction.   2

Solution of problems too complicated for common sense to solve is achieved by long strings of mixed inductive and deductive inferences that   3 weave back and forth between the observed machine and the mental hierarchy of the machine found in the manuals. The correct program for this interweaving is formalized as scientific method.

Actually I've never seen a cycle-maintenance problem complex enough really to require full-scale formal scientific method. Repair problems are not that hard. When I think of formal scientific method an image sometimes comes to mind of an enormous juggernaut, a huge bulldozer—slow, tedious, lumbering, laborious, but invincible. It takes twice as long, five times as long, maybe a dozen times as long as informal mechanic's techniques, but you know in the end you're going to *get* it. There's no fault isolation problem in motorcycle maintenance that can stand up to it. When you've hit a really tough one, tried everything, racked your brain and nothing works, and you know that this time Nature has really decided to be difficult, you say, "Okay, Nature, that's the end of the *nice* guy," and you crank up the formal scientific method. 4

For this you keep a lab notebook. Everything gets written down, formally, so that you know at all times where you are, where you've been, where you're going and where you want to get. In scientific work and electronics technology this is necessary because otherwise the problems get so complex you get lost in them and confused and forget what you know and what you don't know and have to give up. In cycle maintenance things are not that involved, but when confusion starts it's a good idea to hold it down by making everything formal and exact. Sometimes just the act of writing down the problems straightens out your head as to what they really are. 5

The logical statements entered into the notebook are broken down into six categories: (1) statement of the problem, (2) hypotheses as to the cause of the problem, (3) experiments designed to test each hypothesis, (4) predicted results of the experiments, (5) observed results of the experiments and (6) conclusions from the results of the experiments. This is not different from the formal arrangement of many college and high-school lab notebooks but the purpose here is no longer just busy-work. The purpose now is precise guidance of thoughts that will fail if they are not accurate. 6

The real purpose of scientific method is to make sure Nature hasn't misled you into thinking you know something you don't actually know. There's not a mechanic or scientist or technician alive who hasn't suffered from that one so much that he's not instinctively on guard. That's the main reason why so much scientific and mechanical information sounds so dull and so cautious. If you get careless or go romanticizing scientific information, giving it a flourish here and there, Nature will soon make a complete fool out of you. It does it often enough anyway even when you don't give it opportunities. One must be extremely careful and rigidly logical when dealing with Nature: one logical slip and an entire scientific edifice comes tumbling down. One false deduction about the machine and you can get hung up indefinitely. 7

In Part One of formal scientific method, which is the statement of the problem, the main skill is in stating absolutely no more than you are positive 8 you know. It is much better to enter a statement "Solve Problem: Why doesn't cycle work?" which sounds dumb but is correct, than it is to enter a statement "Solve Problem: What is wrong with the electrical system?" when you don't absolutely *know* the trouble is *in* the electrical system. What you should state is "Solve Problem: What is wrong with cycle?" and *then* state as the first entry of Part Two: "Hypothesis Number One: The trouble is in the electrical system." You think of as many hypotheses as you can, then you design experiments to test them to see which are true and which are false.

This careful approach to the beginning questions keeps you from taking   9
a major wrong turn which might cause you weeks of extra work or can even hang you up completely. Scientific questions often have a surface appearance of dumbness for this reason. They are asked in order to prevent dumb mistakes later on.

Part Three, that part of formal scientific method called experimenta-   10
tion, is sometimes thought of by romantics as all of science itself because that's the only part with much visual surface. They see lots of test tubes and bizarre equipment and people running around making discoveries. They do not see the experiment as part of a larger intellectual process and so they often confuse experiments with demonstrations, which look the same. A man conducting a gee-whiz science show with fifty thousand dollars' worth of Frankenstein equipment is not doing anything scientific if he knows beforehand what the results of his efforts are going to be. A motorcycle mechanic, on the other hand, who honks the horn to see if the battery works is informally conducting a true scientific experiment. He is testing a hypothesis by putting the question to Nature. The TV scientist who mutters sadly, "The experiment is a failure; we have failed to achieve what we had hoped for," is suffering mainly from a bad scriptwriter. An experiment is never a failure solely because it fails to achieve predicted results. An experiment is a failure only when it also fails adequately to test the hypothesis in question, when the data it produces don't prove anything one way or another.

Skill at this point consists of using experiments that test only the hy-   11
pothesis in question, nothing less, nothing more. If the horn honks, and the mechanic concludes that the whole electrical system is working, he is in deep trouble. He has reached an illogical conclusion. The honking horn only tells him that the battery and horn are working. To design an experiment properly he has to think very rigidly in terms of what directly causes what. This you know from the hierarchy. The horn doesn't make the cycle go. Neither does the battery, except in a very indirect way. The point at which the electrical system *directly* causes the engine to fire is at the spark plugs, and if you don't test here, at the output of the electrical system, you will never really know whether the failure is electrical or not.

To test properly the mechanic removes the plug and lays it against the   12
engine so that the base around the plug is electrically grounded, kicks the starter lever and watches the spark-plug gap for a blue spark. If there isn't

any he can conclude one of two things: (a) there is an electrical failure or (b) his experiment is sloppy. If he is experienced he will try it a few more times, checking connections, trying every way he can think of to get that plug to fire. Then, if he can't get it to fire, he finally concludes that *a* is correct, there's an electrical failure, and the experiment is over. He has proved that his hypothesis is correct.

In the final category, conclusions, skill comes in stating no more than   13
the experiment has proved. It hasn't proved that when he fixes the electrical system the motorcycle will start. There may be other things wrong. But he does know that the motorcycle isn't going to run until the electrical system is working and he sets up the next formal question: "Solve Problem: What is wrong with the electrical system?"

He then sets up hypotheses for these and tests them. By asking the   14
right questions and choosing the right tests and drawing the right conclusions the mechanic works his way down the echelons of the motorcycle hierarchy until he has found the exact specific cause or causes of the engine failure, and then he changes them so that they no longer cause the failure.

An untrained observer will see only physical labor and often get the   15
idea that physical labor is mainly what the mechanic does. Actually the physical labor is the smallest and easiest part of what the mechanic does. By far the greatest part of his work is careful observation and precise thinking. That is why mechanics sometimes seem so taciturn and withdrawn when performing tests. They don't like it when you talk to them because they are concentrating on mental images, hierarchies, and not really looking at you or the physical motorcycle at all. They are using the experiment as part of the program to expand their hierarchy of knowledge of the faulty motorcycle and compare it to the correct hierarchy in their mind. They are looking at underlying form.

EXERCISE 7A

Analyzing Pirsig

1. According to Pirsig, what is the most important part of the mechanic's work?

2. How does Pirsig define induction and deduction?

3. Which method of reasoning—induction or deduction—does the scientific method rely on?

4. Return to the statement by mathematician and philosopher Alfred North Whitehead (1861–1947), which begins this chapter, and explain its meaning.

EXERCISE 7B

Distinguishing Inductive from Deductive Reasoning

A. Read the following passages carefully to determine which are based on deductive reasoning and which on inductive. Briefly explain your answers.

1. Only eighteen-year-old citizens can vote, and Felix is not a citizen so he can't vote in the upcoming presidential election.

2. The United States Supreme Court nominee received excellent grades throughout his school career and made law review at Harvard Law School. Add to these excellent credentials, the fact that everyone who has ever known him says that he is kind and fair. I think he will make an excellent Supreme Court justice.

3. Marie must be out of town. She hasn't answered her phone in a week, nor has she returned the messages that I have left on her answering machine. When I drove by her house last night, I noted that the lights inside and out were off.

4. Cat lovers do not care for dogs, and since Colette had numerous cats all of her life, I assume she did not care for dogs.

5. According to polls taken prior to the national convention, the candidate I support held a substantial lead in the presidential race. I am now confident that he will win in November.

6. Every Frenchman is devoted to his glass of *vin rouge*. Philippe is a Frenchman, so he too must be devoted to that glass of red wine.

7. Bill Clinton lied to the American people about his relationship with a White House intern. Richard Nixon lied about Watergate. Lyndon Johnson lied about the Gulf of Tonkin and the Viet Nam War. I'll let you draw your own conclusions.

8. As an expert testified on the *News Hour* following the *Challenger* space shuttle disaster, the solid rocket booster had proved safe in over 200 successful launchings of both space shuttles and Titan missiles. It was reasonable to conclude that the same rocket booster would function properly on the *Challenger* mission.

9. Over time the only investment to keep pace with inflation is an investment in the stock market. So despite the current economic crisis, responsible retirement fund managers should continue to buy stocks.

10. When people are confident and cheerful, they are generally inclined to spend more freely. With this in mind, we have designed these ads to project a feeling of cheerful confidence that should encourage viewers to spend more freely on your product. [Ad agency pitch to a potential client]

B. Read the following passage taken from Arthur Conan Doyle's story "A Study in Scarlet." Some critical thinkers have presented this passage as an example of deduction, others as induction. What do you think? Explain your decision.

A Study in Scarlet

"I wonder what that fellow is looking for?" I asked, pointing to a stalwart, 1
plainly dressed individual who was walking slowly down the other side of the street, looking anxiously at the numbers. He had a large blue envelope in his hand, and was evidently the bearer of a message. "You mean the retired sergeant of Marines," said Sherlock Holmes.

"Brag and bounce!" thought I to myself. "He knows that I cannot verify 2
his guess."

The thought had hardly passed through my mind when the man whom 3
we were watching caught sight of the number on our door, and ran rapidly across the roadway. We heard a loud knock, a deep voice below, and heavy steps ascending the stair.

"For Mr. Sherlock Holmes," he said, stepping into the room and hand- 4
ing my friend the letter.

Here was an opportunity of taking the conceit out of him. He little 5
thought of this when he made that random shot. "May I ask, my lad," I said, in the blandest voice, "what your trade may be?"

"Commissionaire, sir," he said, gruffly. "Uniform away for repairs." 6

"And you were?" I asked, with a slightly malicious glance at my 7
companion.

"A sergeant, sir, Royal Marine Light Infantry, sir. No answer? Right, sir." 8

He clicked his heels together, raised his hand in salute, and was gone. 9

I confess that I was considerably startled by this fresh proof of the prac- 10
tical nature of my companion's theories. My respect for his powers of analysis increased wondrously. There still remained some lurking suspicion in my mind, however, that the whole thing was a prearranged episode, intended to dazzle me, though what earthly object he could have in taking me in was past my comprehension. When I looked at him, he had finished reading the note, and his eyes had assumed the vacant, lack-lustre expression which showed mental abstraction.

"How in the world did you deduce that?" I asked. 11

"Deduce what?" said he, petulantly. 12

"Why, that he was a retired sergeant of Marines." 13

"I have no time for trifles," he answered, brusquely; then with a smile, 14
"Excuse my rudeness. You broke the thread of my thoughts; but perhaps it is as well. So you actually were not able to see that that man was a sergeant of Marines?"

"No, indeed." 15

"It was easier to know it than to explain why I know it. If you were   16
asked to prove that two and two made four, you might find some difficulty,
and yet you are quite sure of the fact. Even across the street I could see a
great blue anchor tattooed on the back of the fellow's hand. That smacked
of the sea. He had a military carriage, however, and regulation side
whiskers. There we have the marine. He was a man with some amount of
self-importance and a certain air of command. You must have observed the
way in which he held his head and swung his cane. A steady, respectable,
middle-aged man, too, on the face of him—all facts which led me to believe
that he had been a sergeant."

"Wonderful!" I ejaculated.   17

"Commonplace," said Holmes, though I thought from his expression   18
that he was pleased at my evident surprise and admiration.

DEDUCTIVE REASONING

Class Logic

Having established the differences between deductive and inductive reasoning, we can now examine each in greater detail. Underlying both forms of reasoning is an understanding of class logic. In fact, good reasoning in general often depends on seeing relationships between classes. A **class** in logic is all of
the individual things—persons, objects, events, ideas—that share a determinate property, a common feature. What is that determinate property? Anything under the sun. A class may consist of any quality or combination of qualities that the classifier assigns to it. A class may be vast, such as a class
containing everything in the universe, or it may be small, containing only one
member, such as Nick's last girlfriend. Making classes and assigning members
to those classes is an essential part of everyday reasoning—it's how we order
our experience. Indeed, each word in the language serves as a class by which
we categorize and communicate experience. We can then take these words in
any combination to create the categories or classes that serve our purpose.

A recent article in the *Journal of the American Medical Association*, for example, features a piece titled "Risk of Sexually Transmitted Diseases Among Adoles-
cent Crack Users in Oakland and San Francisco." This title, which identifies one
class (and the subject of the article), was created by combining seven classes: the
class of things involving risk, the class of things that are sexually transmitted, the
class of disease, the class of adolescents, the class of crack users, the class of persons living in Oakland, and the class of persons living in San Francisco.

Relationships Between Classes

There are three possible relationships between classes: **inclusion, exclusion,** and **overlap.**

INCLUSION   One class is included in another if every member of one class is a member of the other class. Using letters, we can symbolize this relationship as all As are Bs. Using circle diagrams, also called Euler diagrams after Leonhard Euler, an eighteenth-century mathematician, we can illustrate a relationship of inclusion this way:

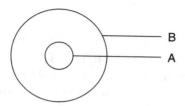

For example, the class of professional basketball players is included in the class of professional athletes because all professional basketball players are also professional athletes. The following diagram illustrates this relationship:

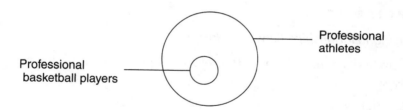

EXCLUSION   One class excludes another if they share no members, that is, if no As are Bs. Such a relationship exists between handguns and rifles:

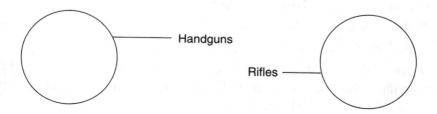

OVERLAP   One class overlaps with another if both have at least one member in common—if at least one A is also a B—for example, students at this university and students who like classical music:

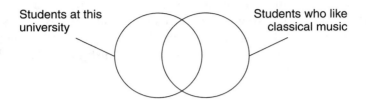

Students at this
university

Students who like
classical music

The way our public institutions classify relationships between groups of people can have a significant impact on their lives. The federal Department of Housing and Urban Development (HUD) is authorized to allocate housing funds to individuals with disabilities. People with AIDS argued that they were entitled to such funds, but HUD, until recently, had denied them any such subsidy. Clearly, HUD saw the relationship between disabilities and AIDS as one of exclusion, whereas those with AIDS saw their relationship to those with disabilities as one of inclusion, a relationship they were, over time, able to convince HUD of.

EXERCISE 7C

Identifying Relationships Between Classes

Using circle diagrams, illustrate the relationships between the following pairs of classes:

1. witches and women
2. cantaloupes and watermelons
3. judges and lawyers
4. Saabs and convertibles
5. mollusks and amphibians
6. cosmetics and hairspray
7. the homeless and the mentally ill
8. euthanasia and suicide
9. concession and Rogerian strategy (see Chapter 4)
10. What is the meaning of the following diagram, which appeared on the *New York Times'* editorial page?

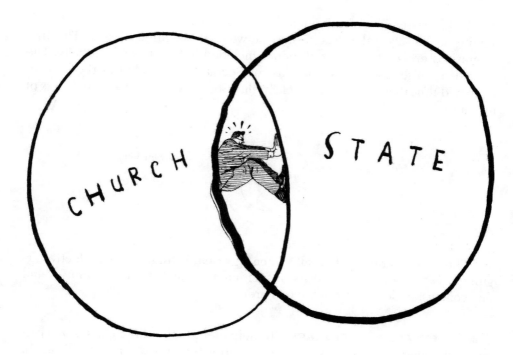

Now create your own classes:

1. Identify two classes, one of which is inclusive of the other.
2. Identify two classes that are exclusive of one another.
3. Identify two classes that overlap one another.

Class Logic and the Syllogism

Both inductive and deductive reasoning often depend on supporting a conclusion on the basis of relationships between classes. Let's look first at deduction. Deductive arguments usually involve more than two classes; in fact, the simplest form of deductive argument involves three classes. Remember this famous argument?

All men are mortal.

Socrates is a man.

∴ Socrates is mortal.

The three classes are "men," "mortality," and "Socrates." We can use circle diagrams to illustrate the relationship between these three classes. The first premise asserts that the class of men is included in the class of mortality. The second premise asserts that the class of Socrates is included in the class of men; and thus the conclusion can claim that Socrates is included in the class of mortality.

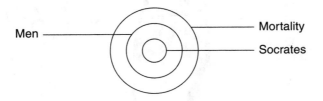

This type of argument is called a **categorical syllogism**—a deductive argument composed of three classes; such an argument has two premises and one conclusion derived from the two premises.

THE SUBJECT AND THE PREDICATE   To help identify the three classes of a categorical syllogism, you may want to identify the subject and predicate of each premise. Categorical propositions, and indeed all English sentences, can be broken down into two parts—the subject and predicate. These terms are shared by both grammar and logic and mean the same thing in both disciplines. The subject is that part of the sentence about which something is being asserted, and the predicate includes everything being asserted about the subject. In the first premise above, "all men" is the subject and "are mortal" is the predicate; in the second premise, "Socrates" is the subject and "is a man" is the predicate. The subject identifies one class; the predicate, the other.

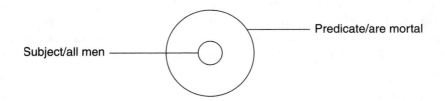

Note: If the premise stated "men are mortal" rather than "all men are mortal," the meaning would be the same because, if a class is not quantified in some way—*some, many, few, one*—it is assumed that the assertion refers to the entire class.

TRUTH, VALIDITY, AND SOUNDNESS   If the conclusion follows of necessity, inescapably, from the premises, as it does in the syllogism about Socrates, then it is a **valid** argument.

We frequently use the term "valid" in everyday language. For example, we say, "That's a valid point." But in logic **validity** has this very precise meaning: The conclusion follows of necessity from the premises, the form of the argument is correct, the line of reasoning conforms to the rules of logic. When we learn to evaluate the validity of a deductive argument, we can see what it means for a conclusion to follow inescapably from the premises.

Validity, however, is not the only requirement for a successful deductive argument; the premises must also be "**true**" or "**acceptable.**" Logicians use the term *true,* appropriate when a proposition can be evaluated by absolute or mathematical standards. But proof must often fall short of what can be claimed as true, an absolute term too imposing, even intimidating, for many assertions that we would nonetheless be inclined to accept. In most of our arguments, we must settle for what is **reasonable to believe,** what has been adequately supported and explained. Oliver Wendell Holmes, Supreme Court Justice (1902–1932), skirted the issue when he said, "What is true is what I can't help believing." We prefer the term "acceptable" to "true."

An important point here is that to evaluate an argument successfully, we must begin by evaluating the premises, one by one, rather than moving in on the conclusion first. The conclusion will only be as acceptable as the sum of its premises.

To summarize, two requirements must be met for us to accept the conclusion of a deductive argument:

1. The structure of the argument must be *valid*—that is, the conclusion must follow of necessity from the premises.

2. The premises must be *acceptable* (true).

A deductive argument whose premises are acceptable and whose structure is valid is a **sound** argument—a successful deductive argument. Put another way, if the argument is valid and the premises are acceptable, then the conclusion cannot be false. Keep in mind that the terms validity and soundness can refer only to the argument as a whole. In contrast, individual statements can only be described as acceptable or unacceptable (true or false). In logic, we don't describe an argument as being true or a premise as valid.

Some examples of sound and unsound arguments:

1. A sound argument—the premises are acceptable and the structure valid.

   Drift-net fishing kills dolphins.

   Mermaid Tuna uses drift nets.

   ∴ Mermaid Tuna kills dolphins.

2. An unsound argument—one of the premises (in this example the first one) is false or not acceptable, even though the structure is valid.

All Latins are volatile.

Jesse is a Latin.

∴ Jesse is volatile.

3. An unsound argument—the premises are acceptable but the structure is invalid.

All athletes are people.

All football players are people.

∴ All football players are athletes.

Note that in example 3, all the statements are acceptable, both the premises and the conclusion, but because the structure of the argument is invalid—the premises do not lead inescapably to the conclusion—the argument is unsound. Sketch this argument with circle diagrams to illustrate the principle.

Unreliable syllogisms turn up as accident and as humorous intent in a variety of places. Writer and critic Donald Newlove once claimed that, because he fell asleep while reading Harold Brodkey's *Runaway Soul,* which he also did his first time through literary classics *Moby Dick* and *Ulysses, Runaway Soul* must also be a great work of literature. Writer Ian Frazier found the following graffiti on a library table at Columbia University:

Bono is supreme.

God is supreme.

∴ Bono is God.

GUILT BY ASSOCIATION   Let's look at another example of an invalid argument with acceptable premises.

Members of the Mafia often have dinner at Joe's Place in Little Italy.

My neighbor frequently dines there.

∴ My neighbor is a member of the Mafia.

Most of us would reject this argument, but this pattern of reasoning, erroneous as it is, is fairly common. One famous example took place in 1950 when communism was referred to as the "red menace," and Senator Joseph McCarthy and the House Un-American Activities Committee were beginning their witch hunt against anyone who had ever had an association, no matter how slight or distant, with communism. It was in this climate of national paranoia that Republican Richard Nixon, running against Democrat Helen Gahagen Douglas for a California senate seat, presented the following argument, allowing the voters to draw their own conclusions:

Communists favor measures x, y, and z.

My opponent, Helen Gahagen Douglas, favors these same measures.

∴ [Helen Gahagen Douglas is a Communist.]

This kind of reasoning, based on guilt by association, is faulty (but often effective—Douglas lost the election) because it assumes that if two classes share one quality, they share all qualities. Such reasoning is a source of much racism and sexism; it assumes that if two people are of the same sex or race, they share not only that characteristic but an entire set of characteristics as well. But simple diagrams can illustrate where the logic fails:

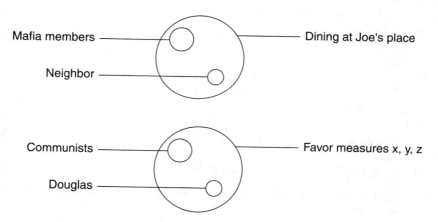

MORE ON SYLLOGISMS   Before you examine some syllogisms on your own, we need to look once again at exclusion, overlap, and inclusion. Examine the following example and use circle diagrams to illustrate the relationship between each of the classes to determine the validity of the reasoning.

All Alice's friends are business majors.

Deborah is not a business major.

∴ Deborah is not a friend of Alice.

Were you able to illustrate by exclusion that this is a valid argument? Can you do the same for this one?

None of Alice's friends are business majors.

Deborah is not a friend of Alice.

∴ Deborah is not a business major.

Can you illustrate why this reasoning is not reliable, why the argument is invalid?

So far we have been dealing with what we call a **universal proposition,** an assertion that refers to all members of a designated class. What happens when we qualify a premise with "some" and then have what logicians call a **particular proposition?** Let's look at an example:

All gamblers are optimists.

Some of my friends are gamblers.

∴ Some of my friends are optimists.

A diagram illustrates that because the conclusion is qualified, it can follow from one qualified, or "particular," premise. Although it's possible for some friends to fall outside the class of gamblers and thus, perhaps, outside the class of optimists, the second premise guarantees that some (at least two) of my friends are included in the class of gamblers.

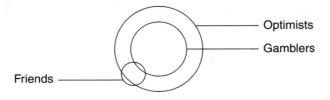

EXERCISE 7D

Determining the Validity of Categorical Syllogisms

Use Euler diagrams to determine the validity of the following categorical syllogisms.

Example

1. Stealing is a criminal act.

   Shoplifting is stealing.

   ∴ Shoplifting is a criminal act.

VALID Inclusion

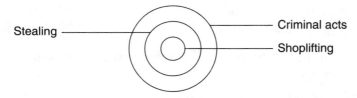

1. Liberals want to ban offshore drilling.

   Conservationists want to ban offshore drilling.

   ∴ Conservationists are liberals.

2. A cautious pilot wouldn't drink before a flight.

   Maxine is a cautious pilot.

   ∴ Maxine wouldn't drink before a flight.

3. All Jose's parrots understand Spanish.

   Pepe is his favorite parrot.

   ∴ Pepe understands Spanish.

4. Gauguin's paintings of Tahiti have brilliant and unrealistic colors.

   "Starry Night" has brilliant and unrealistic colors.

   ∴ "Starry Night" is a Gauguin painting of Tahiti.

5. Young men with shaven heads and swastikas tattooed on their arms are racists.

   John is a young man who doesn't shave his head or have a swastika tattoed on his arm.

   ∴ John is not a racist.

6. Nations that do not respect human rights shouldn't receive favored nation status.

   Tiananmen Square demonstrated China's complete lack of respect for the rights of its citizens.

   ∴ China doesn't deserve its favored nation status.

7. Every pediatrician knows that each child develops at his own rate.

   Dr. Haskell knows that each child develops at his own rate.

   ∴ Dr. Haskell is a pediatrician.

8. Some artists are completely self-absorbed.

   Frida Kahlo was an artist.

   ∴ Frida Kahlo was completely self-absorbed.

9. Members of the Christian Coalition believe in family values.

   Carlos and Maria believe in family values.

   ∴ Carlos and Maria are members of the Christian Coalition.

10. Killing the innocent is morally wrong.

    Modern warfare always involves killing the innocent.

    ∴ Modern warfare is always morally wrong.

Create three categorical syllogisms of your own—one valid but unsound, one invalid, and one sound.

EXERCISE 7E

Evaluating Deductive Arguments in Everyday Language

Determine whether the following arguments are sound or unsound. For each argument, follow these steps: First, reduce each argument to a categorical syllogism (supplying any unstated premises or conclusions—see hidden assumptions in Chapter 3); then use circle diagrams to determine validity; and finally, discuss the truth or acceptability of each premise.

1. Plagiarism is wrong, and paraphrasing the words of others without proper acknowledgment is the same as plagiarism, so paraphrasing the words of others without proper acknowledgment is wrong.

2. Mafia member Joe Bonano was guilty of criminal activities because he claimed the Fifth Amendment in the course of his trial. The Fifth Amendment, you will recall, is the privilege of a witness not to testify on the grounds that the evidence called for might be incriminating. One may choose not to testify against oneself, but there is a risk attached to this privilege. For we cannot avoid the fact that people who take the Fifth Amendment have something to hide—their guilt. In the case of Joe Bonano, that something to hide was his criminal activities.

INDUCTIVE REASONING

The fundamental distinction between deductive and inductive reasoning lies in the relative certainty with which we can accept a conclusion. The certainty guaranteed when a deductive argument is validly reasoned from acceptable premises cannot be assumed in an inductive argument, no matter how carefully one supports the inference. The terms most appropriate for inductive arguments then are **strong** and **weak, reliable** or **unreliable,** rather than valid and invalid.

Some logicians prefer the categories deductive and nondeductive to deductive and inductive, given the varied forms arguments can take when they don't conform to the rigorous rules of inference required for deduction.

Generalization

Determining cause and effect, formulating hypotheses, drawing analogies, and arriving at statistical generalizations are examples of nondeductive reasoning, or, as we have chosen to call it, inductive reasoning. In this section, we concentrate on the statistical generalization. **Statistical generalizations** are best characterized as predictions, as claims about the distribution of a **projected property** in a given group or population, the **target population.** From the distribution of such a property in *part* of the target population, the **sample,** we infer a proposition, a conclusion that is either strong or weak depending on how carefully we conduct our survey. We make a prediction, an inference, about the unknown on the basis of the known; on the basis of our observations of the sample, we make a generalization about all of the population, including that part we have not observed closely.

Suppose we want to determine whether New York taxpayers will support a tax designated specifically for building shelters for the homeless. Here the projected property would be the willingness to support this particular tax (what we want to find out). The target population would be New York taxpayers. The sample would be that portion of New York taxpayers polled. From their answers, we would draw a conclusion, make a generalization about New York taxpayers in general: unanimous support, strong support, marginal support, little support, no support—whatever their answers warrant. But no matter how precise the numbers from the sample, we cannot predict with absolute certainty what the entire population of New York taxpayers will actually do. When we make an inference from some to all, the conclusion always remains logically doubtful to some degree.

Let's look at another example.

For several years now, scientists and health officials have alerted the public to the increased risk of skin cancer as the thinning of the ozone layer allows more of the harmful ultraviolet rays to penetrate the atmosphere. Imagine that the student health center at your school wanted to find out if students were aware of this danger and were protecting themselves from it. In this case, the projected property would be taking preventive measures to protect oneself from the sun. The target population would be all the students attending your school, and the sample would be the number of students polled. Once again, any conclusions reached by the health center on the basis of its survey would be tentative rather than certain, with the certainty increasing in proportion to the size of the sample—the greater the number of students polled, the more reliable is the conclusion, assuming the sample is representative as well.

The Direction of Inductive Reasoning

The direction of inductive reasoning can vary. We may start by noting specific instances and from them make general inferences, or we may begin with a general idea and seek specific examples or data to support it. The following example moves from specific cases to a generalization:

Observing a sudden increase in the number of measles cases in several communities, public health officials in the 1990s inferred that too many infants were going unvaccinated.

You may notice that our ability to think both deductively and inductively has a way of intertwining the two modes of thought, but the structure of this argument is still inductive, the conclusion being probable rather than guaranteed.

Often we start with a tentative generalization, a possible conclusion called a **hypothesis,** an assertion we are interested in proving.

Rousel Uclaf, the French manufacturers of a revolutionary new pill to prevent pregnancy and avoid abortion, hoped to prove that it was both effective and safe. To do so, they had to conduct elaborate studies with varied groups of women over time. Until they had gathered such statistical support in a sample population, their claim that it was effective and safe was only a hypothesis, not a reliable conclusion. But once they had tested their product, RU 486, on 40,000 women in several European countries and found only two "incidents" of pregnancies and no apparent harm, they were ready to claim that RU 486 is reasonably safe and statistically effective.

Even here, the conclusion remains inductive—it is a highly probable conclusion but not a necessary one as it would be in deduction. Unfortunately, there are examples of such inductive reasoning leading to false (and disastrous) conclusions. Approved for use in Europe, the drug thalidomide, given to pregnant women for nausea in the 1960s, caused many children to be born with grave deformities. And the Dalkon Shield, an intrauterine birth control device of the 1970s, although tested before being made available, caused sterility in many of its users.

Given the degree of uncertainty inherent in any conclusion based on a sample, the Japanese take no chances when it comes to their nation's beef supply. According to the *New York Times*, "Japan tests all the cows it slaughters each year, 1.2 million," while the United States Department of Agriculture relies on a sample, testing approximately one hundred cows a year.

Testing Inductive Generalizations

With inductive arguments, we accept a conclusion with varying degrees of probability and must be willing to live with at least a fraction of uncertainty. But the question always remains, how much uncertainty is acceptable?

CRITERIA FOR EVALUATING STATISTICAL GENERALIZATIONS   *How* we infer our conclusions, the way in which we conduct our surveys, is crucial to determining the strength of an inductive argument. Whether we are constructing our own arguments or evaluating those of others, we need to be discriminating. Many of our decisions on political, economic, sociological, even personal issues depend on inductive reasoning. Scarcely a day goes by without an inductive study or poll reaching the news sections of daily papers or the evening news on TV: Surveys show the president's popularity is rising or falling, Americans favor socialized medicine, one in five nongovernment workers is employed at firms with drug testing programs. A few principles for evaluating such generalizations can help us all examine the conclusions with the critical perspective necessary for our self-defense.

In order to accept a conclusion as warranted or reliable, we need to control or interpret the conditions of the supporting survey.

Two features of the sample are essential:

1. The **size** must be adequate. The proportion of those in the sample must be sufficient to reflect the total size of the target population. Statisticians have developed complex formulas for determining adequate size proportionate to a given population, but for our general purposes common sense and a little well-reasoned practice will serve. The Gallup Organization polls 2,500 to 3,000 people to determine how 80 million will vote in a presidential election and allows for only a 3 percent margin of error. This suggests that the size of a survey can often be smaller than we might initially assume.

2. The sample must be **representative.** It must represent the target population in at least two different ways.

   a. The sample must be selected *randomly* from the target population.

   b. It must also be *spread* across the population so that all significant differences within the population are represented. Such a contrived approach might seem contradictory to a random sample, but some conscious manipulation is often necessary to ensure a sample that is genuinely typical of the target population.

Examine the following diagram to see these principles illustrated:

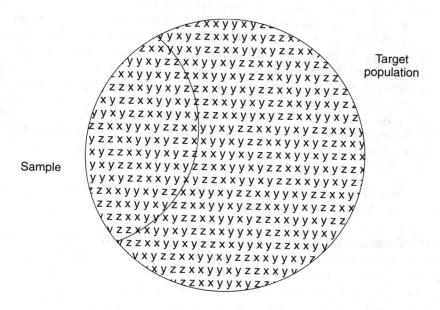

As you can see, we are back to classes (see Class Logic above). The sample is a subclass included in the larger class of the target population. As we make inferences, we move from a conclusion about the smaller class, the sample, to a conclusion about the larger class, the target population.

> *If they remove all the fools from Congress, it wouldn't be a represen-*
> *tative Congress.*
> —POLITICAL COMMENTATOR MOLLY IVINS

Let's evaluate the reasoning in the following argument:

A visitor of modest means from a midwestern city comes to San Francisco for five days and is instructed by her friends to assess the prices of San Francisco's restaurants; some of them are considering a trip there in the near future. Our tourist, let's call her Kate, picks up a guidebook and takes the first five restaurants listed in the book: Masas, Campton Place, Postrio, the Ritz Carlton, and Aqua, all of which are located downtown. Verging on bankruptcy, poor Kate returns home with the report that restaurants in San Francisco are staggeringly expensive. For a resident of San Francisco, the error in her conclusion and the flaw in the reasoning that led to her false conclusion are easy to spot—she has inadvertently chosen five of the most expensive restaurants in the city. Before selecting her restaurants, she should have examined her guidebook carefully to be sure that her survey of restaurants was, to some degree, representative. The book clearly began with a list of the major splurges and that was as far as Kate went.

With only five days, she was necessarily limited when it came to the *size* of her sample, and thus she would have to place a strong qualifier on any conclusions she drew. But, with a little care, she could have aimed for a more *random* sample by investigating different sections of her guidebook, referring to more than one guide, and visiting various geographical areas of San Francisco. Such a sampling would also have helped her arrive at examples spread more effectively over different types of cuisines. A visitor intent on savoring the best fare regardless of cost would have done well following Kate's approach, but one interested in the prices was doomed to a distorted picture.

Can you identify the projected property, the target population, the sample, and the conclusion for this inductive argument?

HASTY GENERALIZATIONS   When, like Kate, we leap to an unwarranted conclusion, we commit the common logical fallacy of hasty generalization. If, for example, after one semester at a university as a student having had two professors who failed to return work, often missed class, or arrived late, you concluded that the university had a rotten faculty, you would be guilty of hasty generalization. The sample is clearly too small to warrant such a conclusion.

Newspaper columnist Jon Carroll "remember[s] one [East Coast] writer who came to California, stayed in the Beverly Hills Hotel for three days and concluded that all Californians were stupid, narcissistic and in the movie business." To discredit this hasty generalization, all one would have to do is find a **counterexample,** one Californian who wasn't stupid, narcissistic, and in the movie business. What mistake did the East Coast writer make with his sample? For further discussion of this familiar fallacy, see Chapter 6.

COUNTEREXAMPLES

With any generalization supported by specific examples, one counterexample can discredit, or "embarrass," the conclusion. Warranted conclusions must be consistent with the data used in their support, and where necessary, qualified appropriately—"most," "some," "usually," "occasionally," "in most cases."

Garfield doubts his conclusion when he finds three counterexamples.

Thinking Critically About Surveys and Statistics

Because surveys and statistics suggest an authority they may not warrant, we must read them critically rather than accept them without question. Statistics should contribute to reasoning, not serve as a substitute for it.

Time magazine ran a recent cover story on the high cost of a college degree entitled "How Colleges Are Gouging You," by Erik Larson. In his article, Larson accused colleges of protecting their endowment funds while charging whatever the traffic will bear for tuition. The piece elicited this angry response:

> To generalize the situation at the University of Pennsylvania and other Ivy
> League schools and apply it to major universities across the board is like using
> the cost of a Lexus to discuss the price of an average family van. In the real
> world of most institutions, faculty members do not average earnings of
> $121,000 a year; they are lucky to make $40,000. And they are teaching larger
> classes with fewer resources and support staff and reduced budgets for essen-
> tial expenses. Unfortunately, Larson's diatribe will probably be used by state
> legislatures as justification to cut budgets of many public institutions.
>
> —JOHN BRUNCH, ASSISTANT PROFESSOR, DEPARTMENT OF MANAGEMENT,
> KANSAS STATE UNIVERSITY, MANHATTAN, KANSAS

This professor from a public university is rightfully concerned that a generalization based on a study of private universities will be applied to public
universities (which often do not have endowment funds), with the conse-
quence of fewer resources for him and his students.

In 1948 Alfred C. Kinsey published *The Kinsey Report,* one of the first
surveys on the sexual mores of Americans. Kinsey concluded among other
things that 10 percent of the population was homosexual. James H. Jones, who
wrote a recent biography of Kinsey, points out that the sample on which this
conclusion was based was not representative of all Americans.

> Kinsey did a great deal of interviewing in prisons, where the incidence of
> homosexuality was higher than in the general population. More damaging
> still to the reliability of his sample was his practice of seeking out individu-
> als on the basis of their sexual tastes and behavior. In compiling his sample
> of the American population, Kinsey targeted gay people, becoming the
> first scientist to study in depth the nascent gay communities in large urban
> areas and elsewhere. In city after city he tapped into gay networks, using
> the contacts he made with gay subjects to generate introductions to their
> partners, lovers and friends. This practice enabled Kinsey to collect a large
> number of gay histories, but, in conjunction with his prison interviews, it
> also skewed his data in the direction of overestimating the percentage of
> gay people in the American population.

Bad science is made worse by the media's often reporting of all surveys in
abbreviated and often sensational ways, frequently giving subtle slants in emphasis to statistics. For example, in the same issue of a major daily newspaper,
the summary caption on page one stated that, "A new poll finds that 1 in 5 Californians still resent Japan for the attack on Pearl Harbor," while the inside
story was headed, "50 years after attack on Pearl Harbor, only 1 in 5 is still re-
sentful, poll shows." What are the different implications of these two captions?

Mistaking Correlation for Causation

Even when a study is carefully done by a reputable institution, the press will
often reduce the results to the most attention-getting headline. The media re-

ported that heavy coffee drinkers had two to three times the risk of heart disease on the basis of a study done at Johns Hopkins University using many subjects over several years. But a careful reading of the study from beginning to end revealed that its authors didn't ask participants about their diet, smoking habits, and exercise levels, mitigating factors in any study of heart disease. The report concluded that there was "a need for further investigation" into the dangers of caffeine, a conclusion the media failed to report. All that one could safely conclude from the Johns Hopkins study is a **correlation** between heavy caffeine use and heart disease, not **causation.** The distinction between correlation and causation is an important one. There is a correlation between home ownership and car accidents. If you are a home owner, you're more likely to own a car, so you're more likely to be in a car accident, but that doesn't mean that home ownership causes car accidents.

To determine causation, researchers must conduct randomized, controlled studies; such studies are difficult to design and complete. Large numbers of people are assigned by chance to different groups. In tests of medications, for example, neither the scientists in charge of the study nor its participants know whether the subjects being studied have been taking a particular drug or a placebo (an unmedicated substance) until the study is completed and the results analyzed.

Observational studies, on the other hand, begin with a hypothesis such as a belief that a low-fat diet protects against heart disease. Researchers then gather relevant patient data, plug this data into computers, which then identify correlations between diet and disease. But mathematical correlations do not necessarily mean causation, a point to remember whenever we see the results of a new study in the headlines or leading the five o'clock news.

AN INTERNET JOKE:

Here's the final word on nutrition.

The Japanese eat very little fat and suffer fewer heart attacks than the British or Americans.

The French eat a lot of fat and also suffer fewer heart attacks than the British or Americans.

The Japanese drink very little red wine and suffer fewer heart attacks than the British or Americans.

The Italians drink excessive amounts of red wine and also suffer fewer heart attacks than the British or Americans.

Conclusion: Eat and drink what you like. Speaking English is apparently what kills you.

RESULTS OF THE
Tropical Fish Sex Survey

Tropical fish who claim to mate two or three times a day.

Tropical fish who, for some strange reason, are under the impression that they never mate.

Tropical fish who would have us believe that they mate two or three times a week.

Tropical fish who think, apparently, that they mate two or three times a year.

Tropical fish who, in their words, mate two or three times a month.

17% 19% 15% 22% 27%

R. Chast

Considering the Source

When evaluating a survey and its conclusions, we must consider the source of the survey—who conducted the survey and who paid for it—to determine if there is a **conflict of interest** or a **hidden agenda.** A recent study of silicone breast implants concluded that there was no link between ruptured implants and connective tissue disease. Lawyer and consumer advocate Mary Alexander criticizes this study, not only for the limited size of its sample and its failure to allow for the 8.5 years of latency between implantation and silicone disease, but also because two of its authors "admitted on the threat of perjury that they were paid consultants of breast implant manufacturers." Furthermore, Dow Corning, the world's largest silicone breast implant manufacturer, had donated $5 million to one of the hospitals involved in the study. Such a study is riddled with conflict of interest. It is not in the best interest of those who benefit directly from Dow Corning to find fault with the company's product.

Recently, class action lawyers filed an $800 million suit against Motorola, claiming cell phones cause brain cancer. This suit motivated cell phone manufacturers to fund studies of their own. These studies, none of which lasted more than three years, concluded that cell phone use did not cause brain cancer. Both the length of these studies and their sponsors cause us to question their conclusions.

The difficulty lies in the reality that sometimes even the most reliable journals and research organizations lead us astray. One of the most respected medical publications, the *New England Journal of Medicine,* has been found guilty of violating its conflict-of-interest policy. In 1989, the journal included an article that played down the risks from exposure to asbestos but failed to inform its readers that the authors had past ties to producers of asbestos. In 1996, the journal ran an editorial claiming that the benefits of diet drugs outweighed the risks but failed to note that the two authors had been paid consultants for firms that made or marketed one of the diet drugs under discussion. And in 1997, the journal featured a negative review of a book connecting environmental chemicals and various cancers, a review written by the medical director of a large chemical company.

CRITICAL READING OF SURVEYS

1. Is the sample representative of the target population? Is it large enough? How long did the study last? Was the study random and controlled or was it observational?

2. Does the media's report on the survey seem fair and reasonable?

3. Does the survey establish causation or correlation?

4. Who wrote or published or called your attention to the survey? Are they impartial or do they have a hidden agenda or conflict of interest? Is the survey cited in advertising or in another context in which the motive is to sell you something?

EXERCISE 7F

Evaluating Inductive Reasoning

In the following studies, identify the **conclusion,** the **projected property,** the **target population,** and the **sample.** Then, drawing on the principles of reliable inductive generalizations, **evaluate their reliability.**

1. The quality control inspector at Sweet and Sour Yogurt removes and tests one container out of approximately every thousand (about one every 15 minutes) and finds it safe for consumption. She then guarantees as safe all the containers filled that day.

2. On November 1, to consolidate his frequent flier miles, businessman Eric Nichols decided to select one domestic airline from his two favorites. He planned to base his decision on each airline's reliability. From November through April he made 20 evenly spaced trips on United, experiencing two cancellations, nine delayed departures, and eight late arrivals. From May through October, he flew American Airlines 22 times, but improved his record with only one cancellation, seven delays, and five late arrivals. Without further consideration, he chose American as the more reliable of the two.

3. Setting out to document her theory on the prevalence of racism on television, a sociologist examines 40 episodes from the new fall prime-time situation comedies and finds that 36 of them contain racist stereotypes. She concludes that 90 percent of television drama is racist.

4. In her book *Women and Love,* Shere Hite claims that a large percentage of American women are unhappy in their marriages and feel that men don't listen to them. She felt confident in her conclusions after mailing out 100,000 questionnaires to women's political, professional, and religious organizations and having 4 percent of the questionnaires returned.

5. The French Ministry of Social Affairs reported that three well-known research physicians at the Laennec Hospital in Paris had observed "dramatic biological improvements" in a group of patients with AIDS. The physicians reported a "dramatic" slowing of acquired immune deficiency syndrome in one of the six patients and a complete halt in the disease's progress in another after only five days of treatment with a compound called cyclosporine. (Hint: The conclusion is implicit.)

6. A recent study by the University of Medicine and Dentistry of New Jersey concluded that "women who were abused [physically, emotionally, or sexually] as children have more health problems and require more hospi-

tal care than women who were not abused." Seven hundred women from a private gynecological practice were interviewed. Mostly white, middle class with college degrees, they ranged in age from 16 to 76.

EXERCISE 7G

Distinguishing Between Correlation and Causation

Read the following essay from the *New York Times* by Dr. Susan Love, a professor of surgery at UCLA School of Medicine, and answer the questions that follow.

Preventive Medicine, Properly Practiced

There are at least 6 million women in this country who are asking themselves, "What happened?" Over the last several years they have read books and magazine articles, listened to TV pundits and talked to doctors and friends—all of whom assured them that taking hormone replacement therapy for the rest of their lives would keep them healthy. Then one bright summer day, their world shifted. Their little daily pill carried not the promise of health but the risk of disease. How could this be? 1

What happened is that medical practice, as it so often does, got ahead of medical science. We made observations and developed hypotheses—and then forgot to prove them. We start with observational studies, in which researchers look at groups of people to see if we can find any clues about disease. But all this observation can do is find associations: it can't prove cause and effect. 2

With hormone replacement therapy, we did many observational studies. We found that women who were on hormone therapy had a lower incidence of heart disease, stroke, colon cancer and bone fracture. And we accepted these findings before we did the definitive research, overlooking the fact that these women were also more likely to see a doctor (which is how they were put on hormone therapy in the first place), and probably more likely to exercise and to eat a healthful diet, than women who were not taking the drug. It wasn't clear whether hormones made women healthy or whether healthy women took hormones. 3

To answer this question we needed randomized, controlled research. The latest study, sponsored by the National Institutes of Health, enrolled 16,608 healthy women from ages 50 to 79 and randomly assigned them to take hormone replacement therapy or a placebo. Much to everyone's surprise, after 5.2 years the study showed that the risks of hormone treatment outweighed the benefits in preventing disease. . . . 4

There is a bigger issue than simply hormone therapy, however. There is a tendency, driven by wishful thinking combined with good marketing and media hype, to jump ahead of the medical evidence. In the 1950's, it was DES, a drug given to pregnant women to prevent miscarriages. It was 5 many years later that a randomized, controlled study showed that it had no effect in preventing miscarriages. Finally, in 1971 it was learned that daughters of women who took DES were at increased risk of developing vaginal cancer.

In the 1990's, the bone marrow transplant—high-dose chemotherapy with   6 stem-cell rescue—was proposed to treat aggressive breast cancers. It was widely used until four randomized, controlled studies showed it was no better than standard therapy, and had far more side effects. Arthroscopic surgery for osteoarthritis was commonly performed but just last week a controlled study showed it had no objective benefit. Hormone replacement therapy is just one more example of this phenomenon. . . .

1. What is the difference between an observational study and a "randomized, controlled" study?

2. Identify the projected property, the target population, the sample, and the conclusion of the National Institutes of Health study of hormone replacement therapy, and then evaluate the reliability of the conclusion.

3. According to Dr. Love, why does medical practice "jump ahead of the medical evidence"? What other examples of this phenomenon, in addition to hormone replacement, does she cite? Can you add to this list?

EXERCISE 7H

Collecting Generalizations

Humorist James Thurber had fun exploiting our tendency to overgeneralize in his essay "What a Lovely Generalization." Many of his examples are absurd, but some suggest the dangers that can spring from such patterns of thought. For those interested in collecting generalizations, he suggests listening "in particular to women, whose average generalization is from three to five times as broad as a man's." Was he sexist or making a joke? He listed many others from his collection, labeling some "true," some "untrue," others "debatable," "libelous," "ridiculous," and so on. Some examples from his collection: "Women don't sleep very well," "There are no pianos in Japan," "Doctors don't know what they're doing," "Gamblers hate women," "Cops off duty always shoot somebody," "Intellectual women dress funny." And so his collection ran, brimming with hasty generalizations.

Your task is to collect two "lovely generalizations" from the world around you, comment on the accuracy, absurdity, and dangers of each, and discuss the implications of your generalizations for those who seem to be the target.

WRITING ASSIGNMENT 15

Questioning Generalizations

Add the two generalizations you chose for Exercise 7H, "Collecting Generalizations," to the following list of generalizations and choose one to write a one-page paper in support of, or in opposition to. This list could be even longer and more diverse if your instructor collects the entire class's generalizations and makes them available to you.

1. Women are better dancers than men.
2. Men are better athletes than women.
3. Everyone is capable of being creative.
4. Nice guys finish last.
5. Appearances can be deceiving.
6. The purpose of a college degree is to prepare an individual for a career.
7. A college graduate will get a higher paying job than a high school graduate.
8. A woman will never be elected president of the United States.
9. All people are created equal.
10. War is a necessary evil.

Audience

A reader who is not strongly invested in the proposition one way or another but who is interested in hearing your point of view.

Purpose

To cast a critical eye on a generalization that people tend to accept without question.

WRITING ASSIGNMENT 16

Conducting a Survey: A Collaborative Project

Conduct a survey at your school to determine something of significance about the student body and then write a report in which you state either a question or a hypothesis, describe the survey, and speculate on the results. (Apologies to statisticians for the oversimplification of a very complex task.)

The class as a whole can brainstorm possible questions to ask the student body, the target population. What do students think about the current administration on campus or in Washington? Our nation's war on terrorism? Or a host of other political issues. How many students take a full academic load and work part-time as well? There are many possibilities.

Choose five or six topics from these many possibilities and divide into groups around them. These groups will then create a survey—a questionnaire appropriate to the topic they are researching—and a strategy for distributing it to a representative sample.

The next step is to collect, tabulate, and discuss the data. Either each student can then write her own report or the group can write a single report, assigning a section to each member of the group.

The report will contain the following:

1. A description of the survey
   What questions did you ask?
   When and where did you ask them?

2. A description of the sample
   Whom did you ask?
   How many did you ask?

3. Evaluation of the survey
   Was the sample large enough?
   Was it representative?
   Were your questions unbiased?
   What could you do to make it better?

4. Analysis of the results
   How does it compare with what you expected the results to be before you began gathering the data?
   What do you imagine are the causes that led to these results?
   What are the implications of the results?

Audience

Your campus community—students, faculty, and staff.

Purpose

To inform your campus community about its student members.

A NOTE ON DEDUCTION, INDUCTION, AND WRITTEN ARGUMENT

Textbooks about writing frequently describe organizational patterns for essays as being strictly deductive or inductive, but we find arguments as they appear in newspapers, magazines, and academic publications seldom take such a restrictive shape. Ultimately, as Pirsig emphasizes in "Mechanics'

Logic," it takes an interplay of the two thinking methods to reflect accurately how we arrive at our conclusions.

Our ability to distinguish between inductive and deductive reasoning enables us to see if a conclusion absolutely follows from the evidence or if it is one possibility among others. Understanding our reasoning and the reasoning of others in these terms increases our ability to both think critically and write logically.

SUMMARY

Inductive and deductive reasoning are distinct from one another in two ways:

1. In a **deductive argument,** the conclusion follows by necessity from the premises if the method of reasoning is valid. In an **inductive argument,** the conclusion can follow with only some degree of probability.
2. In a deductive argument, the inference moves from a generalization to a particular instance or example that fits that generalization. In an inductive argument, the inference usually moves from a series of specific instances to a generalization.

Induction and deduction are interdependent; it takes an interplay of the two thinking methods to arrive at our conclusions.

There are three possible relationships between classes: **inclusion, exclusion,** and **overlap.**

Both inductive and deductive reasoning often depend on supporting a conclusion on the basis of relationships between classes.

For a **categorical argument** to be sound, the structure of the argument must be valid and the premises acceptable.

The **statistical generalization,** based as it is on an inductive leap from some to all, is never as certain as a conclusion drawn from sound deductive reasoning.

The direction of inductive reasoning can vary. We may note specific instances and from them make general inferences, or we may begin with a general idea and seek specific examples or data to support it.

For a statistical generalization to be reliable, the sample must be adequate in size and representative of the target population.

With any generalization supported by specific examples, one **counterexample** can discredit the conclusion.

A **correlation** between two characteristics such as speaking English and having heart attacks does not mean that speaking English causes heart attacks.

KEY TERMS

Categorical syllogism a deductive argument composed of three classes; the argument has two premises and one conclusion derived from the two premises.

Causation anything that directly produces an effect.

Correlation a mutual relationship or connection between two or more things, but not necessarily a direct cause–effect relationship

Class in logic all of the individual things—persons, objects, events, ideas—that share a determinate property.

Deduction a pattern of reasoning in which the conclusion follows of necessity from the premises if the reasoning is valid.

Exclusion a relationship between classes in which classes share no members.

Hypothesis a tentative generalization, an unproved theory or proposition we are interested in proving.

Inclusion a relationship between classes in which every member of one class is a member of another class.

Induction a pattern of reasoning in which the conclusion follows only with some degree of probability.

Overlap a relationship between classes in which classes share at least one member.

Particular proposition refers to some members of a designated class.

Predicate includes everything being asserted about the subject.

Projected property what is to be determined about the target population.

Sample the surveyed members of the target population.

Soundness describes a deductive argument whose premises are acceptable and whose structure is valid.

Statistical generalization a prediction about the distribution of a particular feature in a given group.

Subject that part of the sentence about which something is being asserted.

Target population the group about which the conclusion will be drawn.

Universal proposition refers to all members of a designated class.

Validity the conclusion follows of necessity from the premises; the form of the argument is correct.

CHAPTER 8

The Language of Argument—Style

Style is effectiveness of assertion.

—GEORGE BERNARD SHAW

Some may dismiss style as ornament, as the decorative frills of writing, or as something limited to matters of correct grammar and usage. But an effective style can capture your reader's attention and possibly win the day for your argument. Style certainly includes a carefully proofread, grammatically correct final draft, but it also means **well-crafted sentences** that carry meaning gracefully to your readers, contributing to clear communication.

We address well-crafted sentences in Chapters 3 and 4 when we discuss the value of **logical joining,** and in Chapter 5 when we present **appositives** as a strategy for increasing fluency at the sentence level. In this chapter we introduce **verbal modifiers** and **parallel structure,** and also stress the importance of **concrete sentence subjects** and **active voice verbs.**

VERBAL MODIFIERS

1. In a major new strategy document quoted in *U.S. News & World Report,* the Pentagon is even more specific, ***venturing*** onto delicate ground.

   —GEORGE PACKER

2. The obstacles to a free election in a country with shallow democratic roots, ***suffering*** from years of dictatorship, were immense.

   —SEYMOUR M. HERSH

3. ***Standing*** before reporters, Senator Reid, who had worked behind the scenes for this result, looked euphoric.

   —ELSA WALSH

Note how three political writers turn verbs into verbal modifiers (also known as participles), *venturing, suffering,* and *standing* in the sentences above. Such transformations increase sentence fluency and combine ideas to express logical relationships. Verbal modifiers provide a useful technique for joining choppy sentences and expanding meaning within a sentence and can appear at the beginning, in the middle, or at the end of the sentence, as illustrated above.

A verbal is a verb form that has no subject of its own, but depends on the sentence subject or a noun close to it, to perform its action. In the first sentence, the sentence subject "the Pentagon" is "venturing." In sentence two, "country" is "suffering," and in the third sentence, "Senator Reid" is standing. When you place an idea in a verbal phrase, you can eliminate the repetition of the sentence subject and thus reduce two sentences or clauses to one for a smoother flow of ideas. Hear the difference between George Packer's original sentence, quoted above, and his fluent sentence cut in two parts.

> *In a major new strategy document quoted in* U.S. News & World Report, *the Pentagon is even more specific. It is venturing onto delicate ground.*

We'd get the same result by splitting the other two sentences.

When you use a verbal phrase you express one action in relation to another, often conveying simultaneous action.

> **Standing before reporters**, Senator Reid, who had worked behind the scenes for this result, looked euphoric.

Senator Reid was both standing and looking at the same time. The two ideas move together smoothly in one sentence.

Most commonly, verbal modifiers take the "ing" form of the verb, but they can also take the past participle or "ed" form and the infinitive or "to" form.

ing **form**: hitting, preparing

> **Hitting** better than ever, he hoped for a spot in the majors.

ed **or past participle form:** hit, thought, prepared (the verb form that goes with "had" as in "had hit," "had convinced")

> **Convinced** the criminal was hiding inside, the cop entered the silent building.

to **form:** to hit, to think

> **To think** more clearly, she found herself a deserted room.

Sometimes a verbal phrase can signal a cause–effect relationship, as in the example that follows.

> Lisa was bored by her job. She decided to go back to school.

Rewritten
Bored *by her job*, Lisa decided to go back to school.

You need to keep one rule in mind: Usually, for the sentence to be logical, the doer or agent of the verbal phrase is the subject of the sentence or clause closest to it.

EXERCISE 8A

Creating Verbal Phrases

A. Combine the following sets of sentences by reducing one or more to a verbal phrase.

Examples:

Two choppy sentences
She *thought* critically about the issue. She *recognized* that her opponents had a good argument.

One revision
Thinking critically about the issue, she recognized that her opponents had a good argument.

Another option
She thought critically about the issue, ***recognizing*** that her opponents had a good argument.

1. My aunts thought the shock might kill her. They told her that he had moved to Arizona.

2. We had prepared for this all week. We'd cleaned everything in sight and washed the dust of disuse from the good dishes.

3. They live under unpleasant conditions. They rent rundown apartments. They work in pain for too many hours. They get too little sleep to stay healthy.

4. She caught sight of his long, hopeless, irritated face. She stopped suddenly with a grief-stricken look. She pulled back on his arm.

5. The house was destroyed by the earthquake. The house was rebuilt the following year.

6. American women poured into the workforce during the final decades of the past century. They were inspired by the women's movement. They were prodded by economic necessity.

7. She wanted to learn how to program her computer. She signed up for an advanced class.

B. Expand these sentences using verbal phrases:

1. The angry crowd fell on the assassin.
2. The truck was obviously out of control.
3. The apartment complex was in terrible condition.
4. The crowd began to move forward.

C. In your next essay or a revision of a previous assignment, include and identify at least five verbal phrases. Try to use at least one -*ed* and one *to* form.

Dangling Modifiers

Verbal modifiers can enhance the fluency of your prose, but you need to be careful about their logic. When you use a verbal as a modifier, the person or object serving as the sentence subject must usually also work logically as the agent of the modifier.

In the following sentence **"she"** is "thinking."

Thinking critically about the issue, she recognized that her opponents had a good argument.

In the sentence "she" serves as the logical agent of the verb in the sentence and also of the verbal modifier.

When the logical agent of the verbal is missing from the sentence, it is said to dangle, hence the term **dangling modifier.**

Study the error in logic in the following sentence.

After getting ill last semester and not completing my final paper, you indicated that I should make up the work this spring. [Did "you" get ill?]

EXERCISE 8B

Repairing Dangling Modifiers

Many an experienced writer has lost track of the logic in her sentence. Identify the illogical dangling modifiers in these examples from published writers and recommend a remedy.

1. While writing today's piece, Anna Quindlen's column was lost in the computer. [Did her column write itself?]
2. After passing around pictures of Christopher, the couple's conversation returned to the latest Star Wars movie. [Can a conversation pass pictures around?]

3. By avoiding complex language, the readability of insurance policies can be increased.

4. Instead of treating the illegal alien as a criminal, seasonal immigrations should be allowed.

5. Walking up the staircase to Joyce Carol Oates' office in the Creative Arts building, through the halls that smell of artists' paint, past the neat rows of studios and classrooms, the blood-stained story of her most recent book, *Angel of Light*, seems a tale told on another planet. [Did her blood-stained story walk up the staircase?]

6. Speaking as an old friend, there has been a disturbing tendency in statements emanating from Beijing to question the good faith of our President on the issue of Taiwan. [Did a disturbing tendency speak as an old friend?]

PARALLELISM

In this and previous chapters we discuss strategies for increasing the coherent flow of ideas in your writing. **Parallel structure,** used to organize items in a sentence and even ideas in a paragraph, is another strategy for promoting coherence. The emphasis you achieve by harnessing your points into balanced grammatical structures increases the force of your written arguments.

The Structure of Parallelism

Parallel structure is simply a repetition of like grammatical units—a list of items—often joined by the conjunctions *and*, *but*, or *yet*.
Look at the following two sentences:

I came, I saw, I conquered.
They plan to visit New York, Philadelphia, and Washington, D.C.

Parallelism is a useful rhetorical device, providing a powerful means of emphasizing relationships by organizing ideas into predictable patterns. We hear a repetition and expect the pattern to continue. When our expectations are thwarted, we may falter briefly in our reading or even lose the thread of the writer's thought. In most cases, our ear tells us when a series is wandering off the track, but sometimes it can be helpful to check the grammatical structure. Here is a strategy for examining your own sentences.

Think of parallel structures as lists; in the preceding case, it is a list of cities to visit. We can illustrate this list and the need for it to conform to the principles of parallelism by placing parallel lines at the beginning of the list:

They plan to visit // New York, Philadelphia, and Washington, D.C.

The conjunction "and" joins three proper nouns acting as direct objects of the verb "plan to visit."

We can do the same thing to a more complicated sentence taken from writer Joan Didion's essay on Alcatraz, "Rock of Ages."

It is not an unpleasant place to be, out there on Alcatraz with only // the flowers and the wind and a bell buoy moaning and the tide surging through the Golden Gate. . . . [a list of nouns as direct objects of the preposition "with"]

Now read the next sentence (aloud if possible) and hear how the loss of expected balance or harmony offends the ear.

When I should be studying, I will, instead, waste time by watching television or daydream.

The two verbs are not in the same form and are therefore not parallel. They can be made parallel by simply changing "daydream" to "daydreaming."

EXERCISE 8C

Supplying Parallel Elements

A. Complete these sentences with a parallel element.

1. Writing a good paper is a task that demands // hard work, patience, and . . .
2. She // rushed home, threw her assorted debris into a closet, and . . .
3. Fewer Americans are saving these days // not because they don't think it's wise to save, but . . .
4. The first lady is a woman who // has an open mind but . . .
5. The first lady is a woman who has // an open mind and . . .

B. In the following sentences, identify the misfits—the element of the sentence that is not parallel—and revise the sentence so that all the elements of the list are parallel. Putting slashes where each series starts will help you see where the sentence goes off track.

1. Many influences shape a child's development: family, church, peer groups, economic, social, and school.
2. Michelle lives in a neighborhood where knife wounds, killings, and people are raped are as common as the sun rising in the morning.
3. He helped to wash the car and with cleaning out the garage.

4. Free inquiry in the search for truth sometimes necessitates the abandonment of law and order but which always demands freedom of expression.

5. Pineapple juice is my favorite because it is a good source of energy, it isn't artificially sweetened, and because of its low cost.

6. The mayor launched a campaign against drunk driving and promoting the use of seat belts.

C. Read the following passage taken from *The Road from Coorain,* an autobiography by Jill Ker Conway, the first woman president of Smith College, and note the rhetorical effect. Use our system of notation to mark off the different series or lists. How many did you find?

Those night train journeys had their own mystery because of the clicking of the rails, the shafts of light pouring through the shutters of the sleeping compartment as we passed stations, and the slamming of doors when the train stopped to take on passengers. In the morning there was the odd sight of green landscape, trees, grass, banks of streams—an entirely different palette of colors, as though during the night we had journeyed to another country. Usually I slept soundly, registering the unaccustomed sounds and images only faintly. This time I lay awake and listened, opened the shutters and scanned unknown platforms, and wondered about the future.

D. Now write three of your own sentences—one with three or more verbs sharing the same subject, one with three or more adjectives, and one with three or more nouns. Use as your subject a topic you are currently writing about.

Logic of the Parallel Series

The items in a list, however, must not only be **grammatically** similar but also relate **logically** to one another. Sometimes faulty parallelism offends not only our ear but also our reason.

People who have "book smarts" usually work in places like // *libraries* or *assistants* to attorneys.

Though the writer has joined two nouns (grammatically compatible elements), an assistant of any kind cannot be a "place." He has lost control of the sentence because he has forgotten where the list begins. There is more than one way to fix this sentence, to make it logical and balanced. How would you correct it?

To understand further what we mean, look at the following sentence:

We will have to look at the language used in the text for sexism, racism, and bias.

The list in this sentence is "sexism, racism, and bias." The list is *grammatically* parallel because all three words in the list are nouns, but not *logically* parallel since sexism, racism, and bias are presented as three separate and distinct categories when in fact sexism and racism are particular forms of bias. They are included in what we can call the class or group of *bias*, not separate from it. (Remember class logic in Chapter 7.) One way to correct this faulty logic would be to replace *"bias"* with "other forms of bias" and thus illustrate the logical and actual relationship that exists between the three terms.

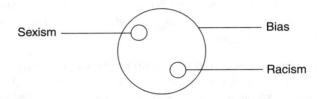

EXERCISE 8D

Editing the Illogical Series

Revise the following sentences for logical parallel structure.

1. In their attempt to excel, our employees often work extra hours and work through many lunch hours.
2. I have seen city ordinances that do not allow smoking popping up all over the place: in offices, in buildings.
3. I asked Linda if she had any materialistic aspirations such as living in a mansion, having a nice car, or being extremely wealthy.
4. The customers at the bank where I work are wealthy depositors, checking account holders, cooperative individuals, and those who are thoughtlessly rude to me.
5. For the most part, he is handsome, active, well dressed, and wears a suit and tie.

Emphasizing Ideas with Parallelism

As we mentioned above, parallelism can be a powerful rhetorical device, especially in argument. Beyond the sentence, parallelism can provide emphasis and organize major ideas in paragraphs, even throughout an entire essay.

In a column on the Israeli withdrawal from Gaza and the West Bank, Thomas L. Friedman, a respected reporter and a specialist on Middle Eastern affairs, adds force and passion to his prose with parallel structures. Read the passage aloud to hear the effect of his style.

> . . . In sum, Israel should withdraw from the territories, not because it is weak, but because it must remain strong; not because Israel is wrong, but because Zionism is a just cause that the occupation is undermining; not because the Arabs would warmly embrace a smaller Israel, but because a smaller Israel, in internationally recognized boundaries, will be much more defensible; not because it will eliminate Islamic or European anti-Semitism, but because it will reduce it by reducing the daily friction; not because it would mean giving into an American whim, but because nothing would strengthen America's influence in the Muslim world, help win the war of ideas and therefore better protect Israel than this. . . .

EXERCISE 8E

Creating Parallel Structure

In your next essay or in an assignment you are revising, construct a paragraph with a series of parallel sentences to emphasize a point you are making.

SENTENCE FOCUS—TECHNIQUES FOR SHARPENING THE FLOW OF IDEAS

> *He draweth out the thread of his verbosity finer than the staple of his argument.*
> —SHAKESPEARE, *LOVE'S LABOUR'S LOST*

We are all familiar with the confusion and obfuscation of much official prose—political, bureaucratic, academic. Some of this muddled language may be deliberate, to conceal meaning. But often it is inadvertent, a result of writers surrendering to the abstractness of language. We refer to such writing as "unfocused," in much the same way that fuzzy, confused thought is often unfocused. Think of a fuzzy, unfocused photograph.

Look at this example of unfocused writing:

> Agreement on the overall objective of decision usefulness was a prerequisite to the establishment of a conceptual framework. Now, at least, we know where we are headed. (The Week in Review, newsletter of Deloitte Haskins & Sells)

Do we know where they are going?

Compare the following memo from the Internal Revenue Service and a possible revision.

Original

Advice has been requested concerning tax deductions for research expenses, including traveling expenses, incurred by college professors.

Revision

College professors have requested advice about tax deductions for their research expenses, including traveling expenses.

Which version is clearer, easier to read? We assume that the majority of readers will prefer the second. What are the differences? The possible revision is shorter by two words. But is this the only distinction? Make your evaluation before reading on.

Calvin and Hobbes   by Bill Watterson

Concrete Subjects

Look at the grammatical subjects in the two sentences above—"advice" in the first, "professors" in the second—and notice what kinds of nouns they are. One is an **abstract noun,** the other a **concrete noun.** Because the sentence subject tends to reflect what a passage is about, the subject is where the **focus** of a sentence usually sits. A concrete noun is capable of producing a visual picture and thus can also focus a reader's attention more closely. When that concrete noun is a person or people, readers can visualize an action and so more readily follow the precise progression of ideas in a sentence. Hence, "professors" as the subject of the second sentence is preferable to the "advice" of the original. The reader can see the "professor" but not the abstraction "advice."

Active and Passive Verbs

Now look at the verbs. In the original sentence on tax deduction, the verb is "has been requested" while in the revision the verb is "has requested." The first is **passive voice,** the second, **active voice.** The basic distinction is:

With a passive verb, the subject is acted upon; the subject is not doing anything in the sentence—it is passive.

"Advice" is being requested, not, obviously, doing the requesting.

When the verb is active, its subject is performing the action of the sentence.

Thus the reader can see a subject **doing** something. The "professors" are doing the requesting.

We must wade through the original IRS memo to understand the point, whereas in the revision we see from the beginning that professors are requesting advice, people are doing something. Bureaucrats, often writing about vague or abstract subjects in which they have little invested interest or feeling, can easily fall into the passive verb trap. They are rarely the ones actually *doing* anything they are writing about. Don't let your academic writing succumb to this danger.

Sentences written in the passive are easy to spot because they always follow a grammatical pattern:

subject + a form of the verb "to be" (*am, is, are, was, were, has been*)

+

the past participle of the verb (usually with an *-ed* ending) + a "by" phrase (sometimes implied) which contains the agent of the verb

(subject)	(to be)	(past participle)	(by phrase)
Advice	has been	requested	by college professors

The following two sentences say essentially the same thing, but note how the change in the form (voice) of the verb shifts the emphasis from the concrete subject, "J. Robert Oppenheimer," to the abstract, "elemental danger."

Active: J. Robert Oppenheimer, one of the creators of the atom bomb, **felt** the elemental danger loosed on the earth.

Passive: The elemental danger loosed on the earth **was felt** by J. Robert Oppenheimer, one of the creators of the atom bomb.

Which version do you prefer? Why?

Passive Verbs and Evasion

Politicians have a tendency to rely on the passive to evade responsibility. William Safire in his *New York Times* column, "On Language," comments on this predilection, focusing on a former White House chief of staff, who, when asked at a press conference about the use of government funds for personal expenses, replied, "Obviously, some mistakes were made."

Safire notes that "the passive voice acknowledges the errors, but it avoids the blame entirely. . . . When deniability is impossible, dissociation is the way, and the [passive voice] allows the actor to separate himself from the act."

When the Passive Is Appropriate

Aiming for direct, assertive prose, careful writers usually prefer active verbs. But, on occasion, when one wants to emphasize someone or something not performing the action in a sentence, the passive is useful. Scientists and social scientists, for example, must often focus on the content of their research rather than on themselves as researchers. Under such circumstances, the passive serves a useful purpose.

> This research *was undertaken* with a grant from the National Science Foundation.

rather than

> I *undertook* this research with a grant from the National Science Foundation.

In this case the **focus,** the emphasis, of the sentence falls on *research* rather than on *I.* Thus *research* should be the grammatical sentence subject.

Sharp Paragraph Focus

Central to good **paragraph focus** is the logical progression of ideas within a paragraph. Read the following paragraph closely to see how research physician and writer Lewis Thomas maintains consistent sentence subjects, emphasizing the topic of the paragraph—how **we** relate to the concept of **death.** Note how the grammatical subjects provide a coherent line of reasoning even though at the heart of the passage lies an abstract idea.

> **We** continue to share with our remotest ancestors the most tangled and evasive attitudes about death, despite the great distance **we** have come in understanding some of the profound aspects of biology. **We** have as much distaste for talking about personal death as for thinking about it; it is an indelicacy, like talking in mixed company about venereal disease or abortion in the old days. **Death** on a grand scale does not bother us in the same special way; **we** can sit around a dinner table and discuss war, involving 60 million volatilized human deaths, as though **we** were talking about bad weather; **we** can watch abrupt bloody death every day, in color, on films and television, without blinking back a tear. But when the numbers of

dead are very small, and very close, **we** begin to think in scurrying circles. At the very center of the problem is the naked cold **deadness** of one's own self, the only reality in nature of which **we** can have absolute certainty, and **it** is unquestionable, unthinkable. **We** may be even less willing to face the issue at first hand than our predecessors because of a secret new hope that maybe **it** will go away. **We** like to think, hiding the thought, that with all the marvelous ways in which **we** seem now to lead nature around by the nose, perhaps **we** can avoid the central problem if **we** just become, next year, say, a bit smarter.

Revising for sharp sentence and paragraph focus helps to maintain the clear, direct expression you and your readers demand, no matter what your academic or professional discipline. Keep in mind, however, that revising is often most effective at a late stage in the writing process. We may expect a first draft to have several poorly focused sentences and paragraphs. Look back at Chapter 1 to refresh your memory on the writing process.

EXERCISE 8F

Sharpening Sentence Focus for Clear Expression and Fluent Style

A. Revise the following sentences for good focus, combining where appropriate for a smooth, logical flow of ideas. Think in terms of assertive sentences, ones that use strong verbs and say directly who is doing what.

Example:

First Draft
Feeling in good spirits, it was unanimously concluded by the students that Accounting 400 was a good class. [Note how poor focus has also led to a dangling modifier.]

Revision
Feeling in good spirits, the students concluded that Accounting 400 was a good class.

1. A strike is used when employees want things their employers are unwilling to provide.

2. When it is seen that a criminal act is being committed, a call should be placed to the police.

3. Fear of brutality from customers is a concern many prostitutes have.

4. The leaders have determined that the spiritual initiate has no need of worldly things, so only minimum wages are paid.

5. There is a much bigger emphasis placed on the role of the individual in this generation than in our parents' generation.

6. Teenagers are easily influenced by TV. Specific violent acts have been committed by teenagers after such acts have been shown on prime time.

7. The people of this tribe are literate, given that they have twenty terms for "book." There also may be several kinds of artwork they create, since they have nine words for "artist."

8. Having developed a complex social order, cultural patterns have been shown by the people of this tribe. These patterns are reflected in their arts and their theatre.

B. Now try your hand at revising this student paragraph with the same strategies in mind. Note how difficult it is to follow the writer's reasoning in this poorly focused paragraph.

There are many ways to be a bad teacher. There are mistakes made by bad teachers that come in a variety of forms. Assignments are given unclearly so that when papers are graded it isn't known what students are graded on or what the grade means. Grading by the ineffective teacher is according to arbitrary standards, so students think their grades are unfair. There are problems with explanations given by bad teachers and understanding is hard to arrive at. This disorganization can be seen by students when the poor teacher fails to bring all materials to class. There are many explanations given, but the dissatisfaction of students is clearly not done away with. In such cases it is not clear who is responsible for a bad grade—the student or the teacher.

WRAP-UP ON WRITING STYLE

1. To increase the flow of ideas, expand your sentence repertoire with verbal modifiers in addition to appositives (Chapter 5) and logical joining (Chapters 3 and 4).

2. Use parallel structure to increase coherence, organize lists, and emphasize relationships.

3. When logically possible, use concrete, consistent grammatical subjects which reflect the subject you are writing on.

4. Choose active verbs that allow for direct, vigorous expression of your ideas, unless you have compelling reasons for preferring the passive voice.

Caution: Do not think about these writing strategies until you have completed a first draft. Content and organization must come first.

REVISION

Review Chapter 1 for discussion of **audience** and **purpose** and the **writing process.** In particular, the section on writing first drafts provides essential material on revising your papers.

As a final step, you always need to proofread carefully for mechanical errors—typographical and spelling errors, omitted words—as well as for appropriate verb tenses, subject/verb agreement, and pronoun reference. After reading through your final draft with close attention to detail, try reading it aloud, slowly, perhaps to a critical friend or classmate. Reading pages in reverse order can help you find small technical mistakes easily overlooked when you read straight through for meaning.

WRITING ASSIGNMENT 17

Revising an Essay

Choose one of the assignments you completed earlier and reread it critically. Now is the time to revise it after reviewing material covered in this chapter particularly and in the book in general, especially Chapter 1. Consider your word choice carefully in light of Chapter 5, "The Language of Argument—Definition," and review the "wrap-up on writing style" above for a refresher on polishing your prose. You may also want to look back to Chapter 6 to see if your arguments contain any logical fallacies.

Going back to a paper after time has elapsed can give you a useful new perspective. Consider whether you have changed your mind about the issues and whether you have discovered new material relevant to your topic. Whichever assignment you choose to revise, the skills we cover in this chapter and also the passage of time will help you strengthen the draft when you return to it.

SUMMARY

Style as well as correctness is an essential part of effective written argument.

Combining and expanding sentences with **verbal modifiers** increase the logical flow of ideas.

Parallelism is a useful rhetorical device, providing a powerful means of emphasizing relationships by organizing ideas into predictable patterns.

For a vigorous and concise writing style, writers prefer **concrete subjects** and **active verbs.**

Revising a manuscript plays an important role in strengthening any writer's prose.

KEY TERMS

Active voice   a sentence construction in which the subject performs the action of the sentence. [Example: The Supreme Court ruled on the constitutionality of the 1991 civil rights legislation.]

Focus   concrete, consistent sentence subjects that reflect the rhetorical subject of the writing.

Parallel structure   a repetition of like grammatical units, often joined by the conjunctions *and, but, yet.*

Passive voice   a sentence construction in which the subject is acted upon, not doing anything in the sentence. [Example: The constitutionality of the 1991 civil rights legislation was ruled on by the Supreme Court.]

Verbal modifier   participles—verb forms usually ending in *-ing*—used as sentence modifiers. [Example: *Before resorting to violence,* we must thoroughly investigate all other means of resolution.]

CHAPTER 9

Research, Summary, and Documentation

RESEARCH

In Chapter 4, you learned the value of narrowing your topic to a particular question at issue. This focus will make it much easier for you to conduct your research since the Internet provides access to an overwhelming amount of information, not all of it reliable.

Where to Begin

For this reason, we urge you to begin your **electronic search** with **your school's library Web site.** Libraries subscribe (at significant cost) to many indexes and databases covering a wide range of disciplines. Here are a few of the indexes and databases your library will most likely subscribe to:

InfoTrac Expanded Academic. The Gale Group's general periodical index covering arts and humanities, the social sciences, and sciences as well as national news periodicals. It includes full-text articles.

LexisNexis Academic. An index of news and business, legal and reference information, with full-text articles. *LexisNexis* includes international, national, and regional newspapers; newsmagazines; and legal and business publications.

Wilson Databases. A collection of indexes including *Business Periodicals Index, Education Index, General Science Index, Humanities Index, Readers' Guide to Periodical Literature,* and *Social Sciences Index.*

Another great place to begin your research is **Librarians Index to the Internet, lii.org.** The stated goal of this Web site is "to provide a well-organized point of access for reliable, trustworthy, librarian-selected Internet resources." In other words, this Web site and your school's library Web site have been prescreened by professionals. This is not the case when you use the following three search engines, all popular choices for general information. *Google,* www.google.com; *Yahoo!,* www.yahoo.com; and *Ask Jeeves,* www.askjeeves.com. These search engines are perfect for finding the best pizza in town, the cheapest airline ticket, or the biography of a public figure, but for academic work you should rely primarily on academic Web sites. *Google,* however, is branching out. Their more recently established site, scholar.google.com, enables you to search specifically for a wide range of scholarly literature. And print.google.com is making it possible to search the entire text of an increasing number of books. Neither site should be considered as a complete source, at least not yet.

Check the Address

Note the .com that is part of the **URL** (Uniform Resource Locator), the Web address, for *Google, Yahoo!,* and *Ask Jeeves.* The **com** assignation indicates a commercial site. You may find those sites whose addresses include **edu** (an educational institution), or **org** (a nonprofit organization), or **gov** (a government site) more reliable. Still, careful evaluation is needed since an *edu* site may consist of unedited student work or an *org* site may champion a sexist or racist agenda.

Refine Your Search

Once you have chosen a site for research, you will be asked to enter a subject or key word. Refine your search by providing more than a single word. Make the terms of your search as precise as possible. The word *AND* indicates that you want all the terms to appear in your search; for example, *selling AND embryos.* On some sites, a + sign attached directly in front of a word will accomplish the same thing. The word *NOT* indicates that you want to exclude irrelevant words; for example, *"Dolphins NOT Miami."* This will exclude needless references to the football team when you want to research only the mammals. Like the + sign above, using a – sign before a word means that you don't want a word used in your search.

Don't Forget Books

The Internet is vast but not unlimited. It provides only limited information on sources prior to the 1980s. And many books and periodicals are only available at the library, so don't restrict your research to electronic sources.

Take Notes

Copy by hand, print out, or photocopy material you think you will use in your paper. Include all the necessary bibliographical material. A **bibliography** is simply a list of sources. An **annotated bibliography,** which your teacher may ask for, is a sentence or two summarizing the material taken from the source cited. Many articles have **abstracts,** a summary of the content, which will prove helpful in assembling your notes and an annotated bibliography should it be required.

Necessary Bibliographical Material

For a Book

> Library call number
> Name of author or editor
> Title and subtitle
> Publisher's name, place and date of publication

For an Article

> Name of author
> Title and subtitle of article
> Title of periodical
> Date of issue
> Page numbers of article

For Electronic Sources

> Name of author
> Title and subtitle
> Publication data for books and articles (see above)
> Date of release, online posting, or latest revision
> Medium (online, CD-Rom, etc.)
> Format of online source (Web site, Web page, e-mail, etc.)
> Date you consulted the source
> URL (electronic address)

This information will also allow you to retrace your steps should you lose material or want to return to a book or site for more information. Don't rely on memory. Like Garfield's friend below, write down important information.

Three Options for Including Research

Once you have completed your research, you have three choices for incorporating it into your paper:

Direct quotation: A word-for-word transcription of what an author says, requiring quotation marks and documentation. For the most part, keep quotations short. It is your paper, not the words of others, that your instructor wants to read. Reserve direct quotations for those times when the author's precise language is important, either because it is colorful or exact or cannot be paraphrased without distorting the author's original intent.

Paraphrase: A restatement of an idea in language that retains the meaning but changes the exact wording. Such references require documentation but not quotation marks.

Summary: A short restatement in your own words of the main points in a passage, an article, or a book. Because writing a summary is an important skill for the classroom and the workplace, we return to it later in this chapter, outlining how to write a good summary step by step.

Integrate Research into Your Own Writing

If you want your paper to read smoothly, you must take care to integrate direct quotations and paraphrases into the grammatical flow of your sentences. Don't just "drop" them with a thud into a paragraph. Rely, rather, on a ready supply of introductory or signal phrases with which to slide them in gracefully, for example, "As Freud **discovered**," "Justice Scalia **notes**," and "**according to** the *Los Angeles Times*." What follows is a list (incomplete) of verbs with which to ease the ideas of others smoothly into your sentences:

believes

claims

comments

contends

describes

explains

illustrates

mentions

notes

observes

points out

reports

says

suggests

Sometimes, to make a quotation fit in smoothly with your own writing, you must revise the original by adding or deleting a word. Whenever you change the original, you must indicate the change by using brackets:

> "I [can't] imagine a more crucial skill than summarizing; we can't manage information, make crisp connections, or rebut arguments without it."
>
> —MIKE ROSE

Make the Purpose Clear

As well as introducing quotations and paraphrases smoothly into the syntax of your sentence, you must also pay attention to the meaning of your sentence. Don't assume that the relevance of the quotation is self-evident. Make its relationship to your reasoning explicit. Is it an example? An appeal to authority? Premise support? A counterargument? A concession? Whatever the case, the purpose of the quotation—how it relates to the point you are making—should be made clear.

Punctuation and Format of Quotations

Periods and commas are placed *inside* quotation marks unless the quotation is followed by a parenthetical citation, in which case the period follows the citation.

> "Writing, like life itself, is a voyage of discovery," said Henry Miller, author of *Tropic of Cancer*.

> "Thinking is the activity I love best, and writing to me is simply thinking through my fingers."
>
> —ISAAC ASIMOV

> "The true relationship between a leader and his people is often revealed through small, spontaneous gestures" (Friedman 106).

Colons and semicolons go outside quotation marks.

> Read Tamar Lewin's essay, "Schools Challenge Students' Internet Talk"; we'll discuss it at our next class meeting.

Use single quotation marks [' '] for quotations within quotations.

> "In coping with the violence of their city, Beirutis also seemed to disprove Hobbes's prediction that life in the 'state of nature' would be 'solitary'" (Friedman 210).

If the prose quotation is more than four lines long, it should be indented, about 10 spaces for MLA (Modern Language Association) format, 5 spaces for APA (American Psychological Association) format, and double-spaced as in the rest of the text. Drop the quotation marks when you indent.

Omitting Words from a Direct Quotation—Ellipsis

Sometimes we don't want to include all of a quotation, but just certain sections of it that apply to the point we are making. In this case, we may eliminate a part or parts of the quotation by the use of *ellipsis* dots: three spaced periods that indicate the intentional omission of words. If the *ellipses* conclude a sentence, add a final period.

1. Something left out at the beginning:

   > ". . . a diploma from Harvard or Emory nearly guarantees a financially rewarding career," says columnist Cynthia Tucker of the *Atlanta Constitution*.

2. Something left out in the middle:

   > Explaining the desperation of a writer, William Faulkner once said, "Everything goes by the board: honor, pride, decency . . . to get the book written. If a writer has to rob his mother, he will not hesitate; the 'Ode on a Grecian Urn' is worth any number of old ladies."

3. Something left out at the end:

   > As Henry Lewis Gates says, "The features of the Black dialect of English have long been studied and found to be not an incorrect or slovenly form of Standard English but a completely grammatical and internally consistent version of the language. . . . "

SUMMARY

As you conduct your research, you will come across articles and books that you will want to summarize for your notes and for possible inclusion in your paper. Educator Mike Rose sees summarizing as an essential writing skill: "I [can't] imagine a more crucial skill than summarizing; we can't manage information, make crisp connections, or rebut arguments without it. The great syntheses and refutations are built on it."

Summaries come in many lengths, from one sentence to several pages, depending on the purpose of the summary and the length of the piece to be summarized. Note, for example, the brief summaries at the conclusion of each chapter in this text.

A good summary is both **complete** and **concise.** To meet these conflicting goals, you must convey the essence of the whole piece without copying whole passages verbatim or emphasizing inappropriate features of the argument. Background information, detailed premise support, and narrative illustrations are usually omitted from summaries. Paraphrases of ideas, rather than direct quotations, are preferred (except for a critically important phrase or two). A summary should also be **objective,** excluding inferences and opinions. These are reserved for argument analysis.

Strategies for Writing a Summary

1. Read the piece you are to summarize carefully to determine the writer's main point or conclusion. Write this conclusion **in your own words.**

2. Write a sentence expressing the most important point in each paragraph **in your own words.**

3. Write a first draft by combining the conclusion with your one-sentence summaries of each paragraph, **making sure the beginning of the summary includes the title and author of the piece.**

4. Edit your draft by eliminating repetition and any details that are not **essential** to the writer's argument. If you decide to include a significant sentence or phrase from the original, use quotation marks.

5. Check this edited draft against the piece being summarized to make sure you haven't overlooked an important idea or included an opinion of your own.

6. Revise for coherence by combining sentences and inserting transitional phrases where necessary. (Refer to Chapter 3 for joining strategies.) Edit for conciseness by eliminating all "deadwood" from your sentences. Check grammar and spelling.

An Example of a Summary

Following the steps outlined above, we have summarized "Could It Be That Video Games Are Good for Kids?" an editorial included in Chapter 4, page 94.

Steven Johnson in his editorial "Could It Be That Video Games Are Good for Kids?" argues that children are not negavitvely affected by playing video games. In fact, he believes high school football encourages more violent thoughts and behavior than video games. As for explicit sexual content, Johnson recommends appropriate ratings.

He contends that children have always played games and most children are not giving up reading the classics to do so. He also maintains that video games are much more challenging than traditional board games. Video games "force kids to learn complex rule systems, master challenging new interfaces, follow dozens of shifting variables in real time and prioritize between multiple objectives," all skills which will prove useful in the workplace. Johnson also points out that teenagers are watching fewer televised sporting events and that playing video games is more demanding than passively watching television.

Violent games are plentiful, but kids today are less violent than in the past according to the Duke University's Child Well-Being Index, a fact which suggests that these games act as a safety valve. And SAT scores are improving as well. Johnson does concede that children don't get exercise when playing video games and that the rising obesity among children is a serious problem.

In this summary, the sixteen paragraphs of the original have been reduced to three paragraphs that reflect the essence of the original. If summarizing for note-taking purposes only, you may want to limit yourself to steps one and two of summary strategies listed above.

> Summaries should be objective, concise, complete, and coherent, and written in your own words.

WRITING ASSIGNMENT 18

Constructing a Summary and Response

a. First, read the following essay by high school senior Nathan Yan carefully, and write a summary of the article (approximately 150–200 words). You may want to compare summaries with classmates.

b. Then write a letter to the editor of the *San Francisco Chronicle* where the essay appeared in which you express your opinion of Yan's essay and your position on the issues he raises. Discuss the premises he presents, and if you think of others not mentioned in the article, include them. Letters to newspapers, like summaries, are usually compressed, so you will need to be economical and selective with words here, limiting yourself to between 100 and 200 words.

Audience

Readers of the daily newspaper who will need the key points of the original argument before they move on to your response.

Purpose

To present an insightful analysis of an argument in order to illuminate the issue for your readers.

AP Courses—Mounting Burden, Declining Benefit

NATHAN YAN

For many high school juniors and seniors, this school year has been the year   1
of the AP, a nonstop rush of drills, flash cards and night-before cramming.
In every advanced placement class, students devote an immense effort to
studying for these tests; they buy prep books, stay excessive hours after
school and spend a disproportionate amount of time on AP over their regular classes.

As one of many AP students, I've experienced the madness myself. Per-   2
haps it is part of our natures, as "top tier" students dedicated to success, but
at its core, the work ethic of the majority of AP students represents an un-
healthy obsession with the AP test.

The AP tests are nationwide standardized tests administered by the pri-   3
vate College Board Association. Successfully passing an AP test will count
toward college credit and, depending on the college or university, may
grant exemptions from certain general education courses. For many high
schools it represents the highest class level for students taking a particular
course.

While preparing for AP tests is not so much of a problem, the issue for   4
almost any AP student is that their focus on passing the test takes prece-
dence over the subject matter of the course. Students spend days and days
practicing how to manage their time on the essay prompts, and learning
the grading process that AP scorers use, and listening endlessly to the use-
less "guessing is good if you can eliminate one answer choice" rubbish. Interest in understanding the actual subject takes a backseat, and worst of all,
confined by the College Board defined AP curriculum, teachers are stripped
of the power to direct the AP crazed students toward actual subject comprehension. School administrators, with their "pass the AP" mandate, are about
as inclined to teach the subjects as students are to learn it.

All of the time wasted and knowledge lost in studying for the AP test   5
aside, if a student actually needed nighttime and weekend study sessions,
third party prep books and a specialized class *just to pass a test*, one must
wonder if passing the AP exam really means anything. Those who have im-
mersed themselves in this AP trap of test drills and endless study are fooling

themselves into a false sense of security that a score of 3 or 4 or 5 on some AP test means that they're "smart," that they can get into a University of California campus, that they're ready for the University of California.

As for teachers, have they blindly accepted this "pass the AP" mantra as   6 simply part of the job description? Any teacher who has ever taught an AP class knows every hour wasted on explaining how AP graders score essays is an hour that could have been used to educate students on something of real substance. Every AP teacher knows that the AP syllabus, mandating what must be taught, restricts the teachers' freedom in what the class can learn. Despite this, teachers seem willing to approach the standard AP formula as simply another quirk in the education system that must somehow be accommodated.

As students, we shouldn't buy into this "failing AP equals Apocalypse"   7 paranoia, this "Oh my God, this AP seems so hard and if I fail I've got no future, I've got to do everything humanly possible to prepare for it!" This is what puts us into a black-or-white, "will this help me on the AP or not?" perspective that distracts us from real education. We don't need AP prep books or daily after-school study sessions, and if any students still feel they do, they need to reassess their ability to handle an AP course.

Teachers, similarly, need to realize that they don't need to gear their   8 classes to training for a test; teaching it like any other non-AP class, they will discover that those students who understand the material will be able to pass it, and others will not, simply because they're either lazy or unable to grasp the subject. Both teachers and the administration need to realize that a student will never fail an AP test for a lack of test preparation.

Maybe the best solution, then, is to completely drop the college credits   9 and the AP test itself, thereby eliminating all the competitive pressure and failure anxieties of today's AP courses. We would return classroom autonomy to the teachers, and, with a de-emphasis on competition and achieving a good score "on paper," the administration, teachers and, most especially, the students can get back to an environment where we're more concerned with learning about a subject, rather than learning how to pass a test on the subject.

PLAGIARISM

In a summary, you paraphrase another writer's ideas, putting them into your own words. When writing a paper of your own, you must be circumspect in giving credit to the sources you consult and place quotation marks around the words of others. **To pass off someone else's ideas or words as your own is to plagiarize.** The word *plagiarism* is derived from the Latin *plagiarius*, meaning kidnapper. Now, there are ideas or facts that are part of the public domain, they belong to all of us, such as the Latin root of *plagiarism*. No one person "owns" that information; it's (almost) common knowledge. But if we went on to trace history's most famous cases of plagiarism, research would be required, and we would have to document all of our sources and place quotation marks around sentences taken from these sources.

The Internet, while it has been an enormous help to students and teachers alike in its ability to provide us with an abundance of information on any subject, also makes it easier for students, and others, to plagiarize. According to Donald L. McCabe, founder of the Center for Academic Integrity at Duke University, in 2003, 40 percent of college students admitted to Internet plagiarism, up from 10 percent in 1999. In response to the problem, colleges subscribe to Web sites like Turnitin.com, which allows professors to submit students papers which are then analyzed for plagiarism.

Read the words of Gillian Silverman, an English professor at a public university, whose essay on plagiarism appeared in *Newsweek* magazine:

> The thing my students don't seem to realize, however, is that as easily as they can steal language from the Web, I can bust them for it. All it takes is an advanced [Web] search. . . . Plug in any piece of questionable student writing and up pops the very paper from which the phrase originates.

Silverman goes on to say that she uncovered eight cases of plagiarism in one semester, "a new record," and failed each of the offenders. Failing a class that a student has invested time and money in is a serious penalty, but the larger penalty is one that does not show up on a college transcript. The loss of skills in reading, writing, and thinking that writing assignments are designed to develop is a much larger penalty, one that can have a significant impact on one's life and career.

Two very prominent and successful historians, Stephen Ambrose and Doris Kearns Goodwin, whose credentials and literary skills are well established, were accused of plagiarism. They took sentences for their books from works by other writers and did not place the material in quotation marks. As a result, their reputations have been severely damaged, forcing Goodwin to leave her position as a public commentator on National Public Television's *News Hour*. The following essay, *Other People's Words*, by Paul Gray, which appeared in *Smithsonian Magazine*, addresses this literary scandal.

Other People's Words

PAUL GRAY

Though some writers may shrug it off as the sincerest form of flattery, plagiarism is hardly a minor menace.   1

Imagine yourself a high school history teacher who has been handed a   2
research paper on air combat during World War II by one of your better students. In it, you come upon the following sentence, without quotation
marks: "No amount of practice could have prepared the pilot and crew for
what they encountered—B-24s, glittering like mica, were popping up out of
the clouds over here, over there, everywhere." A footnote identifies your
student's source: *Wings of Morning* (1995), by Thomas Childers, page 83.
You're conscientious about your work, so you check the reference against
the Childers book, where you read: "No amount of practice could have prepared them for what they encountered. B-24s, glittering like mica, were
popping up out of the clouds all over the sky."

Since it boggles the notion of probability to believe that these nearly   3
identical sentences could have been written independently, you, dear
teacher, are stuck with two possible explanations: either your student forgot
the rule that the use of someone else's language must be identified as such
by quotation marks—that is, that a footnote alone is not enough to indicate
a word-for-word appropriation of material—or the student assumed that
you wouldn't bother to track down the original passage. If you decide that
sloppiness is the cause, you flunk the paper and hope the lesson will stick,
this time; if you have reasons to believe that deceit was the motive, you report your student to the responsible school authorities.

But what should be the response when the malefactor isn't a teenager   4
but rather Stephen E. Ambrose, 66, who has become over the past eight
years probably the most famous and widely read historian in the United
States? For, as the *Weekly Standard* reported in early January, Ambrose's
best-selling *The Wild Blue* (2001) reproduced, footnoted but without quotation marks, the "glittering like mica" passage cited above, and two others as
well, from Thomas Childers' book. Given Ambrose's prominence—he's appeared in photographs flanked by Tom Hanks and Steven Spielberg—the
hunt was immediately on for other examples of apparent plagiarism in his
works. Sure enough, other examples turned up: passages in *The Wild Blue*
that are suspiciously similar to two other sources in addition to Childers,
plus unacknowledged quotations in at least three of Ambrose's earlier books
dating back to *Crazy Horse and Custer* in 1975.

A front-page story in the *New York Times* reporting the growing furor   5
over Ambrose's methods included a truculent mea culpa by the historian: "I
wish I had put the quotation marks in, but I didn't. I am not out there stealing other people's writings. If I am writing up a passage and it is a story I
want to tell and this story fits and a part of it is from other people's writing,
I just type it up that way and put it in a footnote. I just want to know where
the hell it came from." This explanation baffled most academic historians,
not to mention most readers of it. Even those who had defended Ambrose
on the grounds that the former professor—with the help of his five grown
children—churns out best-selling books so rapidly that slipshod mistakes
were inevitable had to reconsider. Ambrose hadn't said he'd been careless
through haste, but that, by his lights, he hadn't been careless at all.

While the Ambrose story still percolated in late January, the *Weekly Stan-*   6
dard (yes, again) published some passages from Doris Kearns Goodwin's *The*
Fitzgeralds and the Kennedys (1987) that, without quotation marks, almost
exactly reproduce passages in three earlier books about the Kennedys.
Asked to comment on these similarities, Goodwin, whose book on Franklin
and Eleanor Roosevelt won the 1995 Pulitzer Prize for history, told the
Weekly Standard: "I wrote everything in longhand in those days, including
the notes I took on secondary sources. . . . Drawing on my notes, I did not
realize that in some cases they constituted a close paraphrase of the original work." Yep, that is certainly one way of committing what looks like plagiarism, and it's a way that beginning students are repeatedly reminded
not to take.

What, if anything, should the reading public make of the Ambrose and   7
Goodwin dustups or of the many similar cases of plagiarism-spotting, real or
fanciful, that have cropped up so often over the past few decades? Some
have had real consequences. Alex Haley paid author Harold Courlander
some $600,000 to settle a plagiarism suit for material Haley appropriated
for *Roots* (see "New Routes to Old Roots"); Senator Joseph Biden's bid for
the Democratic presidential nomination in 1988 hit a wall when it was
demonstrated that he'd lifted a stump speech, virtually verbatim, from then
British Labour Party leader Neil Kinnock. Other accusations of plagiarism
have dragged prominent names through headlines with inconclusive results: historian Stephen B. Oates, authors Susan Sontag and Jay McInerney.
Is any of this of more than academic interest?

Certainly, if you believe that an author's words unencumbered by quota-   8
tion marks have been conceived of and arranged solely by that author. . . .
That Ambrose and Goodwin have offered readers some ostensibly original sentences that are not of their own is assuredly a lapse rather than a crime. These
talented, industrious historians did not plagiarize their way into eminence. But
the lapses remain troubling, as do the rather blithe, dismissive self-defenses expressed by both authors. Unintentional theft remains theft, whether committed by those who know better or by those who are in the process of learning.

EXERCISE 9A

Defining Plagiarism

1. What is Stephen Ambrose's response to those who accuse him of plagiarism? What is your opinion of his defense? Do you think he is guilty of
   plagiarism even though he footnoted the sentences in question? Explain
   your answer.

2. What is Doris Kearns Goodwin's explanation for using the words of others without documentation in her book, *The Fitzgeralds and the*
   Kennedys? Do you see her as guilty of plagiarism? Explain your answer.

DOCUMENTATION

Once you have completed your research, remember that the paper is going to be yours, written in your own words, and expressing the opinions you have developed during the course of your research. To avoid charges of plagiarism, you must correctly attribute all the ideas and information you gather from outside sources. For an example of MLA documentation, see the student essay, "College Athletes—Special Admissions?" page 101.

What Information Should Be Documented?

1. All direct quotations.
2. All indirect quotations in which you summarize the thoughts of others without quoting them directly. For example:

   Science writer Gina Kolata notes that infertile couples are willing to spend large sums of money for fertility treatments (418).

3. All facts and statistics that are not common knowledge. If we were to state that half of all marriages in the United States end in divorce, documentation would not be necessary because the assertion reflects common knowledge. But if we state that only one out of seven college students in the United States will graduate, we must provide documentation; our readers would want to know the source of this exact conclusion to evaluate for themselves its reliability.

How to Document Information

Although each discipline has its preferred style of documentation, four standard styles prevail.

MLA (Modern Language Association). *MLA Handbook for Writers of Research Papers*. Use for English, foreign languages, and some other humanities. http://www.mla.org.

APA (American Psychological Association). *Publication Manual of the American Psychological Association*. Use for psychology and other social sciences. http://www.apastyle.org/faqs.html.

The Chicago Manual of Style. Use for history, art history, and philosophy. http://www.press.uchicago.edu/Misc/Chicago/cmosfaq.html.

CSE or CBE (Council of Science Editors, formerly Council of Biology Editors). *Scientific Style and Format: The CBE Manual for Authors, Editors, and Publishers*. Use for life sciences, physical sciences, and mathematics.

The MLA and the APA have evolved a system of parenthetical references—author and page number cited in the text of the paper—with a list of cited works or electronic sources and all relevant publishing information at the end of the paper. Chances are you will be following the MLA style for the writing assignments in this text and in many of your general education courses, but it's wise to consult your instructor about which style he or she requires.

Given the constraints of length, we cannot include here a complete listing of appropriate documentation for the four styles listed above. We illustrate with examples from the MLA style, offer the basic distinctions of the APA system, and introduce electronic documentation.

Should you need more information than we offer here, please refer to the Web sites listed above or visit www.ablongman.com/littlebrown for added help as well as exercises on using MLA, APA, and *Chicago Manual of Style* documentation methods.

The MLA Style of Documentation for Printed Sources

CITATIONS WITHIN YOUR TEXT   In many cases, you can slide a reference into the text of your paper without disturbing the flow of your ideas. Introduce the material being cited with a signal phrase, usually the author's name, and use a parenthetical citation stating the page number where the material can be found. Readers can then turn to the list of works cited at the end of the paper to discover the title and publishing information, which are listed under the author's or authors' last names.

1. **A book by one author**

S. I. Hayakawa points out that advertising and poetry are alike in that "they both strive to give meaning to the data of everyday experience" (162).

When the author is not identified in the text—when there is no signal phrase—the author is identified in the parenthetical citation.

Consumers want to identify with the happy, attractive people featured in advertisements (Hayakawa 164).

Note that there is no punctuation between the author's name and the page reference.

2. **A magazine article**

Once again, you may identify the work and/or author in a signal phrase, placing the page number in a parenthetical citation.

In "Reinventing Baltimore," author Tony Hiss tells us, "A city [Baltimore] that was almost two-thirds white in 1960 is now almost three-fifths black" (41).

Or, in the absence of a signal phrase, identify both the author and page number in a parenthetical citation.

Baltimore, "almost two-thirds white in 1960 is now almost three-fifths black" (Hiss 41).

3. **More than one author**

When the source is a book or a magazine with two or more authors, list all their last names in either the text or the parenthetical citation. If there are more than three authors, you may list all their last names (within reason) or cite one last name followed by *et al.* and the page number. If an author has more than one work cited, you need to provide a shortened version of each title in the text reference, relying on the concluding list of works cited for the full title.

Sometimes you will be quoting a writer who is cited by another author you are reading. If you are unable to find the original source yourself, acknowledge both sources: original author in the body of your text, followed by (qtd. in Hiss 68). Note that MLA now suggests abbreviations in their parenthetical references.

Here is an example of multiple authors quoted from an essay from a collection:

The authors reason that "since gene selection is not limited to cloning, what we have to say about the demand for cloning may well have implications for other reproductive technologies" (Eric A. Posner and Richard A. Posner, "The Demand for Human Cloning," qtd. in Nussbaum and Sunstein 235).

First names are included here because the authors' last names are the same. Usually only last names are used.

Place your parenthetical citations close to the material quoted or referred to, sliding them in at the end of grammatical units in the sentence and thus making them as unobtrusive as possible.

Consumers want to identify with the happy, attractive people featured in advertisements (Hayakawa 164), and thus you will find that advertising models are forever young, healthy, and slender.

The idea in the first part of the sentence belongs to Hayakawa, the comment in the second half reflects the idea of the student writing the paper.

Although disciplines that follow the *Chicago Manual of Style* may still use traditional numbered footnotes at the bottom of the page or the end of the paper, this is rare in literature or the social sciences.

List of Works Cited: MLA

This list, to be titled "Works Cited," will be the final page of your paper and include all of the works cited in it, documented according to the examples that follow:

1. The information comes in three units—author, title, and publishing information—each separated by a period.
2. List, in alphabetical order, the authors by last name, with first names following. If there is more than one author, all *additional* authors are listed first name and then last name.
3. Capitalize the first word and all important words in a book's title. Underline titles of books and periodicals; place titles of articles in quotation marks.
4. For the publisher, write the place of publication, followed by a colon, the name of the publisher, followed by a comma, and the date of publication. Dates now follow the European form: day, month, year. Example: 29 April 2003.
5. If the book has an editor, write *Ed.* and the editor's name before the title of the book, following the article or chapter taken from it.
6. Double-space and indent the second line 5 spaces under the first.

1. **Book by one author**

   Hayakawa, S. I. *Language in Thought and Action.* Orlando: Harcourt Brace Jovanovich, 1990.

   You can find the publishing information on the reverse side of the title page of the book.

2. **Excerpt from a collection or anthology**

   Posner, Eric A., and Richard A. Posner. "The Demand for Human Cloning." *Clones and Clones: Facts and Fantasies about Human Cloning.* Ed. Martha C. Nussbaum and Cass R. Sunstein. New York: Norton, 1998. 233–61.

3. **Magazine article**

   Toufexis, Anastasia. "Seeking the Roots of Violence." *Time* 19 April, 1993: 53.

4. **Professional or academic journal article**—(same format as for a magazine article)

Reiss, David. "Genetic Influence on Family Systems: Implications for Development." *Journal of Marriage and the Family* August 1995: 547.

5. More than one author

Use the last name and then the first name of the initial author followed by additional authors' names in reverse order—first name, then
last.

Specter, Michael, and Gina Kolata. "After Decades and Many Missteps,
Cloning Success." *New York Times* 3 Mar. 1997: A1.

When a magazine article is unsigned, list the title of the article first, al-
phabetized by the first letter of the article, followed by the title of the
magazine, appropriate dates, and the page number.

If an entry refers to an editorial or letter to the editor, cite the author,
or if there is no author, cite the title, followed by either the word "Editorial" or "Letter" set off by periods.

The APA Style of Documentation for Printed Sources

Because this book is intended primarily for classes in the humanities, we concentrate on MLA style, but for quick reference we include an introduction to
the fundamentals of APA documentation.

Citations Within Your Text

1. Book by one author

Introduce the quotation using the author's name followed by the date of
publication in parentheses. Place the page reference in parentheses at
the end of the passage, using *p.* before the number.

Semanticist S. I. Hayakawa (1990) points out that advertising and poetry
are alike in that "they both strive to give meaning to the data of everyday experience" (p. 162).

2. Paraphrase

If paraphrasing rather than quoting directly, include the author's name
in a signal phrase followed by the publication date in parentheses, similar to the example above. If the author is not identified in a signal
phrase, place his or her name and the publication date in parentheses at
the end of the sentence. A page number is not required for a paraphrase.

3. Magazine article

For a quotation taken from a magazine article, follow the same format required for a book by one author.

According to Toufexis (1993), the roots of violence are complex and diffuse.

List of Works Cited: APA

In APA style, the alphabetical list of works cited is entitled "References" and conforms to the following guidelines (you will note several distinctions between APA and MLA):

1. List the authors by last names, and use initials instead of first names.
2. Capitalize only the first word of a book's title and proper names. Italicize the title of books and journals.
3. If there is more than one author, separate their names with a comma and the symbol &.
4. Place the publication date in parentheses after the author's name.
5. Omit quotation marks around the title of an article.
6. Where there is an editor, place the editor's name before the title of the book, write (Ed.), followed by a comma and the book's title, the pages in parentheses, location of publication, and name of the publisher.

1. Book by one author

Hayakawa, S. I. (1990). *Language in thought and action.* Orlando: Harcourt Brace Jovanovich.

2. Book by more than one author

Nelkin, D., & Lindee, S. (1996). The DNA mystique: The gene as a cultural icon. In P. Brown (Ed.), *Perspectives in medical sociology* (pp. 415–433). New York: Waveland.

3. For a magazine article

Hiss, T. (1991, April 29). Annals of place: Reinventing Baltimore. *New Yorker*, pp. 40–73.

Electronic Sources

Precise information about author, date, and other source details is not always consistent on the Internet, but the **MLA** and **APA** have established guidelines for documenting online sites. When you are not able to find all the information desirable for complete documentation of electronic sources, provide as much as possible. The point is to provide easy Web access to your readers, acknowledging that addresses and sites change.

Under most circumstances, you need the following information from an Internet site:

1. Author (if one is named).
2. Name of the specific page(s), usually in quotation marks.
3. Name of the main page, usually underlined or in italics. Sometimes this and the previous citation are the same.
4. Date when source was posted online.
5. Date you accessed the site.
6. URL in angle brackets at end of the entry.

Citations Within Your Text

You may refer your reader directly to a Web site without including it in your list of works cited. The form follows the same guidelines for printed sources listed above, reflecting either MLA or APA style as appropriate.

> For a complete legal brief prepared by the National Legal Center, visit the Web site <www.filteringfacts.org/>.

List of Works Cited: MLA

The author's last name comes first. If there is more than one author, the first author's last name comes first, with additional authors listed first names first, in the same form they appeared under List of Works Cited for print sources (see above under MLA). Next comes the title in quotation marks, and then the **source and date** of publication or posting. This material is followed by the **date you accessed the site** and then the Web address or **URL** in angle brackets (for MLA). It is particularly important to make a note of the address before leaving the site because, if you wanted to recheck your documentation, you need that address. When a line break occurs in the middle of an address (some can be astonishingly long), make the break immediately following a punctuation mark, not between letters or numbers. Printing a hard copy from the Internet can also be helpful, especially if you want to quote a substantial passage. Again, list the documentation information; printed pages often omit it.

1. **Source directly from the Web**

> Beeson, Ann, Chris Hansen, and Barry Steinhardt. "Fahrenheit 451.2: Is Cyberspace Burning? How Rating and Blocking Proposals May

Torch Free Speech on the Internet." *ACLU Whitepaper* 16 Jul. 1997. 26 Aug. 1997 <http://www.aclu.org/issues/cyber/burning.html>.

2. **Article from the World Wide Web that has also been published in print magazines.** Include that source before the electronic address.

Morton, Oliver. "Overcoming Yuk." *Wired* Jan. 1998. 20 Mar. 1998. <http://www.wired.com/wired/6.01/Morton.html>.

Wilmut, I., A. E. Schniek, J. McWhir, A. J. Kind, and K. H. S. Campbell. "Viable Offspring Derived from Fetal and Adult Mammalian Cells." *Nature* 27 Feb. 1997. 19 Jul. 1997 <http://www.nature.com/Nature2/serve?SID=90209795&CAT=NATGEN&PG=sheep/sheep3.html>.

3. **Article in a newspaper or from a newswire**

Wade, Nicholas. "The Genome's Combative Entrepreneur." *New York Times* 18 May 1999. 19 May 1998 <http://www.nytimes.com/library/national/-science/051899sci-genome-venter-html/>.

4. **Electronic mail**

Todd, Alexandra. Status of the human genome project. E-mail to the authors, Cooper and Patton. 2 June 2005.

List of Works Cited: APA

Here is an example of an article from the Web to show how APA differs from MLA.

Inada, K. (1995). A Buddhist response to the nature of human rights. *Journal of Buddhist Ethics, 2,* 55–66. Retrieved July 23 1996, from http://www.cac.-psu;edu/jbel/twocont.html.

Sources on CD-ROM. Cite author, title, magazine or journal if applicable, and specific disk publication information.

Information received through e-mail (electronic mail). Give the name of the writer, give the title or describe the transmission with name of receiver, and give the date the e-mail was sent.

FORMATTING YOUR PAPER

When you prepare the final draft of your paper, some matters of format will vary according to whether you are following MLA or APA guidelines. In general, however, you should double-space and have margins of at least 1 inch all around, and for APA allow a margin of 1 1/2 inches on the left. Beginning with the title page, number each page. If you are including an abstract, place it on a separate introductory page.

For MLA, you have a choice of using a title page for your title, name, class name and number, and date **or** of placing identifying material at the top left of page one with the title centered on the page below it, immediately above the opening paragraph. In general, you will omit section headings within the paper unless called for on a technical subject.

For APA, put identifying material and title on a title page and place your name and a short version of the title at the top right-hand margin of every page. Scientific disciplines tend to be more demanding on specifics of format than the humanities, so when writing papers that require the APA style, consult your instructor about details of format.

Verb Tenses

Verb tenses in English are complex, but when writing in the humanities, you should usually use the present tense when referring to matters discussed in the writings of others. This is a convention and not all disciplines follow it. The APA prefers past tense. Try to be consistent when selecting a verb tense, although logic sometimes requires a shift. Trusting your ear and depending on common sense will usually serve you well.

An example of the *present tense* used in a paper about a book:

> "In *Zen and the Art of Motorcycle Maintenance,* Robert Pirsig *breaks down* the steps of motorcycle repair into logical components."

An example of the *past tense* to express a contrast in time:

> "Richard Epstein, in his essay 'A Rush to Caution,' *warned* against a quick ban on all cloning, but today he might approve of cloning under some circumstances."

A REMINDER

This chapter contains a great deal of detailed information that we don't expect you to memorize. Before each paper that requires research, we suggest you look over the chapter to refresh your memory on the basic principles of generating ideas for a research project, finding material, and documenting sources. Once you have gathered your information and are ready to start writing, use the chapter as a reference, consulting Web sites and research handbooks for more complete technical support.

TEXT CREDITS

INDEX